Cover Image:
Cocoon House (Healey House), Sarasota, FL
Architect:
Paul Rudolph and Ralph Twitchell
Photographer:
Ezra Stoller / Esto

Title Page Image:
Holmes Residence, Tampa, FL
Architect:
Dwight E. Holmes
Photograph courtesy of:
Jan Hochstim

First published in the United States of America in 2012 by The Center for Urban & Community Design, University of Miami, School of Architecture, 1223 Dickinson Drive, Coral Gables, Florida 33146-5010.

To order directly from The Center for Urban & Community Design, please call 305-284-3439.

Library of Congress, ISBN 0-9754506-3-8

UNIVERSITY OF MIAMI
SCHOOL of
ARCHITECTURE

ART WORKS.
arts.gov

UNDER THE SUN

Traditions and Innovations in Sustainable Architecture and Urbanism in the Sub-Tropics

Editor
Sonia R. Cháo

Introduction
Elizabeth Plater-Zyberk

Contributing Writers
Sonia R. Cháo
Jaime Correa
Thorn Grafton
Jorge L. Hernandez
Jan Hochstim
Becky Matkov
Carolyn Mitchell
Gustavo Sanchez-Hugalde
Allan T. Shulman

UNDER THE SUN

Traditions and Innovations in Sustainable Architecture and Urbanism in the Sub-Tropics

Editor
Sonia R. Cháo

Introduction
Elizabeth Plater-Zyberk

Contributing Writers
Sonia R. Cháo
Jaime Correa
Thorn Grafton
Jorge L. Hernandez
Jan Hochstim
Becky Matkov
Carolyn Mitchell
Gustavo Sanchez-Hugalde
Allan T. Shulman

This book is dedicated to Adrian and Max, for their patience, encouragement, and love; to my mother Abigail for sharing her appreciation of the built and natural patrimonies of two locations dear to her - Cuba and South Florida; to John for his moral support and finally, in loving memory of my father Felix, for a lifetime of devoted guidance and to my colleague Jan Hochstim, a dedicated architect and academic, for his example and his mentorship.

UNDER THE SUN: TRADITIONS AND INNOVATIONS IN SUSTAINABLE ARCHITECTURE AND URBANISM

10 **Preface**
Sonia R. Cháo

12 **Introduction**
Elizabeth Plater-Zyberk

SUSTAINABLE URBANISM: CREATING ROOTED AND ENDURING PLACES

16 **Sustainable Urbanism: a traditional agenda beyond science and business development**
Jaime Correa

24 **Stupid Is As Stupid Does**
Part I - Climate Change: an intensifying voice amongst the din of political Pollyannaism
Part II - At the Intersection of Sprawl, Poverty, and Climate Change
Part III - The DNA of American Cities: the good, the bad and the ugly
Part IV - Climate Change: cities lie at the crux of the problem and of the solutions
Sonia R. Cháo

56 **City of Habitats**
Gustavo Sánchez-Hugalde

SUSTAINABLE ARCHITECTURE: UNDER THE SUN AT MID-CENTURY

78 **Architecture Under the Sun: a lifelong conversation across the straits reaches its zenith at mid-century with a Tropical Modern Regionalism**
Sonia R. Cháo

166 **Greener Than Green: mid-century Florida sensibility - a precursor to present day sustainability**
Jan Hochstim

182 **The Tropical Home in Florida: minimalism, modernity and sustainability**
Allan Shulman

192 **Traditions of Sustainable Green Architecture in South Florida**
Thorn Grafton

HISTORIC PRESERVATION - A 'GREEN' ALTERNATIVE: CASE STUDIES

202 **Historic Preservation: a green alternative**
Sonia R. Cháo

210 **The Coral Gables Museum: a lesson in sustainable stewardship**
Jorge Hernandez

212 **Endangered 1920's Bungalow: saved from demolition and restored by Dade Heritage Trust**
Becky Matkov

COMPLIMENTING PASSIVE DESIGN STRATEGIES

218 **What is LEED?**
Carolyn Mitchell

PREFACE

Sonia R. Cháo
Symposium Chair, Editor and Contributing Writer

Arquitectura Magazine, 1956

In January 2006, a 2 ½ day symposium was held at the University of Miami School of Architecture, entitled *Under the Sun: Traditions and Innovations in Sustainable Architecture and Urbanism*. The articles in this publication summarize some of the primary concepts presented at the event. The underlying concept for the symposium evolved over a period of time, inspired by my first hand experiences in the Caribbean Basin and South Florida, which reawakened my interest in traditional approaches to sustainability.

Several years of working with impoverished neighborhoods and later collaborations in the Caribbean, served as a reminder that individuals living in walkable communities and in climatically attuned buildings, irrespective of style, have easier access to transit, markets and jobs, and live with a degree of comfort and dignity, which permit them to more readily and affordably confront the challenges of daily life. Conversely, families living in mono-zoned communities or less regionally calibrated buildings meet greater challenges, limitations and/or costs. Equally interesting was to observe that in some of these same cities where affordable housing is scarce, nonetheless, structurally stable buildings - devoid of operable windows- sit vacant, often the by-product of a lack of energy resources or monetary funds to turn on the needed mechanical systems, thereby rendering them inhospitable. Needless to say, their architects did not contemplate that "cheap oil" and personal or national economies might wane.

These are snapshots of current and possible future scenarios, which can easily extend beyond the realm of third world countries or our own impoverished neighborhoods, into mainstream society, should irresponsible energy consumption and building continue to outpace sound practices and designs, and, the dependence on mechanical systems not be tempered by or partnered with passive 'alternatives'.

Currently, in several countries, very effective standards encourage architects to develop projects which embrace recycling, reuse and innovations. Valuable as those standards remain, their heavy reliance on technologies make them less relevant in the context of people and places that can ill afford to purchase and/or over time maintain those systems. By elevating the fundamental role of typological and morphological decision-making - of 'passive design' - all projects and places can benefit, irrespective of current or future economies, impacting not only our environment but our spirit, - that of individuals and society. For this reason, present benchmarking standards should further embrace, better value and reward the inclusion of 'passive' methods; as for example has been accomplished with LEED-ND.

The *Under the Sun* symposium underlined the camaraderie between tradition and innovation and among the intertwined macro and micro scales of sustainability - the city and its increments. The symposium's title was a nod to a conference held in West Palm Beach Florida in 1947, when then President of the *Colegio de Arquitectos de La Habana*, lectured at an AIA event at the Norton Museum, on the necessity for Modern Architecture to 'adapt' to the Tropics *(Arquitectura Bajo el Sol)*. Several of the articles in this publication focus precisely on the post-war era of Modern Regionalist architecture in the Caribbean Basin, a period that exemplifies how architecture can handsomely combine conventional wisdom, originality and technical advancements.

The purpose of the symposium was to promote and discuss sustainable building techniques and practices, relating the topic to the traditions of vernacular architecture and sustainable urbanism. The symposium served as a forum for all interested in 'green' design for temperate and sub-tropical climates, as well as to enhance their knowledge of and to promote 'green' building as a part of a gamut of inherited, 'sustainable' design values. The event was held in collaboration with the University of Miami Law School's Center for Ethics and Public Service and the U.S. Green Building Council - South Florida Chapter. Participants included academics, professionals, government leaders and students from various areas of South Florida, in addition to speakers from around the nation and region, including New Urbanism founders Dean Elizabeth Plater-Zyberk and Jaime Correa; architect Peter Brown and mid-century practitioners Alfred Browning Parker, George Reed and Thomas Jefferson; Carolyn Mitchell, then president of the local US Green Building Council chapter and US Department of Energy consultant, Michael Myers. Lectures 'bridged' between tradition and innovation, looking at 'green', not as a trend, but rather as part of a historical continuum, allowing for the retrieval of design values that have naturally and traditionally accompanied building design-- thus expanding on current mainstream thinking. The lectures pointed to lessons from our past and more recent history that are relevant to present and future generations of designers and offered alternative concepts, to current technologically oriented methods, proposing that 'sustainable design' embrace urban and building traditions that conserve energy and materials, which often also represent more financially viable alternatives.

INTRODUCTION

Elizabeth Plater-Zyberk

South Florida lies in the sub-tropics, latitudes that mediate the tropical equatorial circumference and the hemispheric temperate bands. The southern quarter of peninsular Florida is the only part of the United States that belongs to this global climate belt.

The region's native residents thrived as a rural society, hunting, farming, and trading, with lightweight shelters responsive to local climate including periodic destruction by tropical storms. Early twentieth century settlers from the continent to the north and from islands to the south, at first emulated native methods of survival, but soon sought permanence with structures and commerce related to more distant sources. Wood buildings and citrus farms represent the region's inaugural image. Other influences followed: the wood frame house evolved into the wood and stone bungalow, developed under similar climate conditions in India. We are still the only part of the U.S. in which concrete and masonry bearing wall construction dominates. Miami builders continued to emulate practices of similar climate until the mid-century when technological inventions, in particular air-conditioning, increased the comfort of habitation in the sub-tropics.

A century after its first climate-sensitive buildings, South Florida is re-examining the relationship of the built and natural environments. Concerns about energy use, its carbon after-effects, and a growing understanding of the adaption needed for a warming climate, encourage study of alternatives to recent design and building modes. Thus, this series of essays explores what might be learned from design and building practice that preceded cheap energy and mechanical air-cooling, and that can guide the future.

The authors of these eleven essays have been immersed in studies/examination of building design and construction methods characteristic of our region. The region here is not just the South Florida we live in, but indeed the greater Caribbean basin, with its numerous islands and surrounding continental shores that share the characteristics our buildings respond to - heat, sun, rain, humidity, tropical force winds, et cetera. Looking to history for experience gained before widespread energy use for climate mitigation, these essays look to that period of South Florida building when there was a recognition by architects that designing with the climate instead of against it, could produce a lyrical and unique character that would identify this emerging place and their work in a world of intentionally universal modernism.

This collection of essays serves a broad audience. For the student of architecture en route to a professional career it spans the breadth of professional studies – history, theory, design and practice. For the South Florida resident, it describes design, building, living and behavior appropriate for our climate. For the historian it describes that part of the history of our region evidenced in the cultural production of architects.

Following a symposium several years ago, chaired by Sonia Cháo, in which the authors first gathered to share and discuss their research, this knowledge is now presented with the intention that it be a continuing inspiration for community and building design as South Florida continues to grow and adapt to its evolving climate.

Jindee, Fruit Vendor Oblique, Australia, Jaime Correa

SUSTAINABLE URBANISM:
creating rooted and enduring places

SUSTAINABLE URBANISM:
a traditional agenda beyond science and business development

Jaime Correa

Figure 1. Public Space in Finca Sasay, Plan, Northern Guatemala, Jaime Correa
Figure 2. (Opposite Page) Public Space in Finca Sasay, Perspective, Northern Guatemala, Jaime Correa

"More than any other time in history, mankind faces a crossroads. One path leads to despair and utter hopelessness; the other, to total extinction. Let us pray we have the wisdom to choose correctly." -Woody Allen

Publishing a transcript of a speech given years ago is not easy. A prior record of the content of our minds makes us nauseous about our own deliverance and conclusions; not that the ideas seem to be scientifically wrong, but they appear to be trivial in contrast to the compassion and understanding we hold in the present. So, I am writing this document because my conscience leaves me no other choice; however, it is not intended to be a mirror of self but, the latest compilation of findings regarding the future of urbanism in an age of collapse.

A prediction of the future requires a prophetic approach; and, I am certainly not endowed with such a precious gift. Prophets are generally offended by those who don't listen, pessimistic by their predicament, and reproachful of their unappreciative audiences. I would much rather think that my audience is intelligent and that I can easily bring about awareness while raising our collective voices in order to make social and physical transformations occur, at a time when they are really needed. As Rev. Martin Luther King remarked, "There comes a moment when silence is betrayal" and, that time has come for all of us.[1]

SASAY
BIBLIOTECA
1225
1301

When looking into a crystal ball for future scenarios, whether we are futurologists or fortune tellers, the scope of the experience is likely to make humble men and women of all of us. "Trying to predict the future," business consultant Peter Drucker once said, "is like trying to drive down a country road at night, with no lights, while looking out the back window."[2] That's why it is particularly meaningful when someone steps out and bets its professional reputation on a limited amount of controversial scenarios; and, as far fetched as it may sound, I am willing to do so in the context of this document.

Nature as a Receptor of American Urbanism

At the foundation of the modern environmentalist program is the notion that there is an intrinsic human connection with nature; this proto-Buddhist belief was shared, in the nineteenth century, by the members of the Transcendentalist Movement of Massachusetts. Nature, with its symbolic and spiritual content, was considered to be a source of guidance and a mirror reflecting back the mystery and inner intelligence of the universe. The works of Ralph Waldo Emerson and Henry Thoreau helped established the American notion of nature as a teacher of majestic lessons and as an ideal place for the location of the human abode. Emerson described our relationship with nature in terms of seven fundamental components supporting our human intuition: commodity, beauty, language, discipline, idealism, spirits, and prospects – principles which were also essential for the enhancement of our civic experience and the creation of a new enlightened society.[3] Thoreau, his friend and disciple, took greater risks to define a simple existence while carrying a self-sufficiency experiment in a small wooden hut next to Walden Pond near Concord, Massachusetts. In his words, "I wished to live deliberately, to front only the essential facts of life, and see if I could not learn what it had to teach, and not, when I came to die, discover that I had not lived."[4]

Although a cycle of learning was completed by the philosophers of the Transcendentalist Movement, the nineteenth century also marked the beginning of the Industrial Revolution and its three most important corollaries: first, the social alienation and despair caused by rapid urbanization; second, the unbridle consumption of our natural resources; and third, the greatest financial and economic greed in the history of human civilization. In this context, the transcendental pastoral vision of simplicity gained much appeal to those for whom life was full of confusion, distraction, and complexity. Cities were repelled as places of damnation while suburbia gained impetus through the manifestation of transcendental moral principles.

The invention of the oil-powered automobile engine and the car suburb strained the capacities of individuals, organizations, agencies, and administrators in ways both strange and overpowering. With the Industrial Revolution, and its dependency on fossil fuels, urban and rural areas were certainly stepping off into a precipice and into an era of extraordinary change. And to add greater tensions into the modern recipe for urbanization, a legal 1926 precedent (*Ambler v Euclid*) made it illegal to put houses, stores, and businesses in close proximity within the same neighborhood. As a result, America ended up with standard boiler-plate zoning laws which advocated car dependency and devastated the traditional notion of anthropometric design; despite the fact that everything in America was measured in feet, we could not get anywhere on foot anymore.

Since 1950, America has built more than 50 million suburban homes, the equivalent of 38 million football fields covered with asphalt for roads and parking lots, billions of square feet of malls and office parks, and about 30 million acres of suburban lawn. Suburbia has become an oil-dependent, land-hungry, conglomeration of secured homes isolated from schools, shopping areas, workplaces, and civic centers. On the opposite side, and to make matters worse, urban centers have lost their collective appeal and, despite their numerous redevelopment efforts, they are still populated by poor migrants, the racially discriminated, or simply occupied by dull towers symbolizing the conglomeration of economic power of greedy developers and financial institutions. In our country, more than 12 million people live in gated communities, 8 million people live in secured apartments, and 2 million people are incarcerated; in other words, approximately 22 million people live behind bars. Little by little, our sense of community has been eroded and our abundance of physical barriers has made it impossible to create the "perfect neighborhood" where everyone knows your name.

Seven Trends Shifting the History of our Civilization

In the current Urban-to-Rural confrontation, we have lost our ability to think about the public interest and the common good; as we continue destroying and displacing wildlife and potential food resources with suburban development, a population explosion is threatening the fundamental principles of our status-quo and our commitment to democratic justice. A confluence of economic, social, cultural, ecological, technological, geopolitical, and military advances is compounding slowly to form our current predicament and its potential for disruptions of unprecedented magnitude.

The world is about to experience a shift unlike anything seen before. Whether our forecast is one of a "heavenly state" -typically associated with exponential advances in technology, or the so-called "hell scenario" – represented by the "gloom-and-doom" of our civilization, we are in for a major upheaval that will likely shake our institutions, our socio-economic arrangements, and our political systems. Our civilization is witnessing transformations that require us to think about humans, nature, and the configuration of urbanism in ways which we never dare to imagine. Seven indicators are already pointing a direction towards a new frontier. Let's take a look at what is happening:

1. *Population Growth*: More people have been born during the last one hundred years than in all the preceding five thousand. Humanity threatens to achieve what living systems almost never do, suffocate itself. Between the years 1900 and 2009 the planet's population grew a little bit under seven times to an estimated 6.8 billion people; at the current rate of growth of 2.5 people per second, there will be 7.3 billion by 2016 and approximately 9.0 billion by 2050.[5] But, these figures don't become a challenge until one realizes that first, approximately half of the population is younger than 25 and the other half is aging rapidly to reach a life expectancy without precedent; when the average life expectancy in 1950 was approximately 45 years of age, the current world population life expectancy is 70, and by 2050 it is estimated to be 150 years of age.[6] Secondly, in the developed world there are more elderly than young people; and, in the less developed world more youngsters than elderly –to our demise, this young population is basically illiterate and survives on less than one dollar a day. In this quandary, the remaining question is: who will take care of whom?

2. *Carrying Capacity*: As human population continues to expand, and finite resources are divided among larger numbers of people, it will become more difficult to maintain our existing levels of prosperity and quality of life. Our current global population is being maintained only through the exhaustion and dispersion of our limited natural resources. This rapid depletion of essential resources, coupled with a worldwide degradation of urbanized land and atmospheric quality, indicates that the human enterprise has not only exceeded its current carrying capacity, but it is actually reducing the same potential for future generations. Clearly, human numbers can not continue to increase indefinitely. The usual consequence for an animal population that exceeds its biophysical carrying capacity is its population decline, brought about by a combination of increased mortality, reduced fecundity, and massive migration. Resources are already severely limited, and there is emerging evidence that natural forces are beginning to control human population numbers through malnutrition and other severe diseases. As reported by Professor David Pimentel and his colleagues, at Cornell University, "more than 3 billion people worldwide are already malnourished, and 3 billion are living in poverty; grain production per capita started declining in 1984 and continues to decline; irrigation per capita declined starting in 1978 and continues; arable land per capita declined starting in 1948 and continues; fish production per capita started declining in 1980 and continues; supplies essential for food production started declining in 1989 and continues to do so; loss of food to pests has not decreased below 50% since 1990; and pollution of water, air, and land has increased, resulting in a rapid increase in the number of humans suffering from serious, pollution-related diseases."[7] Humanity is approaching a crisis point with respect to the interrelated issues of population, food production, water, air, energy, urbanization, economic equity, global security, and sustainability.

3. *Informal Urbanization*: Crowded together in the phantasmagoria of the metropolis or separated by artificial moats in the loneliness of suburbia, we no longer recognize the face of our neighbors or the scale of our territorial enterprises; with rare exceptions, our current notion of community is blurred and inhuman. In the suburban territory, and within the last ten years of inefficient land use planning, the U.S. has paved more than 6 million acres of top-quality farmland and about 5 million acres of agricultural land - the approximate size of the State of Maryland;[8] meanwhile, the generational gap described above and the current imbalance of population distribution is contributing to high growth in some areas and acute depopulation in other. To make matters worse, a little bit over fifty percent of humanity (3.5 billion) lives in informal peripheral cities where strenuous economic conditions promise a bleaker future than the present.

4. *End of Cheap Oil*: In 1956, Marion King Hubbert, a geoscientist who worked at the Shell Research Laboratory in Houston, predicted that oil production in the United States would peak around 1970 and, he turned out to be right. By 1974, Hubbert predicted, once again, that worldwide oil production would peak around 1995; but, this time, it did not happen due to the crisis of the late 1970's. However, scientists supporting Hubbert's calculations predicted that global oil production would peak by no later than 2015, and possibly already did as early as 2004. In fact, oil production has already peaked in 50 countries around the world.[9] Global energy supply and consumption is becoming less and less sustainable. We appear to have initiated the end of the "Cheap Oil Era" and with it, the end of the fossil fuel based civilization we built within the last one hundred and fifty years.[10]

5. *Climate Change*: Our planet has a fever. As Fred Pearce, a New Scientist author, stated, "earth is already as warm as at any time in the last 10,000 years, and is within one degree of being its hottest for a million years".[11] Meanwhile, James Hansen, the popular NASA mad-scientist, has insisted that, if the planet gets one degree warmer, it could trigger the irreversible melting of the Greenland ice sheet; the melted ice would cause a dramatic rise in sea levels (2-3 meters) and the flooding of all major coastal cities would require us to draw a new map of the world while creating human migrations of unprecedented proportions. Altered climate patterns would result in severe droughts, crop failures, famine, and possible mass starvation. Desperate wars could erupt over dwindling supplies of food and other resources. And, equally importantly, if the mountain glaciers of the Himalayas, Andes, and Rockies disappear, the billions of people who depend on them for fresh water would be left dry and desolate while the prodigious frozen deposits of the highly potent greenhouse gas methane would be released from permafrost and even from below the Arctic Ocean. Violent conflict over vanishing sources of water could very well become the "oil wars" of the future.

6. *Technological Advances*: We are definitely experiencing an inflection point in history. Technology is allowing us to transcend seemingly impossible physical and mental barriers at an exponential rate. Four interrelated technologies are modifying our understanding of nature and are collectively creating a "new S curve" of change unlike anything we humans have ever seen: electronic information, genetic engineering, nanotechnologies, and robotics. Computation is no longer a discrete experience but a matter of achieving new frontiers at the current 1,000 trillion calculations per second. The completion of the Genome Project, advances in artificial intelligence, and the production of microchips of molecular or atomic size are moving us into a true era of information and scientific development. We are entering an age in which entertainment, working, and learning will be one and the same.

7. *Global Interdependence*: The current socio-economic crisis demonstrates that a genuine global system is coming out of age. As the current government deals with a dead financial structure, economic power is shifting massively and permanently to the European Union and Asia, breaking the link between economic primacy and liberal democracy. As stated by John Petersen, "these changes seem to be driven by an inexorable movement to higher rates of complexity and interdependence that are intrinsic to the human and planetary development process. Globalization is not just an artifact of airplanes and the internet. No, globalization and the knowledge and communications that enable it are what happen to organisms as they move from simpler to more complex forms."[12]

A Sustainable Vision for the Future of Urbanism

In the face of the seven converging indicators above, there seems to be a need for a pragmatic vision; a vision which will blend ethical, moral, political and aesthetical principles in order to produce brand new systems with their own internal coherence. Additionally, our current predicament will force us to consider holistic epistemological and metaphysical approaches, underlying trends in science and technology, and radical social transformations reflecting the re-localization of economic resources and the inevitable urban contractions implied in current development trends. If fully realized, then and only then, a *Novus Homo* will emerge triumphantly from the ashes of the industrial society and its environmental chaos.

The following strategic list can provide a starting point for our venture into a sustainable future:

1. *Clear differentiation between human settlements and countryside*: The countryside is the only kind of nonurban land in existence; its protection is vital to the survival of the human species. We should confine our physical territories to limited geographic areas and expand our mental boundaries to include water, plants, soil, animals and the natural wilderness.

2. *Resolution of the big city v. small village paradox*: While the metropolis may be a cultural asset, the rural settlement is a place of self-sufficiency. Facing the depopulation of large urban areas -due to economic and environmental crises, the decentralization of the global population, and the contraction of sprawling cities across the planet, both cities and villages can coexist as interrelated places of economic, social and political exchange.[13]

3. *Small increments of development*: The neighbor-hood unit shall be the defining element of the urban composition and the small lot its genetic material. Citizens must be able to find everything they need for their daily living at walking distance -including local areas for food and renewable energy production.

4. *Death of functional zoning*: A diversity of land uses is an important key to the ecological health and anthropometric dimensions of human settlements. In an age of sustainability and pollution control, disparate land uses may coexist without damage to human fitness or real estate economic values.

Figure 3. Jindee, Block Oblique, Australia, Jaime Correa

5. *Preservation of agricultural valleys*: The protection of agricultural valleys should become a development priority – even if they are not presently cultivated. Retaining prime farmland near the places where people live shall become the most important re-localization strategy of the future.

6. *Reforestation of wild peripheral gardens*: Since up to a quarter of the existing carbon emissions come from deforestation, the fastest, cheapest way to reduce them is the protection of existing forests and the initiation of a disciplined reforestation of the periphery of human settlements.

7. *Re-localization of food production*: The failure of global supply chains will initiate a reliance on local food suppliers. Fresh, healthy food will be a necessity for sustaining the physical and mental requirements of a new self-sufficient world.

8. *Edible landscapes*: Edible landscapes are an alter-native to conventional ornamental urban landscapes. Edible landscapes should combine fruit and nut trees, berry bushes, vegetables, herbs, edible flowers and ornamental plants into aesthetically pleasing designs for the free use and consumption of the public.

9. *Configuration of civic and open spaces*: Shapeless residual space will be replaced by positive configurations with a certain degree of convexity. Partly enclosed and bounded outdoor open spaces will provide a medium for political participation and social interaction.

10. *Mix of housing types*: A combination of building types will insure a democratic distribution of human and economic assets while providing for a healthier ecological diversity.

11. *Re-localization of jobs*: Large concentrations of jobs will be forbidden. There will be a shift towards small local jobs and community cooperation and away from economic competition and the migratory nature of surpluses.

12. *Reconfiguration of commercial enterprises*: A decentralization and re-localization of jobs will allow the production of live-work units at the neighborhood scale. Due to advances in communication technologies, people will still be able to produce goods and services of enormous complexity while jobs are scattered throughout the globe or the local community.

13. *Cradle to Cradle Industrialization*: Inspired by nature, a new set of design principles are making industry more prosperous and sustainable. According to William McDonough and Michael Braungart, "when designers employ the intelligence of natural systems – the effectiveness of nutrient cycling, the abundance of the sun's energy, they can create products, industrial systems, buildings, even regional plans that allow nature and commerce to fruitfully co-exist."[14]

14. *Light imprint design*: Innovations in sustainable engineering sciences may offer great environmental benefits in the detailing of public and private infrastructure as well as in the preservation of natural hydrological and ecological processes.[15]

15. *Appropriate technologies*: Once a renewable-energy-based world is achieved, we will be inclined to use those technologies designed with consideration to the environmental, ethical, cultural, social and economical aspects of the community they are intended for. These technologies will have a lower overall cost, less impact on the environment, will require fewer resources, and will be easier to maintain.

16. *A redefinition of the notion of mobility*: A pedestrian redefinition of the urban territories will be supported by advances in private transportation technologies and mass transit. Whether the car industry converts quickly to renewable energies or not, conventional hybrid engines, plug-in hybrid electric vehicles, and compressed air technology automobiles are currently shifting the market preferences of consumers all over the globe; in this context, Transit Oriented Development (TOD) will become a priority of the future.

17. *Advances in medicine and a new sense of mortality*: A new era of exponential medical discoveries will allow us to enhance our minds and bodies in ways exceeding the most optimistic forecasts of science fiction. As a result, new life-expectancy thresholds will evolve – and, so will do the corresponding ethical controversies around the topic of human mortality.

18. *Decentralized education*: A traditional system of education will enable the younger generations to learn fundamental crafts and scientific lessons. Schools and universities will disperse classrooms throughout the city to form small urban workshops and spatial clusters where masters and apprentices can work and meet together.[16]

19. *Politics of cooperation and justice for all people*: An equitable global yet local civilization will be worked out. The cultural character of individual societies will relate effectively to the larger world but will not be forsaken in the name of progress or development.

20. *Individual self-realization*: A new understanding of oneself and our untapped metaphysical potentials will allow us to achieve self-realization in all aspects of human activity.

Conclusion

We still have a brief window of opportunity to ensure the continuity of human life on this planet. If we understand the processes of urbanization and sustainable development in their real context, beyond science and business development, we will realize that we just cannot afford to compromise the needs of future generations.[17] And, if we do, it is time to hear their voices begging for leadership, wisdom, and compassion.

Let's not let them down.

Endnotes

[1] King, Martin Luther Jr. *A Testament of Hope: the essential writings and speeches of Martin Luther King Jr.* James M. Washington, Editor. Harpers Collins Publishers, New York, 1991.
[2] Drucker, Peter F. *The Essential Peter Drucker: the best of sixty years of Peter Drucker's essential writings on management.* Harpers Collins Publishers, New York, 2001.
[3] Richardson, Robert Jr., ed. *Ralph Waldo Emmerson: selected essays, lectures and poems.* Bantam Books, New York, 1990.
[4] Krutch, Joseph Wood, ed. *Walden and Other Writing by Henry David Thoreau.* Bantam Books, New York, 1962.
[5] United Nations Development Program. *Human Develop-ment Reports: population indicators*, 2009.
[6] Garreau, Joel. *Radical Evolution: the promise and peril of enhancing our minds, our bodies - and what it means to be human.* Broadway Books, New York, 2006.
[7] Pimentel, D., X. Huang, and A. Cardova. *Environmental Management in Practice, Vol. 1.* Routelage, London, 1998.
[8] American Farmland Trust. *Farming on the Edge: sprawling development threatens America's best farmland,* 2002.
[9] Heinberg, Richard. *Peak Everything: waking up to the century of declines.* New Society Publishers, Canada, 2007.
[10] Kunstler, Jim Howard. *The Long Emergency: surviving the converging catastrophes of the twenty-first century.* Atlantic Monthly Press, New York, 2005.
[11] Pearce, Fred. *Climate Change: one degree and we are done for.* New Scientist, Environment, September 27, 2006.
[12] Petersen, John L. *A Vision for 2012: planning for extraordinary change.* Fulcrum Publishing, Colorado, 2008.
[13] This argument plays an important role in the context of the *Transect Theory* and the *SmartCode* epistemology promulgated by Andres Duany, Elizabeth Plater-Zyberk, et al., as follows: "Urban and Rural areas should coexist along the Transect."
[14] McDonough, William and Michael Braungart. *Craddle to Craddle: remaking the way me make things.* North Port Press, 2002.
[15] Low, Thomas E. *Light Imprint Handbook: version 1.2.* New Urban Press, 2008.
[16] Alexander, Christopher, et al. *The Pattern Language: towns, buildings, construction.* Oxford University Press, New York, 1977.
[17] The most remembered quote of the so-called "Brundtland Worldwatch Institute Report" of 1984 states that, "(sustainable development is) a type of development that meets the needs of the present without compromising the ability of future generations to meet their own needs"; and it adds, "it requires meeting the basic needs of all and extending to all the opportunity to fulfill their aspirations for a better life."

Image Sources

All images courtesy of Jaime Correa.

"STUPID IS AS STUPID DOES" - *Forrest Gump*
Part I - Climate Change: An Intensifying Voice Amongst the Din of Political Pollyannaism[1]

Sonia R. Cháo

Santa Clara, Jaime Correa

Physical scientists and environmentalist shun at the prospects that once again, as occurred in the early 1980's, cheap but now 'unconventional' oil options will sidetrack politicians, economists, and the layperson - including architects and urban designers, from the overriding implications of climate change, thereby protracting global marches towards a zero-carbon planet reliant on renewable resources.

Doomsday sociologists, employing data from physical scientists, predict that the offspring of increasing fossil fuel demands, largely resulting from irresponsible agricultural and industrial practices, and lax public policies, but also due to distended land use patterns and mind-less consumerism, have already set off a ripple effect that in the coming decades will result in untenable and nationwide economic and social tumbles.

Indications of such a scenario first percolated in 1956, when prominent geophysicist M. King Hubert warned of "peak oil"[2] and its impact on the US economy. At the time, he was ridiculed by his peers, elbowed out of the petroleum industry by its leaders, and shunned by his later boss at the U.S. Geological Survey. However, history proved him right as hints of a future energy crisis emerged in the 1960's as demand for electricity in some parts of the country exceeded the 7-to-8% annual growth rate. Some utilities could not build enough capacity, spearheaded by rapid population and industrial growth, resulting in some utility companies reducing voltage output, which in turn resulted in "brownouts" in the summers of 1967 through 1969.[3] The growing problem was further compounded when domestic "conventional" crude oil productions crested in the 1970's.[4]

The energy crisis of 1973-74 was triggered by the U.S. reaching "peak oil" production in 1971 as well as by OPEC's oil embargo of 1973." The United States depended on OPEC oil for under 15% of the country's petroleum needs, but it proved critical for transportation and industrial needs. The price hikes undulated throughout the energy industries and caused alternative fuels, such as coal, to increase in price as well. As one manifestation of the energy crisis, Americans impatiently waited in lines at gas stations to pay higher prices for rationed petroleum products.

As another indicator, the higher energy prices caused the cost of other goods to increase, spurring the inflation rate to jump to about 10% by early 1975. Moreover, investors in the U.S. stock market had little to celebrate. As consumers spent more money on energy and less on other goods, business activity slowed, and the Dow Jones Industrial average dropped 45% from its 1973 high to its 1974 low. President Nixon urged the country to conserve resources and develop new sources of energy, so that the country would become energy self-sufficient by 1980. However, incapacitated politically by the Watergate scandal, Nixon could not lobby successfully with Congress to pass effective emergency legislation in 1973 or 1974."[5] Federal attention on the energy debate in fact waned for a brief period as oil prices leveled off.

Not surprisingly, in 1979, yet another energy crisis arose, the co-mingled by-product of political upheavals in the Middle East and of escalating domestic over-consumption. Directing the predicament were the significant increases in crude oil prices, from $3 to $12 a barrel, the slowing of foreign oil production and increased U.S. dependence on foreign energy resources. President Jimmy Carter reacted in good stead, further empowering the Department of Energy he had already created, issuing a battery of energy-efficiency measures. Congress responded with complimentary incentive programs and restrictions, resulting in the Solar Energy Research, Development and Demonstration Act and the Federal Non-Nuclear Research and Development Act. Carter addressed the American public, saying, "We simply must balance our demand for energy with our rapidly shrinking resources. By acting now, we can control our future instead of letting the future control us."

But, "*stupid is as stupid does.*"[6]

Less than a decade later, as foreign oil prices leveled off and domestic crude oil discoveries increased so too did the nation's shortsightedness, and as prices dropped so too conservation measures declined. The unsexy rallying calls of scientists and environmentalist advocating responsible stewardship of the planet, partially reliant on Americans containing their over-indulgent consumption of goods, energy, and the land, for all intents and purposes fell largely on deaf ears.

Instead, in unabashedly self-serving tenors, Americans in need of their energy fix, rooted for the ventures of oil-seeking 'cowboys' in Texas, Alaska, and the Gulf of Mexico - they in turn, the personifications of the country's reckless and blindly optimistic and self-serving mindset. Mirroring the spirit of the times, Hollywood's very timely fictional and iconic J.R. Ewing, glamorized, and underlined the brashness of the era. Perversely, the nation reveled in the gushing successes of the oil industry and turned a blind eye away from the real underlying problems and their mounting environmental consequences. For the third time in as many decades, swept under the rug were the warning signs, the evidence, and the lessons derived from both science and firsthand experiences. Profit and comfort spoke louder.

In fact, amidst the din of Pollyannaism, but a few voices of reason were heard coming from Capitol Hill during and much since this period. Holding the first congressional hearings on climate change, toxic waste, and global warming in 1976, then U.S. House of Representative Al Gore, became David to the Oil Industry Goliath. The hearings underlined the urgency of climate change and called for cleaner air and water, as well as a reduction in emissions of carbon dioxide and other greenhouses gases. As Vice-president, Gore pushed for the passage of the Kyoto Protocol, only to be defeated by a sclerotic Senate - his ceremonial signage of the Treaty rendered meaningless. When his political platform vanished, Gore collaborated with scientists, economists and entrepreneurs on different occasions,[7] including the 2006 documentary film entitled, *An Inconvenient Truth*,[8] which shed added light on the fundamentally silenced issues related to the 'anthropogenic degradation' of the environment. In 2007, Gore and the Intergovernmental Panel on Climate Change shared the Nobel Peace Prize, "for their efforts to build up and disseminate greater knowledge about man-made climate change, and to lay the foundations for the measures that are needed to counteract such change."[9] That same year, finally leading by example, the U.S. Congress passed the Energy Independence and Security Act with Section 433, requiring that all new federal buildings and major renovations reduce fossil fuel energy consumption incrementally to carbon neutral by 2030. Nonetheless, by and large, U.S. politicians took little other action, lagged behind the international communities already supporting responsible change, and once more ignored mother-nature's call for change.

However, all along, in the shadows of the political limelight and quietly leading progress towards sustainable goals, were scientists and environmental organizations, diligently continuing their research and efforts despite their periodic forced exile from political and national debates. In the field of Architecture, this growing group included the Rocky Mountain Institute, the US Green Building Council and Architecture2030. Their efforts and those of countless other organizations to 'green' the planet, found wind under their sails, in some measure thanks to the 2006 documentary drawing a new audience and group of supporters: politically active, young voters, who increasingly aware that they are inheriting an ailing planet, became a national voting bloc - a force to be reckoned with in the 2007 elections. That said, the 2007-2008 Global Financial Crisis was an equally forceful game changer, on many levels, and itself the result of rampant greed, deregulation, over-consumption and an artificial economy.

Considered by many economists to have been the worst financial crisis since the Great Depression of the 1930's, it resulted in the near collapse of large financial institutions, bank bailouts, and free-falling stock markets. Across the U.S., housing markets also suffered, resulting in foreclosures and protracted unemployment, especially in construction related industries, affecting large swaths of professionals and blue-collar workers. The repercussions devastated key businesses and the ensuing instability affected America's GDP and currency rate.

The economic downturn also resulted in a reduction of consumer spending, sprawling developments, and energy consumption - ironically, from the perspective of scientists and environmentalist, all good things, although brought about by volatile and punitive circumstances that no one welcomed.

The Crisis not only heralded the need to restructure financial institutions, but also underlined the nation's consequent fragile political position on the global stage, again partially attributable to socially and financially unsustainable practices and their undeniable reflections in private sectors, as rising energy costs increasingly affected economic development.

Some limited measures have been introduced in the private and the public sectors including benchmarking tools and incentive programs.

Federal agencies and those they intend to serve are increasingly impacted by the rise of energy costs and they are thusly, albeit sluggishly, instituting new energy policies. For example, in a 2008 report to Congress, HUD outlined the many challenges it faces when it comes to energy policy, referencing its own 2006 report, *Promoting Energy Efficiency at HUD at a Time of Change*, which had identified 25 key actions to accomplish its aims to conserve energy. HUD's Energy Action Plan, provided information, incentives, and technical assistance to HUD consumers, partners, and other housing providers to assist in the development or design of new housing and in the management, maintenance, or operation of existing stock. In addition, in recognition that utility bills burden the poor and can cause homelessness, HUD developed the Home Energy Affordability Gap Index, based on energy bills for individuals below the Federal Poverty Level. The Index illustrates that the burden on the poor is more than four times that of the average 4 percent others pay.[10] Moreover, HUD programs are impacted likewise by energy costs. HUD's own "energy bill" - the amount that HUD spends annually on heating, lighting, and cooling its portfolio of public and assisted housing and section 8 vouchers - reached the $5 billion mark in 2007.

As a result, the cornerstone of HUD's energy programs is the Energy Star label - both Energy Star-qualified products and Energy Star-qualified new homes, are now a widely recognized benchmark of energy efficiency. More recently, HUD has partnered with the Environmental Protection Agency and the U.S. Department of Energy to encourage its affordable housing partners to build to the Energy Star standard for new homes or to buy Energy Star-qualified products and appliances. "The Energy Independence and Security Act, enacted in December 2007, requires HUD to update its minimum energy standards for public, assisted, and insured housing to "meet or exceed" the 2006 International Energy Conservation Code. In addition to these energy-related activities, HUD is beginning to address a broader green building agenda... Intended to complement the growing number of national green housing initiatives, such as the Enterprise Green Communities program, LEED for Homes, the Energy Star Plus Indoor Air Package, and the National Association of Home Builders' (NAHB) Green Building Guidelines."[11] Of equal or greater importance, Congress directed HUD and the Federal Transit Administration to create an interagency Working Group on transportation and housing to encourage the development of 'transit-oriented', affordable housing.

Since 2008, in response to the financial crisis, in addition to industry targeted economic measures, President Obama has promoted innovative energy sources, including wind, solar, biomass, water and geothermal alternatives thereby addressing economic woes by attempting to spur innovative, climate-friendly job sectors. Under his tenure, the production of renewable energy from wind and solar has doubled in the U.S., although these remain a miniscule portion overall.[12] As Carter and Gore before him, the Obama administration has re-focused the nation's political debate onto climate change, instituting reforms at the Federal level, but also encouraging Americans to pursue businesses related to renewable resources and more sustainable practices and visions. Nonetheless, more robust responses are needed to more effectively guide change. Given the magnitude of intersecting environmental, financial and social woes, politicians, scientists, and urban designers/planners should avoid the slippery slope of complacency or denial that previous generations have traveled. The linchpin to future economic, social, and environmental health in the U.S. lies in a comprehensive approach, at all scales of public and private sectors, to incentivize the country's transition towards sustainable practices and a cleaner, energy-efficient economy.

Calibrating Politics, Cities and the Environment

At one end of the spectrum, in lieu of responsible reform, social scientists and economists, promoting consumptionist practices as a method for climbing out of the financial crisis, are selling energy junkies on new forms of potentially cheap, plentiful conventional resources. Their 'fixes' include the 'fracking' of natural gas, already underway in the U.S. and seen by some as a "bridging fuel," to be followed eventually by bounties of *manna* from deep underwater troves of methane-hydrate. Forecasters inside the industry predict that within two decades the needed technologies will have been developed, making methane-hydrate extraction economically viable and capable of yielding quantities vastly surpassing expected demands. This would place countries such as Japan and the United States, both which sit on stockpiles of the methane-hydrate, outside of the quest for conventional fossil fuels, thusly altering current geo-political stances as well. Nonetheless, even in the best of scenarios, methane-hydrate would do little to lessen over-consumption of natural resources and albeit lower, it would remain a source of noxious emissions. In any case, this source of energy only becomes an option - as a growing number of scientists fear - if the warming waters of the ocean don't first melt the methane-hydrate's 'ice-cocoons', releasing potentially lethal amounts of the gas into the atmosphere first.[13]

Physical scientists and environmentalists shirk at the possible repeat of the 1980's scenarios, whereby low-priced but now 'unconventional' fossil fuel alternatives could ostensibly sidetrack decision-makers as well as citizens - including architects and urban designers - from the superseding repercussions of climate change, hence weakening international initiatives towards a zero-carbon planet reliant on renewable resources.

In great measure, the fears of physical scientists and environmentalist are valid and stem from several inter-related forces, which too often direct the currents of public policy: profitability scenarios, uninformed public perceptions, complacency, and the power of special interests. Besides, across contemporary US history, the long-standing relationships between political conflicts, economic boons, and cheap oil notoriously have led to environmental disregard, which in turn has fed misguided notions related to fossil fuel and land consumption. In fact, environmental scientists can plot the correlations between energy consumption and economic outputs, as well as map America's recessions in relation to energy costs and pollution emission patterns.

As recent history has again illustrated, among those factors, America's economy is closely tied to its construction related industries and those sectors in turn effectively rely on energy sources to build, therefore the two arenas are co-dependent and again are confronting each other at the crossroad of America's decision-making.

In either the pessimistic (physical scientists & environmentalists) or the optimistic (social scientists & economists) scenario, current efforts to combat climate change are illusive. Scientists point to a need for a "complete phase out of carbon emissions" within half a century and although that would seem non-negotiable, conventional and unconventional forms of fossil fuels sidetrack attention from the pressing need to focus on renewable energy sources and reduced consumption, as well as the other root causes of emissions.

Whereas optimists predict that emerging types of fuel and energy sources will permit heavily oil-consuming nations to continue their current lifestyle routines, often they do not address how those practices would further impact global warming. Furthermore, "the International Energy Agency (IEA) says production of conventional crude oil peaked in 2006,[14] which for the pessimists signifies an impending global depression, initiating "a chain reaction of various feedback mechanisms in the global markets, with catastrophic consequences for industrial civilization because proactive mitigation measures are becoming less viable."[15]

For more than half a century, the 'doomsayer's' camps, have sustained that staving off the arrival of catastrophic global consequences can only be addressed by a windfall of immediate, measurable, local, and national responses to climate change, to achieve a 'zero-carbon' globe by 2030. That would entail replacing obsolete systems, tools, and energy sources with choreographed 'smart' alternatives, over as short a period as possible. This includes promoting a responsible 'holistic' energy policy that works to increase energy efficiency, investments in alternative and renewable sources, while addressing the culprits driving consumption, including those in the fields of architecture, urban design and planning.

The unanswered questions are: "Have we learned any lessons from recent political history? On this occasion, will the voters of this nation listen to scientists over politicians and mercenary private sector lobbyists? Will we as individuals and as a country react in time, commit for the long haul, with the aim of slowing the rate of temperature rise, decreasing the nation's dependence on foreign resources, and create innovative, economically fervent XXI century industries and places on American soil? Predictably, the self-serving, entrenched fossil fuel industry dinosaurs and their chorus of well-funded lobbyist and enabling politicians are all well positioned to continue distracting and delaying progress along these fronts.

Predictions regarding post-peak oil production, price hikes and the global economy vary greatly, but the rising voice of global warming, with every passing super-storm, tornado, flood, and wildfire is logarithmically amplifying and ringing clearer - waiting for and sparing no one. Until every citizen, in every country across the planet, grasps the range and increasingly negative impacts of climate change on their own life and daily routines, significant responses and action will be slow in coming.

In *The Prince*, Niccolo Machiavelli proclaimed: *"There is nothing more difficult to carry out, nor more doubtful of success, nor more dangerous to handle, than to initiate a new order of things."* Yet, nature continues to remind individuals, professionals, and governments alike that the multifarious impacts of climate change have arrived and are increasing, thereby warranting political, social, and physical modifications, ownership of both individual and collective responsibilities, as well as pro-active action - precisely a 'new order' - now.

There are no miracle pills, Stupid.

Endnotes

[1] This series of four related articles were updated in 2011.
[2] *Peak Oil*, a term coined by Hubert, is the point in time when the maximum rate of global petroleum extraction is reached, after which the rate of production enters terminal decline.
[3] www.history.com/topics/energy-crisis
[4] http://americanhistory.si.edu/powering/past/h3main.htm
[5] Ibid
[6] Popular wisdom from the movie: *Forrest Gump*
[7] Gore established an investment management firm, the web-based *We Can Solve It* organization, and in 2007 partnered with Richard Branson, announcing the Virgin Earth Challenge. In 2008, Gore's Alliance for Climate Protection created the Repower America project to promote a switch towards renewable resources.
[8] The film was accompanied by a publication entitled, *An Inconvenient Truth: The Planetary Emergency of Global Warming and What We can do about it.* New York: Rodale Books
[9] http://www.nobelprize.org/nobel_prizes/peace/laureates/2007/, Retrieved 2008
[10] Ibid
[11] Implementing HUD's Energy Strategy Progress Report *U.S. Department of Housing and Urban Development Office of Policy Development and Research Energy Task Force* Submitted Pursuant to Section 154 Energy Policy Act of 2005
[12] http://www.barackobama.com/environment/
[13] Interview with Dr. Rick Wanninkhof, NOAA/AOML, Ocean CO2 Carbon Dioxide Information Analysis Center, May, 25 2012
[14] "Has the World Already Passed "Peak Oil"?," *National Geographic News*, November 9, 2010
[15] Joe Bel Bruno, "Oil Rally May Be Economy's Undoing," *USA Today Associated Press, 2008*

"STUPID IS AS STUPID DOES" - *Forrest Gump*
Part II - At the Intersection of Sprawl, Poverty, and Climate Change

Sonia R. Cháo

The scientific evidence that our world is warming is unmistakable. According to the Intergovernmental Panel on Climate Change (IPCC) and a majority of scientists, most of the observed warming of the last 50 years is primarily due to the increase in greenhouse gas concentrations. *America's Climate Choices*, a 2011 report requested by Congress, confirms that "communities across the Nation are already experiencing a range of climatic changes, including more frequent and extreme precipitation events, longer wildfire seasons, reduced snowpack, extreme heat events, increasing ocean temperatures, and rising sea levels." The report also "reaffirms that the preponderance of scientific evidence points to human activities - especially the release of carbon dioxide and other greenhouse gases into the atmosphere - as the most likely cause for most of the global warming that has occurred over the last several decades. These trends cannot be explained by natural factors such as internal climate variability or changes in incoming energy from the sun. The report adds that the impacts of climate change on human and natural systems can generally be expected to intensify with warming."[1] With each ton of greenhouse gas emitted into the atmosphere, the risks escalate. Studies including those by the U.S. National Research Council, underscore the urgent need for substantial action by governments to limit the magnitude of climate change and to prepare to adapt to its impacts. Therefore, in the near term, in alignment with scientific data and recommendations, significant decreases of greenhouse gas emissions should be among the highest priorities in the national response, in particular because consequent impacts are not necessarily manifested immediately, yet can persist for centuries afterwards. A coordinated national response, across all levels of government, towards climate change is warranted. Interestingly, the inter-related ways in which humans affect and are affected by climate are engendering inter-disciplinary investigations, from which multi-pronged solutions are possible. In those triangulations, architecture and urban planning are great malefactors, beginning with inefficient buildings and ending with disabled human settlement patterns, yet both can potentially serve as transformational pathways to 'climate compatible development,' adaptation, resiliency, responsibility, along with social, physical and cultural well-being.

Architecture and Climate Change

According to the United States Global Change Research Program, since the mid-1700's at the onset of the Industrial Revolution, concentrations of carbon dioxide (CO2), methane (CH4), and nitrous oxide (NO2) in the atmosphere have increased significantly and caused an increase in global average temperature. Atmospheric concentrations of these three gases are higher at present than at any other time in recorded human history, increasing at exponential rates.[2] The accumulation of natural and anthropogenic sources of greenhouse gases in the atmosphere is driving the increase in global temperature and other climatic changes.

In recent years, conversations related to sustainable design have focused primarily on reducing a building's contributions to greenhouse gas emissions through measurable benchmarks (i.e. LEED). This remains an important pursuit, given that "according to the U.S. Energy Information Administration (EIA), the Building Sector consumes nearly half (48.7%) of all energy produced in the United States (40% for building operations, 8.7% for building construction).[3] Seventy-six percent (75.7%) of all electricity produced in the U.S. goes to operate buildings and, globally, these percentages are even greater. The Building Sector was responsible for nearly half (46.7%) of U.S. CO2 emissions in 2010.[4]

However, in partnership with those assertive benchmarking means to reduce the building industry's consumption of natural resources, inherited passive building design methods represent a cost-friendly 'partner' or even alternative in certain economically restrained circumstances, with equal to if not greater impact on overall consumption needs precisely because they are typically much more affordable. Therefore, a coupling of assertive benchmarking initiatives with greater value placed on passive design methods represents the most efficient manner to promote less consuming, healthier buildings across a wider swath of society while incorporating design features that can converse with local vernaculars and cultural identity. Moreover, also important are the role of historic preservation and projected building trends over the coming decades.

As of 2010, the total U.S. building stock is approximately 275 billion square feet. During normal economic times, approximately 1.75 billion square feet of buildings each year are torn down. Every year, approximately 5 billion square feet are renovated.[5] Every year, new construction accounts for approximately another 5 billion square feet. And, therein lies the silver-lining. "By the year 2035, approximately three-quarters (75%) of the built environment will be either new or renovated. This transformation over the [coming] years represents a historic opportunity for the architecture and building community to avoid dangerous climate change."[6]

Political Posturing vs. The Science of Climate Change

In 1987, the United Nations' Brundtland Commission, defined 'sustainable development' as "the preservation of livable, inspiring, enduring and equitable places, where the quality of life and the long-term quality of human existence will be enhanced rather than depleted." By contrast, since the Industrial Revolution, human activities have increasingly added to the naturally occurring greenhouse gases in the atmosphere thereby worsening the health of the planet.

In recent decades, developing countries experiencing population boons and shifts in their economic base, such as China, India, and Brazil, have logarithmically increased hazardous emissions in the name of economic development, and in conjunction with other countries, such as Japan, Russia, and the European Union are hastening climate change. Curiously, the US, Japan, and the European Union, consume 78% of all Chinese exports, illustrating the interconnectedness of both a global economy and global responsibility.

However, long before these and other emerging countries began their upward climb of emissions, the United States, during the past half century in particular, has consistently been, and to this day is, a leading contributor of CO2 emissions. Presently, the entire globe is reaping the consequences of past and current offences. As the cast of culprit countries increases, so too do the contraventions and the politically driven justifications or finger pointing that have stalled progress.

While politicians posture, debate and negotiate, scientists are overwhelmingly on the same page. According to NOAA's[7] *2009 State of the Climate Report*, "in the coming decades, scientists expect climate change to have an increasing impact on human and natural systems." More than 300 scientists, from 160 research groups in 48 countries, contributed to the report, which confirms that the past decade has been the warmest on record and that the Earth has been growing warmer over the last 50 years. All the carbon dioxide humans have released into the air has warmed the world about 0.8°C above pre-industrial levels.

The quickening pulse of global warming may now be intensifying droughts and other extreme weather events in the United States and across the planet. For example, "satellites that measure the distance from their orbit to the ocean's surface show that global sea level is getting higher. Rising waters threaten ecosystems, freshwater supplies, and human developments along coasts."[8] According to a coastal impact study entitled *Nation Under Siege*, "beginning with just one meter of sea level rise, our nation would be physically under siege, with calamitous and destabilizing consequences."[9]

Cities and Climate Change

There is increasing consensus in global policy and within scientific circles that stabilizing emission at a level associated with a 2 degree C (3.6 F) average warming is essential to avert the most critical impacts of climate change to human and natural systems. In order to remain within this 2 degree C threshold, in the long term, CO2 concentrations must stabilize near current levels.[10] According to the U.S. Environmental Protection Agency, varying manifestations of climate change affect our society, impacting social, cultural, and natural resources, including human health, infrastructure, and transportation systems, as well as energy, food, and water supplies.[11] In a warmer world, accessibility to these basic life-sustaining resource chains, to raw materials, and energy are expected to change further and have a direct impact on human settlements. A settlement's measure of sustainability and impact on the environment can be defined by these yard-sticks as well as by its land-use development patterns, the availability of local and regional mass transit systems, efficient building designs, the production of building goods, industries, availability of open green spaces, as well as its farming and industrial practices. Collectively, these forces influence the consumption of fossil fuels, levels of pollution and the health and availability of natural resources, while influencing the overall quality of life of inhabitants.

An assessment by UN-Habitat,[12] has determined that by the year 2030, 59% of the world's population will live in urban centers with developed countries as the most urbanized at 81%. Cities currently occupy 2% of the surface of the planet, yet they host over 50% of the world's population and are responsible for 70% of greenhouse gas emissions.

The study entitled *Cities and Climate Change: Global Report on Human Settlements 2011*, points out that "while cities [are] energy intensive, effective urban planning could deliver huge savings." Urban areas are set to become the battleground in the global effort to curb climate change," the study warned, predicting a "deadly collision between climate change and urbanization" if no action is taken. How cities manage their impact on the environment lies near the core of the problem. The matter is complicated when in some cases, those urban cores are located in coastal areas that are most susceptible to climate change and sea levels rising. It is the combination of urbanization's fast pace growth and the demand for development that poses the major threat.[13]

"Cities are responsible for the majority of our harmful greenhouse gases. However, they are also places where the greatest efficiencies can be made. This makes it imperative that we understand the form and content of urbanization so that we can reduce our footprint," states Joan Clos Executive Director of UN-HABITAT. "Understanding the contribution of cities to climate change will help interventions at the local level. With better urban planning and greater citizen participation… hot cities can become cool again. To understand and map the impact of cities on climate change, the report highlights the major factors that influence the total and per capita CO2 emissions of urban areas:

- A city's geographic location - influencing the amount of energy required for heating, cooling, and lighting;
- Demographics - the size of the population influences the demand for space and services;
- Urban form and density - sprawling cities tend to have higher per capita emissions than more compact ones;
- The urban economy - types of economic activities and whether these emit large quantities of greenhouse gases;
- The wealth and consumption patterns of urban residents.

The report provided a city-by-city comparison, illustrating how even within countries there are large differences in emissions. For example, in Washington D.C., "overall per capita greenhouse gas emissions are startlingly high compared with other US cities - with a value of 29.7 tons CO2 equivalents per capita each year, compared to a US average of 23.9 tons. Although Washington has very little in the way of industrial activity, it has a relatively small population in relation to the large number of offices for government and related functions thus in this instance, it is not the design of the city but rather the concentration of one use and their consumptive practices that are to blame for the higher emissions. By contrast, New York City's emissions are relatively low for a wealthy city in a developed country. This is the result of high population density, generally small dwelling sizes, an extensive public transport system, and a large number of older buildings that emphasize natural day lighting and ventilation, with an increasing number of which are incorporating energy saving measures.

In further support of mixed-use, pedestrian friendly planning strategies, the report compared US cities to those in Europe and found that the contribution to climate change by urban areas in Europe is relatively low. European cities tend to be more compact and are more apt to have lower car ownership as well as car usage rates, smaller, more fuel-efficient cars, thus reducing emissions related to private transportation. European cities frequently have more effective public transportation networks, which are deemed socially acceptable to a broader range of individuals. Furthermore, urban areas in Europe have higher levels of densification and lower levels of sprawl in comparison to North American cities. "London's overall CO2 emissions in 2006 were 44.3 million tons - representing 8 per cent of the UK's total emissions, and a slight decline from the 45.1 million tons produced in 1990 despite a rise in population of 0.7 million people during the same time period."

Additional studies by the US Green Building Council in 2006 corroborate that many big cities are greener than the average suburb, citing several overlapping reasons:

- Cities are typically compact and have a variety of uses near each other that decrease automobile trips;
- public transit and shorter distances between uses make it easier to get around, including on foot, reducing overall emissions;
- cities have more multifamily housing options, which is usually better for the environment than single-family housing since less land is consumed per dwelling unit;
- in metropolitan areas, open space is generally concentrated for greater public access, and car sharing and communal facilities such as community gardens are more common;
- although urban runoff and industrial pollution can be major issues in metropolitan areas, these are not reduced by sprawl, and
- the segregation of and distance between uses in suburbia make automobiles necessary for most daily tasks, requiring more roads that consume more land and an increasing burden on existing infrastructure networks.[14]

The report concluded that to a sizable extent, the engine of climate change is fueled by the unsustainable characteristics of contemporary human settlements.

Climate Change: Impacts, Planning, Mitigation

In 2010, the International Council for Local Environmental Initiatives (ICLEI),[15] produced a study suggesting that the next step for cities and towns is to understand the assortment of impacts of climate change on local built environments. This in order to manage resources and craft responses, infrastructures and architectural and urban designs today that will be suitable for a range of uncertain futures, mindful of historic trends and current conditions, and with the understanding that energy consumption will increase as climate extremes become the norm.[16] ICLEI introduced a process for climate adaptation planning, similar to its process for climate change mitigation, illustrating a broad scope and comprehensive nature of city climate adaptation plans. These include:

1. Conducting a climate resiliency study,
2. Setting preparedness goals,
3. Developing a climate preparedness plan,
4. Publishing and implementing the climate preparedness plan, and,
5. Monitoring and re-evaluating resiliency.[17]

"Professionals aware of the predicted climate change impacts for their region can incorporate climate adaptation into new buildings and neighborhood designs. Each region of the US will be impacted differently and at varying scales of intensity." Of primary concern is the impact that increasing severity and variability of weather patterns and climate will have on the local built environment.[18] "At the regional scale, numerous elements are susceptible to climate change impacts, including energy(generation, transmission and distribution), water (quality, availability) and transportations systems (cost, reliability) and their future effectiveness. Understanding the drivers of climate change reveals the relationships between cities, neighborhoods and buildings."[19]

Population growth, economic growth, technological development, and energy efficiency improvements make it difficult to predict the long-term climate impacts of greenhouse gas emissions. It therefore makes sense to develop both mitigation and adaptation strategies to reduce emissions and build resiliency.

Suburbia, Emissions and Poverty

What's Driving Emissions?

One of the leading factors in the increase of CO2 levels involves segregated land-use arrangements, specifically, the suburban sprawl that ensued primarily due to XX century Euclidian planning models. The resulting bloated development patterns surrounding cities, has led to car-dependency, longer commutes, and thus increased discharges into the atmosphere. In fact, each US automobile produces on average one pound of CO2 emissions for every mile driven leading to an average US household discharge of 83,000 lbs. per year.[20] The United States has more than 200 million cars traveling almost 4 million miles of road (nationwide roads and parking areas consume 39 million acres of paved surfaces[21]). Every second, these cars travel 60,000 miles, use 3,000 gallons of petroleum products, and add 60,000 pounds of carbon dioxide into the atmosphere - two thirds of the US carbon dioxide emissions.[22] Many of these cars are on the road precisely because 'office parks' are not located near residential 'developments' nor 'shopping malls', and, often in suburbia public transportation networks between these distended mono-use destinations are unreliable and/or infrequent, making them implausible. Furthermore, 90% of the fuel used for transportation is petroleum based, which includes gasoline and diesel, thus in undisputable terms, sprawl spawns additional transportation related CO2 emissions. Thus, by extension, the fragmented and sprawling nature of cities or their expansions are accelerating emissions and climate change. If one of the principal measures of a city's contribution to climate change is its reliance on the automobile, then America's current dependence on the automobile is to be singled-out and largely understood as an incidental by-product of 'conventional' Euclidian zoning, which continues to perpetuate its use and results in overwhelming carbon emissions.

Additionally, gasoline and diesel consumption have geo-political ramifications. "In the early 21st century, Americans continue to rely heavily on foreign oil. The United States consumes about 20 million of the roughly 80 million barrels of oil consumed daily in the world, and three-fifths of that is imported."[23] Conventional fossil fuel reserves are held largely by foreign countries that can fluctuate output to suit their financial or political aspirations and this in turn places the U.S. in a vulnerable position, at times steering its foreign policy and national environmental impact choices towards less than ideal paths.

What's Driving Suburban Poverty?

Place intersects with poverty in ways that can aggravate its challenges. At the private sector end of the economic spectrum, individuals tackle incrementing household expenditures, as energy and gasoline costs rise, exacerbating household finances. According to the 2011 *Confronting Poverty in Suburbia*, study by the Brookings Institution, poverty has catapulted in suburbs as more low-income residents moved to suburbia and as more long-time suburban residents slipped down the economic ladder. The number of poor people in U.S. suburbs rose by 63.6% between 2000 and 2011, from 10 million to well over 16 million people. For the first time, there are now more people living in poverty in the suburbs than in cities.

During the first decade of the XXI century, a number of factors contributed towards these trends, including a global economic downturn as of 2009, but also steering the decline was the continual sprawl outwards of employment opportunities in metropolitan areas. The Brookings study underlines that while "some of the suburban poor enjoy access to quality communities, others face obstacles to economic stability and success that stem from where they live." Poor residents in suburbs must tackle several hurdles, such as '*job mismatch*,' which is when "growth in poverty and growth in employment occur in different parts of the region." This becomes especially problematic for suburbanites dealing with the '*transportation challenge*' that results from limited or absent public transit in many suburban communities, making it more complicated for low-income suburban workers to overcome the '*job mismatch*,' especially if they are unable to afford and maintain a reliable car. Lack of transportation options can also make it more difficult for residents to access critical support services...And many lower-income suburbs include residents who took advantage of programs to expand residential opportunity, but who now find themselves further isolated from social and economic opportunity."[24] According to the findings, policy priorities addressing poverty "must be backed by regional efforts that prioritize and promote equitable development through regional planning" - an essential to sustainable development.

The rapid rise of poverty in suburbs in the first decade of the new millenium, and the fact that suburbs now house more than half the nation's metropolitan poor, should give rise to a serious reevaluation of how poverty is combated and what role segregated land-use patterns play in the equation. If that which ails suburbia remains unchecked, and restricted access to job opportunities and car-dependency persists, the number of suburban poor will rise in the coming decades. "By neglecting suburban poverty's rise, the nation stands to repeat the mistakes of the past and consign millions of new families and communities to a grim future," the study concludes. It therefore stands to reason that suburbia must be retrofitted.

Despite internet and telecommunications innovations, which allow for a degree of 'distant' employment and social interactions - along the same lines that the telegraph and telephone did before them - humans crave opportunities for communal and cultural interaction, furthermore, they are enriched by them. For these added reasons, not only 'geography' matters, but also the psychological and physical aspects, which are conducive to healthy urban environments, prove pivotal. To protect local and national economic engines and society at large, as well as fragile ecosystems entails building 'sustainable communities' that are socially, physically, and environmentally sound as well as resilient to climate change. This can be achieved in great measure by an integrated, climate-literate, responsible approach to the design of cities, towns, and suburbia, coupled with an overhaul of the political and bureaucratic quagmires that too often have slowed progress.[25]

The alternatives are indefensible.

Would the factors driving energy emissions, poverty, isolation, and segregation eventually instigate sub-urbanites to relocate to mixed-use, walkable communities and urban centers, near diversified job centers that are better served by public transport and services? If so, how would the abandonment of the suburbs affect the physical, social, and economic structures of the cities they surround and in turn, how would that reverberate on America's economy? Presently, how can public policy and regulations mitigate the degradation of American cities, towns, and suburbs? Are there ignored lessons in our own recent history both politically and in terms of urban planning?

Endnotes

[1] "Action needed to manage climate change risks; U.S. response should be durable, but flexible." http://www8.nationalacademies.org/onpinews/newsitem.aspx?RecordID=12781
[2] http://www.ipcc.ch/publications_and_data/ar4/wg1/en/faq-2-1-figure-1.html
[3] Prior to 2006, traditional energy data gathering and reporting methods distributed the impact of buildings across various sectors, including industrial, commercial, residential, transportation, and electricity. Architecture 2030 combined the relevant building data contained in each sector, and created a single Building Sector, revealing the extraordinary influence buildings have on energy use, greenhouse gas emissions, and economy.
[4] By comparison, transportation accounted for 33.4% of CO2 emissions and industry for 19.9%.
[5] U.S. Energy Information Administration.
[6] http://architecture2030.org/the_solution/buildings_solution_how#
[7] The National Oceanic and Atmospheric Administration (NOAA) is a federal agency focused on the condition of the oceans and the atmosphere.
[8] http://cpo.noaa.gov/warmingworld/images/TenSignsofaWarmingWorld.jpg
[9] Nation Under Siege-Coastal Impact Study. http://architecture2030.org/hot_topics/nation_under_siege
[10] United States Global Change Research Program
[11] Society Impacts & Adaptation. http://www.epa.gov/climatechange/impacts-adaptation/society.html
[12] The United Nations Human Settlements Programme (UN–HABITAT) is the United Nations' agency for human settlements and promotes socially and environmentally sustainable towns and cities with the goal of providing adequate shelter for all.
[13] Mark Kinver, *UN Report: Cities ignore climate change at their peril.* http://www.bbc.co.uk/news/science-environment-12881779
[14] Larissa Larsen, et al. *Green Building and Climate Resilience: Understanding impacts and preparing for changing conditions*, U.S. Green Building Council, University of Michigan and University of Oregon, 2006 U.S. Green Building Council, 2006
[15] ICLEI is an international association of local governments and national and regional local government organizations, committed to sustainable development, works with local governments across the globe to incentivize international performance-based, results-oriented campaigns and programs. ICLEI USA is the leading membership association of cities & counties committed to climate action, clean energy, and sustainability.
[16] http://www.ipcc.ch/publications_and_data/ar4/wg1/en/faq-2-1-figure-1.html
[17] For more information: and case studies visit: http://icleiusa.org
[18] www.globalchange.gov/ and http://www.globalchange.gov/publications/reports/scientific-assessments/us-impacts/download-the-report
[19] Additional Resource: A. Lowe, OFster and Windkelman. Ask the Climate Question: Adapting to Climate Change Impacts in Urban Regions, 2009, http://www.ccap.org/docs/resources/674/Urban_Climate_Adaptation-FINAL_CCAP6-9-09.pdf
[20] http://www.epa.gov/climate change/ ghgemissions/gases/co2.html
[21] 2006 Statistics, US. Department of Energy
[22] www.epa.gov
[23] http://www.history.com/topics/energy-crisis
[24] Elizabeth Kneebone and Alan Berube, *City Millions: The Rapid Rise of Suburban Poverty.* http://confrontingsuburbanpoverty.org/wp-content/uploads/2013/05/Brookings_Toolkit_Executive-Summary.pdf, The Brookings Institution, 2011
[25] http://cpo.noaa.gov/warmingworld/

"STUPID IS AS STUPID DOES" - *Forrest Gump*
Part III - The DNA of American Cities: the good, the bad and the ugly

Sonia R. Cháo

A Glimpse into Western Place-Making Traditions and their Influence on North American Urban Design Patterns

The design of cities lies among human civilization's greatest achievements, with each new increment a historical reflection of the aspirations of its people. At times, settlements have arisen spontaneously, the product of happenstance, but more often than not, and for better or worse, they have been 'designed'. Across time, in sliding degrees, architects, engineers, politicians, religious leaders, and/or public health officials have guided the envisioning process, focused on spatial form, the interactions between humans, nature and the built environment, commerce and/or defense.

The unique dialogues across history, between human beings and their architecture, town planning practices and the natural realm, provide valuable lessons capable of guiding present thinking. Discerning the DNA of past and present place-making strategies evidences the repercussions of the unchecked consumption of natural resources on the one-hand, and on the other-hand, the value of time-honored planning strategies, which promote self-sufficient, mix-use, walkable communities, thereby identifying what has been lost in the contemporary designs and coding of American cities.

In many instances, older cities in the U.S. can trace their place-making traditions back to European antecedents; often those of English or Spanish lineage, which in turn were informed to a greater or lesser degree, by Greek and Roman traditions.

The early discovery and rediscovery of patterns of order, harmony, proportions, and beauty in nature were consciously incorporated into the design of buildings and towns by multiple civilizations.[1] Religious/political leaders, scientists, astrologers, and/or architects converged their beliefs regarding sophisticated natural patterns with their design principles; seeking either to reflect the higher 'divine' order of the natural realm or to directly engage it through designs and layouts. The layout of early Greek settlements by Hippodamus of Miletus and the planning of ancient cities across Eastern and Western cultures comprise noteworthy early examples of regularized self-sustaining urban communities. In Western cultures, the regularized pattern of Greek settlements informed the organization of Etruscan settlements and eventually Roman encampments and forts (*castra* and *castellum*). As of the 5C BC, their predominant compositional traits were evident across the European continent, organizing cities such as London, Paris, and Barcelona. The earliest recorded advice to architects in ancient architectural treatises pointed to sympathetic siting of settlements and the placement of buildings and their openings for prevailing, benevolent breezes, as well as harnessing or protection from the sun and rain.

In the centuries between the Roman and Spanish colonization periods, arose the more organically composed, yet highly walkable and dense urban centers of medieval towns, the genetic material of which is legible in places such as Venice and Sienna. The irregular layout of such settlements was often a response to topography and/or the quality of sub-soils. Architect and historian Christopher Alexander has argued that the harmony and beauty of medieval towns is directly attributable to the value founders placed on the inherent lessons and cues uncovered in a given location. The precise environment and its logical referencing guided building, informed by a mimicking process, similar to that occurring in 'living structures'.[2]

Since Plato first wrote his philosophical exploration entitled *Republic*, numerous attempts to conceive or develop "Ideal City" plans surfaced. During the Renaissance, the concept resurrects, appearing from the second half of the fifteenth century onward. Renaissance scholars and nobility, seeking to imitate the qualities of Classical civilizations make several attempts to develop ideal city plans along similar lines.

Mindful of Roman antecedents, the planning, regulation and design of 16th - 20th century Hispanic-American settlements[3] are of special note, given their consistency and rigor. Although separated by many centuries, Roman and Spanish place-making strategies share common denominators, including the most evident - a gridiron arrangement, with square or rectangular layouts, according to size of legion or projected population; anchored by civic structures and agricultural lands, in service of a set number of residents. Aqueducts provided water for irrigation and general consumption. Each settlement intended as a self-sufficient unit.

Standardized plans, dimensions, and the types and placement of civic features made way-finding simpler for both Roman and Spanish colonizers. Compositions were centered on a main square, known as the 'forum' or main 'plaza', surrounded by structures for civic and/or military leaders, and from which a plot's distance reflected military or social standings. From the central square, two principal roads, in Roman times denoted as *decumanus maximus* and *cardo maximus*, led to the perimeter gates and defined the composition into quadrants, each in turn centered on its own public space and secondary civic functions. Encampments and towns were typically walkable, dense and flanked by agricultural fields that contributed towards self-sufficiency and commerce.

In both the Roman and Spanish periods, the vast colonization of new territories was guided by precise decrees, ordinances, or "grand strategies," intended to institute order, rule, and predictable expansions, which led to their characteristic geometrical layouts. As described by Vitruvius in his *Ten Books on Architecture* (1 century BC) and defined by the Leyes de Indias (Laws of the Indies, 1573), there were an array of conceptual underpinnings, governing everything between the macro issues of site selection, urban layout and infrastructures, down to the minute details of buildings.

The Laws of the Indies were the first comprehensive legal code focused on town-planning in Hispanic America that expressly alluded to the regularity of the orthogonal grid. The prescription for 'ideal' layouts for new settlements was based on an accrued heritage that reflected centuries of tradition, including the foundational actions during the Iberian Re-conquest. At their core, the Laws imposed a '*form-based*' ordering devise and physical legibility that would facilitate territorial management. The Laws of the Indies prescribed the ideal location and size of the settlements, the dimensions, and shape of plazas, the proportional relationship between street types and corresponding building types, and even the location of public arcades for the convenience of merchants and pedestrian transit, as well as predicating aesthetic unity.

Less evident connections between the Roman and Spanish traditions lie in the remnants of Roman encampments located throughout the Iberian Peninsula that evolved into the foundation of towns during the medieval era. The memory of those compositions influenced the disposition of settlements by early Spanish colonists, until formal decrees, such as Las Leyes de Indias were issued.

The decision by Spanish rulers to adjudicate formal planning principals was moreover steered by the writings of the fourteenth century Franciscan Catalan monk Eiximenis. In his *Dotze del Crestia* - essentially an encyclopedia of medieval life, intent on encouraging theological study - Treatise XXII focused on the fundamental principles for the governing of cities and communities and it in turn was based on descriptions from the Bible's Book of Ezekiel, and according to some scholars, his probable awareness of Vitruvian writings. The Crestia was re-printed in 1484, pre-dating Italian Renaissance treatises on the 'Ideal City', and permitted Spanish rulers to envision an expanded, 'ordered' and 'divinely' ordained kingdom.[4] Additionally, the re-prints of Vitruvius' *De Architettura Libri Decem* in Madrid by Diego de Sagredo in 1526, and the theoretical writings of Leon Battista Alberti in *De Re Aedificatoria*, and Antonio Avelino's (*Filarete*) in *Trattato D'Architettura* likewise have been attributed with influencing subsequent Spanish decrees, which were created to further refine and guide the foundation of new Ibero-American towns with inherent proportions, symbols and signs that transfer meanings.[5] These precepts filtered into the design of new European settlements across North, Central and South America, at times, draped over existing indigenous settlements.

A wide range of pursuits, from military, economic to religious, have produced grid-iron compositions. The supposed quests of some for egalitarian societal ideals often masked real intentions related to security or dominance.[6] Nonetheless, the graphing of those design principles, across vast territories resulted in orderly, legible, sustainable settlements precisely because life's everyday functions were accessible to most inhabitants on foot. The form-based tools commonly employed to govern siting, urban pattern, building disposition and proportions laid the foundation for future legislative tools and visionary plans across the Western Hemisphere, including the seventeenth century Ideal City, and "hygienist' propositions in the following centuries.

Around the late 18th and 19th centuries, emerges another pivotal juncture in the history of Western cities, when concerns for health and public safety mount in densely-populated urban centers and result in new movements and propositions for the design of cities that call for more generously proportioned streets, more sophisticated infrastructures, additional green spaces and the segregation of noxious industrial uses. Architects and engineers, the likes of Haussman, Cerda and Iboleón led the charge that resulted in the expansion of memorable places such as Paris, Barcelona, and Havana.

Urban designers built upon the traditions of formal compositional frameworks and/or the creation or refinement of legislative tools to guide the enlargement of towns and cities. Yet again, those tools often stipulated precise ratios of building heights to street widths, disposition and sizes of windows and doors on building facades, and standardization of material colors to bring unity and harmony to the public environment as well as the consistent planting of street trees. An example of such form-based codes were the 1861 "Ordenanzas de Construcción para la ciudad de la Habana y pueblos de su término municipal."

Sir Ebenezer Howard's publication *Garden Cities of To-morrow* (1898), outlined a utopian city in which society was again intended to coexists harmoniously with nature. The publication gave rise to the formation of the "garden city movement" that resulted in several Garden Cities in Great Britain early on in the 20th century. This movement also brought about the development of several model suburbs in the United States, including Forest Hills Gardens (New York City borough of Queens) designed by F.L. Olmsted Jr. (1909), Radburn, New Jersey (1923), and the Suburban Resettlement Program towns of the 1930s including Greenbelt, Maryland, Greenhills, Ohio, Greenbrooke, New Jersey and Greendale, Wisconsin.[7]

THE CONCEPTION OF NORTH AMERICAN CITIES - ACT I

Between the 16th and early 20th centuries, in the continental United States, handsome, vibrant, and diverse examples of sustainable town plans arose, often paralleling transatlantic trends or precedents. They exhibited an overall internal logic, resulting in memorable places such as St. Augustine, Boston, Philadelphia, Williamsburg, New York, Washington, New Orleans, Charleston, Savannah, Albuquerque, Santa Fe, and San Francisco. These iconic American cities, several amongst the nation's earliest settlements, were conceived with traditional place-making sensibleness, commonplace until around the Second World War, and their mixed-use, pedestrian friendly, compact layouts largely remain as examples of sustainable development. From these early settlements, lessons can be drawn, not so much for their ingratiating dermal features, as for their underlining urban logic and strategies, and at times, for their codification, which resulted in self-sufficient, sustainable towns.

In each instance, the urban fabric was closely woven, distinct and legible, characterized by the predictability and rhythm of the morphology, typologies, and a rich mix of uses. Their dense framework and the common inclusion of agricultural activities in close proximity, contributed to their identity and self-sustaining character. Responding to or producing various social customs and/or economic forces, the conformation of these cities has evolved over time, some more gracefully and sympathetically than others to their original DNA, and/or to their surrounding setting. In each instance, the urban design patterns, which were to shape the dominant cultural strains of the United States as a whole, offer valuable insight, capable of informing present and future sustainable design practices.

Spanish DNA

The Spanish claim to territories that are today the United States rested upon the 16th century exploits of Ponce de Leon, Hernando De Soto, and Francisco Vázquez de Coronado. In 1598, Don Juan Oñante led 500 men from Mexico northward into Pueblo lands in present-day New Mexico. "The invaders brought with them a labor system known as the *encomienda*, which had originally developed in Spain. Under this scheme, large "New World" land grants were structured by the Crown to favor Spanish individuals. The grantees were responsible for the protection and Christian instruction of inhabitants of the lands, and those natives were required to pay tribute - often in the form of crops and labor - to the grantee."[8]

Spanish colonists controlled large areas in the modern-day states of Florida, Texas, California and New Mexico. By the early sixteenth century, they began to establish a network of military and religious outposts across these territories, which were often named after Roman Catholic saints.[9] Many modern-day cities in these states - San Francisco, Los Angeles, Santa Cruz, San Diego, Albuquerque, Santa Fe, and San Antonio - can trace their origins to Spanish colonists.

St. Augustine, Florida

The earliest known Spanish settlement in the continental United States was founded on the eastern seaboard. Explorer Ponce de León claimed the lands of Florida for Spain during his 1513 expedition, and soon after the Spanish Crown identified instrumental point of defense along its coast, hugging the powerful Gulf Stream, to protect trade and transport between the Iberian Peninsula and its newly discovered, gold-laden territories in Mexico, Central and South America. After several failed attempts to colonize Florida, in 1565, Don Pedro Menéndez de Avilés sailed into Matanzas Bay and established the colony of St. Augustine. Due to its strategic siting, across its history, the town would endure several attacks; burned down by Drake in 1586, sacked in 1668, besieged and burned by the South Carolinians in 1702 and bombarded by English troops in 1740. Thus, forty-two years before the English colonized Jamestown, and 55 years before the Pilgrims landed at Plymouth Rock, Spain's St. Augustine became the very first European colony, and it remains the oldest continuously occupied European settlement in what is today the continental United States. St. Augustine endured as the seat of Spanish rule in Florida throughout the 16th, 17th, and 18th centuries.

The town originally served as a military outpost and a base for Catholic missionaries. During its early colonial period, given its tactical significance and because of its strategic siting and the growth of its population, a large fortress, the Castillo de San Marco built in 1672, was to protect the enclave. With further expansion, the town's central Plaza de la Constitución gained importance and the 16th century grid of slender streets evolved into a distinct pattern, at once reminiscent of Iberian precedents, as it was responsive to the hot and humid climate.

A 1603 plan was formulated, based on Spanish colonial city planning codes (Laws of the Indies) that mandated a gridiron with a symmetrical network of streets running both parallel and perpendicular to a central town plaza. The master plan laid out the grid of narrow, thusly shaded, cooler streets that would stretch out from the main plaza throughout the 17th and 18th centuries. Important civic and religious buildings, including the Town Hall, the Bishop's House, a Customs House, Treasury, Arsenal, a hospital, guard-houses and various monuments fronted the central, waterfront plaza and emphasized the preeminence of the church and state; all within walking distance of residences and shops. The courtyard type was prevalently utilized throughout the town during the Spanish colonial era and building designs were adjusted in response to the hot and humid climate, incorporating larger, aligned, vertical openings/windows, porches, and high ceilings. Porches were deep and commonplace, allowing for year-round indoor/outdoor living, as well as social interaction. Early wattle and daub construction methods were replaced with locally quarried coquina stone constructions.[10]

Spanish rule ended with the cession of Florida to the United States in 1821. During English rule, the urban framework remained much the same, but, the courtyard building type was replaced by free-standing, wood-frame, porch-wrapped buildings; modest adaptations of the side-yard and plantation types that tempered the harsh climate equally well, typical of the Deep South.

St. Augustine's existing architectural character spans approximately 500 years, and although it is most renowned for the early Spanish colonial building designs, it's historic district also hosts handsome buildings from the Territorial Period (1821-1845), the Flagler Era (1880's-1890's) and the Florida Boom (1920's).[11] St. Augustine displays a mosaic of architectural styles, materials, and typologies together with traditions and practices inspired by over 500 years of Spanish-Floridian culture and overwhelmingly, the architecture and the urbanism respond to cues from the local context.

English DNA

For the first wave of English colonists, many traveling across the Atlantic in search of religious freedom, life was often crude and difficult. So much so that numerous initial settlements did not succeed and were abandoned. Yet others took root and over time developed into close-knit thriving communities based on mercantile economies. Subsequent waves of colonists would petition to establish new towns, typically granted as 40 square miles (10,000 ha), and located at a practical distance from existing communities, as to facilitate its defense and nurture commerce, trade and social networks. Routes connecting settlements were laid across the Northeast. Through these interconnected processes of defining and then connecting towns, territories under the control of the English throne expanded along the seaboard and more timidly towards interior regions.[12]

Within a settlement, land was distributed by communal agreement in accordance with English customs. Towns were typically compact, with a clear disposition and form, and at times modeled by the terrain. At their nucleus, civic and commercial buildings were placed, including a multipurpose meeting hall, school, tavern, and small shops. The meeting hall was the political and religious center of the community and its prominent siting intentionally underscored the importance of both in daily life. Towns often had a 'village green,' commonly used for public celebrations as well as military regalia and training. Outside a town's center, plots of land were allocated for farming and at times were held communally and were intended to suffice the needs of the town residents at a minimum.[13] The more prosperous towns possessed well-proportioned protected harbors, where land routes met up with navigable routes and commerce flourished.

Boston, Massachusetts

This was the case of Boston. Its earliest grouping of buildings occurred at the harbor, growing over time in a rather organic manner along the crest of the undulating terrain, towards the radial system of roads that linked it to other towns. A large green was set aside on an irregularly shaped plot facing the mud flats. The "Green" was used for public gatherings and accommodated military functions. Boston inherited its organic pattern of growth from the Saxon and Norman traditions of England. That layout was married to a street-defining architecture that would evolve into a more formal, and ordered language as a rising middle class aspired to ascend socially. The city was dotted with public buildings throughout. Colonial Boston's chorus of civic buildings, well-defined streets, and compact character shared common traits with other more formally composed settlements that would follow. Like a phoenix, the city would rise after being the theater of war during the American Revolution, its landmarks multiplying, and its identity evolving gracefully over time, until it was partially mutilated during the urban revitalization efforts of the late XX century.

New Haven, Connecticut

A connection can be drawn between certain North American colonial place-making patterns and earlier Spanish colonial town-planning principles, for their common derivation of inspiration from the Old Testament. Similar scriptures in fact motivated the North American protestant colonization process in the 18th and 19th centuries, by which the territory's expansion was first distributed into regularized portions, shaping the landscape of a burgeoning nation.[14] According to historian Vincent Scully, "the regular grid system which was to become the dominant American scheme appeared very early. The grid was archetypally colonial as well, ideal for impatient settlers… The English had been employing it in ravaged Ireland during precisely the period when their colonization's of America was taking place… New Haven's grid is of a special and distinguished kind. It is a purely Vitruvian figure, a perfect square, canted a little off the north-south axis to adjust to the rivers that mark its site by the shore. It is divided by open streets into nine smaller squares, with the central one reserved as common land, in New Haven called 'Green'."[15] Here again the ideal of consciously designing a city in congress with nature and with the mission of reflecting the innate ordering systems of the natural realm are apparent. The relevance of such a 'spiritual' goal can perhaps be questioned, but the resulting livability of such a layout cannot. New Haven would unfortunately suffer a scaring of its fabric in the late 20th century American zeal to 'revitalize' urban communities.

Philadelphia, Pennsylvania

Although initially missing the baroque radial avenues of Christopher Wren's 1666 plan for London, William Penn's 1682 rectangular grid for Philadelphia was composed of rectangular blocks, stretching between two rivers. Parcels were evenly distributed across the city at one and half acre intervals, moreover facilitating urban agriculture. Two main thoroughfares, Broad and High Streets, crisscrossed the plan, each 100 feet wide, intersecting at 'Centre Square' where sites for civic buildings, including a meeting hall, school, and state house were set aside. Similar to the Roman *cardo* and *decomano* that had informed London's urban pattern, these intersecting roads resulted in four quadrants, each punctuated by a central square and accompanying park. Penn's inclusion of green spaces in each quadrant drew inspiration from his firsthand experiences while living in London during the plague. He described the design for Philadelphia as a "greene towne" and one "which will never be burnt, and always be wholesome… Let every house be in a line, or upon a line, as much as may be."

Savannah, Georgia

The 1734 plan of Savannah introduced a gridiron design distinguished by a rhythmic flow between open spaces and solid blocks, with each expansion and contraction of space culminating in an overall sculptural bacchanalia. In fact, what would increasingly distinguish North American gridded settlements over the coming 200 years from others before them, would be the "gentling effect of its river of trees" within and along public spaces.[16]

FRENCH DNA

Washington, D.C.

Le Notre's plan for Versailles would inspire Pierre Charles L'Enfant's 1791 plan for Washington D.C. with its dominant radial design draped over its gridiron, climaxing on the Capitol and the White House, to underline the rising power of the nation and its institutional anchors. "When the city of Washington was planned under the direct and minute supervision of Washington and Jefferson, the relations that should subsist between the Capitol and the President's House were closely studied. Indeed the whole city was planned with a view to the reciprocal relations that should exist among public buildings. Vistas and axes: sites for monuments and museums; parks and pleasure gardens; fountains and canals; in a word, all that goes to make a city a magnificent and consistent work of art were regarded as essentials in the plans made by L'Enfant under the direction of the first President and Secretary of State. Nor were these original plans prepared without due study of great models. The stately art of landscape architecture had been brought oversea by royal governors and wealthy planters; and both Washington and Jefferson were familiar the practice of that art. L'Enfant, a man of position and education, and an engineer of ability must have been familiar with those great works of the master Lenôtre which are still the admiration of the traveler and the constant pleasure of the French people. Moreover, from his well-stocked library Jefferson sent to L'Enfant plans "on a large and accurate scale" of Paris, Amsterdam, Frankfort, Carlsruhe, Strasburg, Orleans, Turin, Milan and other European cities, at the same time felicitating himself that the President had "left the planning of the town in such good hands." The later 1902 plan prepared with the consultation of leading architects of the time including Burnham, Olmstead, and McKim had the objective "to prepare for the city of Washington such a plan as shall enable future development to proceed along the lines originally planned- namely, the treatment of the city as a work of civic art."[17] The city's early vibrancy was quieted over time as residential and commercial uses were sacrificed to expand the presence of government institutions; a detrimental trend for the life of the city, which only recently has begun to change.

New Orleans, Louisiana

Sited along the banks of the sinuous Mississippi River, New Orleans is a mélange of gridded expansions, already evidenced in its plans of 1815 and 1841. That physical collage, seamed together by radiating avenues, reflects New Orleans' contrasting cultures. Each neighborhood is legible, walkable, with an architectural syntax stemming from diverse cultural heritages, at times fused, and adapted to the hot and humid climate. The city's renowned cross-pollinated cultural richness resulted from its once exuberant public life, in turn facilitated by its public spaces and graced by a palette of building types. Since its foundation in 1718, New Orleans experienced explosive bursts of growth because of three factors: its waves of European immigrants from Germany, Italy, and Ireland, the traffic of African slaves, and the 1809 arrival of 10,000 refugees from Haiti. The city flourished because of its geographic location along the Gulf of Mexico and due to the exploitation of outlying fertile lands and of human resources. The city grew to host the largest population in the Deep South until WWII. Interestingly, although the physical characteristics of the terrain made inland expansion of the city initially implausible, mid-twentieth century swamp draining techniques opened the floodgates for suburbia. That resulted in the segregation of the city's population - 'white flight' - and a decline in its economic activities and educational investments. More recently, natural disasters, such as Hurricane Katrina, have placed into question the ancestral choice of founding a city in such a precarious, low-lying, and vulnerable terrain. But the price of logic - its abandonment - is unfathomable. Therein lies a clue as to the power of shared identity, of community and the role of design in shaping both, and whereas it does not justify its ill-conceived siting, it does explain the insistent attempts to restore, better protect, and preserve it.

Hybrid Strains

Manhattan, New York

Early Dutch settlements at the tip of the island of Manhattan, then known as New Amsterdam, were a hodge-podge of intersecting grids built over time. In 1861, the city's expansion northward from Wall Street broke away from the initial irregularly patterned settlement as well as its more intimate scale. A rectangular gridiron, relentlessly extending, far beyond the limits of then populated areas was proposed, initially conceived with few public spaces or buildings. Thankfully, the later inclusion of a "Central Park" would provide the much-needed 'green' lung that both the scale of the city and its increasing population logically called for; thereby in some measure ameliorating the endless march of its persistent grid and the large proportions of its blocks.

Salt Lake City and the New Territories

That increasingly monotonous, endlessly repetitive model often devoid of significant public spaces and buildings, would occur throughout the 19th century, all across the new territories as the country expanded towards Oklahoma and Salt Lake City, thereby 'ordering' and proclaiming control of new lands and incentivizing their homesteading. The predilection for geometric designs would even find a manifestation in the delimitation of states, including Arizona, Colorado, New Mexico, and Utah. This westward-ho application of the urban grid layout would intersect with those that had already emerged as the Spanish colonizers had moved north from Mexico and west from Florida and somewhere along the way it lost both its significance and usefulness.

The Unrelenting Application of a Pattern Devoid of Essential Civic Features and Life

For centuries, across the continental United States, the gridiron would be utilized frequently, but increasingly with unabated speculation as its driving force (i.e. New York City), and exploding modulations (i.e. Salt Lake City). The swollen dimensions of blocks, in places such as Salt Lake City, no longer sustained walkable scales of development, and a decreasing presence of public squares or parks as organizing elements and centers for communal gatherings, made public life and civic engagement less accessible and fluid.

Furthermore, the organic urban patterns that ingratiated places such as Boston, which were always accompanied, as in the English countryside, with civic spaces and buildings, where not emulated adeptly by modern planners and developers, which instead generated dysfunctional places that were in addition fragmented, cul-de-sac ridden, contrived, sprawling suburban enclaves, with equally disastrous effects on cities and the environment.

Worsening matters, many early settlements and best samples of sustainable development in the United States eventually fell victim to twentieth century 'city planning' principals and/or redevelopment programs, while historic neighborhoods have been consumed by unsympathetic 'revitalization' initiatives and/or isolated by strangling stretches of highways. The morphologies and typologies of many American cities have been raped or exterminated, and all in the name of modernizing progress and an insidious lust for economic gain through predictably 'zoned' investments. The legibility and grain of towns and cities and the intensity and mix of uses characteristic of earlier sustainable settlements, both informal and formal in composition, have yielded to the needs of the automobile, private sector development interests, as well as unbridled suburban expansion patterns.

How did town-planning patterns that so effectively served Western civilization with great effectiveness for over 4000 years, become so meaningless and useless in less than a century? What 'steered' their demise? The balance and syncopation between civic buildings, public spaces, and streets was lost, while speculation, segregation, and the automobile took over planning objectives.

The Rise of Planning and the Demise of Place-making

Following the Industrial Revolution's chorus of increasing socials ills and escalating public health concerns, the first university 'city planning' curriculums emerged in the U.S., imparted by a collective of architects, landscape architects and architectural historians. Over the last century, those curriculums progressively veered away from spatial design gauges and instead primarily focused on technological needs and responses to planning that influenced the emerging profession of "city planning" and the related codifying instruments that would be developed. A trend, which early on, John Nolan, and other practitioners and scholars feared.

As one of the results of that new direction, late twentieth century expansions surrounding historic urban cores and new cities were increasingly characterized by suburbs, which over time developed a sprawling and/or fragmented nature as their attributes became generic and their mono-use footprints were less inter-connected.

This contrasts with the first American suburbs that appear in the late nineteenth century, in places such as Brooklyn and Llewellyn Park, New York and Gross Park in Chicago. Suburbs at the time, are essentially extensions of existing cities, and feature physical characteristics similar to their 'parent'. Horse-drawn streetcars connect less affluent suburbs to urban cores and in the case of New York City this leads to the development of new settlements not only across the East River, but also within the island of Manhattan to its north, which tend to be denser than the more picturesque suburbs farther afield. During this period, new building increments also appear, as suburbs located within vast natural settings evolve, away from the denser row-house type to the side-yard and eventually the single-family dwelling; this last type contemplated as a happy medium between "town and country".

With the advent of the electric streetcar, in particular between 1890 and 1930, distances between the urban core and its off-spring are ever more distended and so too their morphologies grow apart. The urban patterns and the building character of suburbs leads to an emerging larger-scale of development and an independent identity. Prolonged commercial strips, today referred to as 'Main Street,' were drawn-out along the path of the electric trolley, resulting in a new way of organizing retail activities, unlike the patterns that had defined the commercial cores of cities until then. During this same period, the automobile appears more frequently on city streets and as it becomes more affordable, soon imposing its presence.

Following the Great Depression and the availability of Federal Housing Loans, the middle-income bracket of society aspires to move out of congested, polluted urban cores where population density outpaces infrastructure improvements. Suburban developments, constructed all at one time flourish. Post-WWII developments such as Levittown are recognized for their relentless use of the same house "model." The era of mass-production gives rise to generic, formulaic housing, devoid of the customization features that were possible, and at times had been the norm, in previous centuries. The stretched out 'ranch-house' type later becomes the iconic image of suburbia. In parallel, commercial and retail strategies continue to morph, away from Main Street and towards large air-conditioned, inward focusing malls, essentially islands surrounded by vast and convenient seas of parking, distending urban increments, yet also managing to usurp life from Main Streets. The whiplash effect on 'Main Street' eventually leads to its death.

History reveals that American suburbs, some slowly, others more quickly, assimilated the freedom and mobility that the automobile offered, and around mid-century often bridged between the traditional city and the technological innovations of the time. Yet, in short-measure, this would give way to increasingly dispersed patterns of development and additional inward focusing building types, such as office parks, retail malls and eventually, a couple of decades later: the proverbial McMansions - reflections of the nation's increasing segregation of uses or the population's insatiable appetite for material goods. Also of significance around this period is the expansion of the inter-state highway system, which eventually laid the path towards a new "sub-urban dominated metropolis."[18] In the XXI century, the suburban 'Edge City,' is in some areas of the country, in particular in the Northeast where major cities are located in close proximity to each other, meeting up with other 'Edge' cities. The result is often a jumbled sea of walled communities characterized by cartoonish cookie cutter-houses, generic large box retail malls, islands of office parks and enormous parking lots surrounding just about everything. Each use disconnected from the others, assembled as if a quilt composed of irregular scraps, usually lacking public spaces or buildings, and primarily connected by endless ribbons of highways and collector roads - a mess.

These more recently developed suburbs of the late twentieth and early twenty-first century are unlike their late nineteenth through mid-twentieth century suburban ancestors. The overall scale, proximity to a variety of uses and public transportation of older suburbs were accompanied by more modestly scaled building increments, resulting in healthier built and natural environments, more compact, walkable neighborhoods, albeit not always completely self-sufficient. Metropolitan areas, such as Atlanta, Houston, Las Vegas, and Miami are the poster-children of unbridled suburbanism; in each instance, leading to a loss of identity, crippled infrastructure systems, increased pollution, and energy consumption, not to mention the decimation of natural resources. That type of suburbia is typified by its ravenous consumption of open land and dysfunctional infrastructures and has created social, economic, and physical burdens that now jeopardize the survival of many American cities as well as the environment.

In conclusion, the construction of cities is one of the prime achievements of civilizations throughout history, and America has produced some memorable examples. But, in the last sixty years in particular, the frenzied growth of human settlements without sustainability criteria, underscored by a lack of logically scaled patterns, a mixed of uses, civic buildings, public spaces and green areas, has become a significant threat to the survival of communities and by extension mankind. Modern suburbanism's disregard of place-making traditions of the past has dissolved public space, rejected all connections to the admirable concepts that historically guided the growth of cities, ignored the specific realities of place, while ballooning the dimensions of streets and plots, relegating the role of pedestrians in public life to the background, while idolizing modern engineering and compartmentalizing society. Planning became servant to the car and its indiscriminate use of bloated and/or fragmented designs responsible for urban and environmental blights. XXI century planners and government leaders cannot continue to evolve under a regime of public policies that ignore the needs of citizens, the environment, or the impact of their unsustainable practices on third parties beyond their borders - be they a mile or a continent away.

Endnotes

[1] Gyorgy Doczi, *The Power of Limits: Proportional Harmonies in Nature, Art, and Architecture*, 1981, Shambhala Publications,Inc. Boston, MA
[2] Christopher Alexander, *The Nature of Order: An Essay on the Art of Building and the Nature of the Universe, Book II*, The Center for Environmental Structure, Berkeley, CA.
[3] From the first voyages to the Americas in 1492 until the loss of its last African colonies in 1975.
[4] Ibid
[5] *La Ciudad Hispano-Americana: El Sueño de un Orden*, Centro de Estudios Históricos de Obras Públicas y Urbanismo, Ministerio de Obras Públicas y Urbanismo, 1989
[6] Spiro Kostof, *The City Shaped: Urban Patterns and Meanings Through History*
[7] Robert Stern, *The Anglo American Suburb*, London: Architectural Design Profile, 1981, pgs. 84-85
[8] United States History: Spanish Colonization of North America. http://www.u-s-history.com/pages/h438.html
[9] The word for saint in Spanish is "san" or "santa."
[10] Albert Manucy, *The Houses of St. Augustine 1565-1821*, St. Augustine: St. Augustine Historical Society, 1962
[11] http://palmm.fcla.edu/fhp/outline.shtml
[12] Benjamin Woods Labaree, *Colonial Massachusetts: A History*, KTO Press, 1979, pg. 83-91
[13] Ibid, pgs. 51, 59
[14] Interview between Vincent Scully and author, 2006
[15] Vincent Scully, *American Architecture and Urbanism*, Praeger Publishers, Inc. New York, N.Y., 1969
[16] Ibid, pgs. 32-36
[17] Charles Moore (ed.) (1902), *The Improvement Of The Park System Of The District of Columbia: Report by the United States Congress: Senate Committee on the District of Columbia and District of Columbia Park Commission*, Washington, D.C.: Government Printing Office, pg. 12, Fifty-Seventh Congress, First Session, Senate Report No. 166, pgs. 11-12, 35-36, Google E-book.
[18] Robert Lang, Jennifer LeFurgy, and Arthur C. Nelson, "The Six Suburban Eras of the United States Research Note," *Opolis: An International Journal of Suburban and Metropolitan Studies*, Vol. 2: No. 1, Article 5. http://repositories.cdlib.org/cssd/opolis/vol2/iss1/art5, 2006

"STUPID IS AS STUPID DOES" - *Forrest Gump*
Part IV - Climate Change: cities lie at the crux of the problem and of the solutions

Sonia R. Cháo

The Modern American City: "New Towns for Old"

As far back as 1921, in stark contrast to the emerging Modern trends in urban planning promoting distended and disconnected designs, prominent landscape architect and town planner, John Nolan, "concluded that re-planning the American city was hopeless." The nation's cities, he wrote, were "cursed... with nearly insolvable social and political problems." Thus, Nolen, philosophically indebted to Raymond Unwin, designer of the first *Garden City*, began the planning of 'new towns' based on *Garden City* ideals, in an effort to recuperate those design principles that would lead to more livable and viable communities. By 1927, Nolan published *New Towns for Old*, tracing the lineage of American towns and proposing a recuperation of some of its characteristic features in the design of new developments, but in a manner that also addressed contemporary health and infrastructure concerns. Nolan wrote:

"It now looks as if the industrial future would lie with the city or town of moderate size - of about fifty thousand inhabitants, or perhaps thirty thousand as an average - rather than with the huge million-peopled aggregations that modernity has produced. A few gigantic cities have doubtless been necessary. It is quite possible that other and more flexible conditions of organization and transportation will change the present tendency towards concentrations. The Garden City and Garden Suburb movements in Great Britain have been significant indications, as was also the remarkable attention paid to the planning of minor industrial centers in Germany before the World War - doubtless already resumed as an element of the new day of a German democracy... American emphasis, also, seems to be placed more and more on the desirability of smaller cities... Another indication that in recent years has been pointing more and more in like directions is the policy of various great manufacturing enterprises - such as the General Electric, Co, Westinghouse Electric and the General Chemical Co. for instance - to locate plants in minor centers of population all over the country. This is being done for various reasons: better social conditions, insuring a higher class of workers - more prosperous, intelligent and contented; the location of workers' home more convenient to shop or mill, thus demanding less expenditure of time and energy in going to and fro; opportunities for the economical manufacture of various parts, for which the raw materials to be worked exist in, or are produced in, a given region, or to which special activity the class of skilled workers residents in given localities is best adapted; economies in transportation affected by manufacturing in the neighborhood of important markets... Transportation problems are basic considerations for all community planning. The widespread civic awakening is no vague movement, with vague and indefinite aims. It seeks to provide convenience in streets and buildings, to meet the requirements of public health, to recognize the true function and place of art, to regard obligations to future generations, to supply the imperative needs of children, to satisfy the love of nature and the desire for outdoor life. The form of this civic awakening that is most significant and promising is the recognition of the need of comprehensive planning and replanning, especially of smaller cities."[1]

In his own professional practice, Nolan met initial success applying his theories in the master-planning of Mariemont, Ohio. Soon afterward, in 1922, John Nolen designed the town of St. Petersburg, Florida. He defined the setting as a "site blessed by a benevolent Nature." Within a year, Nolen completed a comprehensive plan for this resort city of 15,000, with a "form and flavor unlike that of other places... A greenbelt of preserves and parks encircled the lower third of the peninsula, defining the city's 'natural boundaries'." Nolan proposed plans to improve traffic connections, provide a Civic Center, mixed-use neighborhood centers, a system of parkways, pedestrian access to parks and local neighborhood centers, retail, churches, and public buildings.

"Nolen's plan rested on the "adequate control of private development." He proposed a series of land use controls to ensure that development followed the efficient outlay of public facilities, rather than outline speculative desires. Without these regulations, Nolen was hardly sanguine about the city's future. "It has been said and with reason," he wrote, "that man is the only animal who desecrates the surroundings of his own habitation."[2]

John Nolen's *Garden City* Plan for Florida

The St. Petersburg project was not executed for a variety of reasons, not the least of which were speculative interests and then a busting economy. But, Nolan's firm went on to design 54 projects in Florida, including city plans for Clearwater, Sarasota, and West Palm Beach, new town plans for Clewiston and Bellaire, and neighborhood plans for University Park (Gainesville) and San Jose Estates (Jacksonville).[3] In 1925, Nolen claimed to have finally found in "Venice an opportunity better... than any other in Florida to apply the most advanced and most practical ideas of regional planning." He planned Venice, Florida for the Brotherhood of Locomotive Engineers (BLE), a labor union aiming to profit from state's next land boom. And yet, the Brotherhood also understood their investment as a long-term financial commitment, and aimed to create a regional center for agriculture and light industry, "a place where the ordinary man could have a chance to get all that the rich have ever been able to get out of Florida."

"Nature led the way" and the plan, Nolen wrote, "followed her way." Greenbelts protected important natural features, with parkways connecting them to Venice's downtown. These greenbelts circumscribed the town to the east and south, as did the Gulf and bay to the north and west. A waterfront linear park provided picturesque settings, punctuated by an amphitheater and beachfront park. At the core of the composition, a main 'plaza' anchored the town, dotted with a sequence of parks and public buildings that offered visual connections to natural features beyond. In keeping with traditional planning, secondary public spaces and buildings were located strategically in each neighborhood. The overall plan was mindful of contemporary trends as well, evidenced by the inclusion of expansive open spaces and hotels catering primarily to potential tourist, while accommodating the automobile and pedestrians with a variety of street types/sections, and setting aside parcels for needed infrastructures and networks. Nolan's greatest challenge working in the Deep South, was his contrasting views on segregation. Although in this sense, he "failed to fight the southern caste system directly," he remained adamant that African-Americans receive the benefits of good planning and so he laid out Harlem Village, just across the railroad tracks along similar lines, with "the hope of uniting diverse people through nature" and for, Nolen wrote, "the brotherhood of man."

In Venice, Nolen successfully mediated his design between two visionary aims - Nature and Civic Engagement. To date, Venice stands as the most complete example of the *Garden City* movement in Florida. As Nolen himself wrote, Venice would remain "an inspiration to those who would make this world a better place to live." Sadly, only a handful of Nolen's contemporaries would share his vision of the American City, while the majority and for much of the balance of the century, abandoned the defensible models of the past, in search of modern efficiency, which in turn quickly led to unsustainable development patterns across the nation.

THE MODERN AMERICAN CITY - ACT II (PUBERTY)

The typical late twentieth and twenty-first century bloated mono-use suburb generates sprawl and disconnections. Lacking a web of connections, they are often designed as a fractured maze of cul-de-sacs, littered with the exact same or very similar housing models. Although cul-de-sacs are safe havens for young children to play in, their splintered character results in added congestion on main (collector) streets and necessitates the use of a vehicle for most daily activities, both resulting in greater pollution. Drivers and pedestrians regularly face detours to get around walled communities. This 'incomplete urbanism' is aggravated by a usual lack of dedicated sidewalks and bicycle paths, although space for both are usually available. Generally, sprawling patterns of development are the artifact of a twentieth century instrument: Conventional (alias Euclidian) Zoning.

Conventional Zoning emerged at the beginning of the twentieth century as a means to remove noxious uses from cities. However, it wound up segregating all uses, including those that were compatible and thereby changed the substance of cities and the structure of urban codes across the US, primarily by regulating development through land-use classifications that in effect separate uses and thus people. Typical land-use classifications include single-family residential, multi-family residential, commercial, industrial, recreational, and institutional. Accompanying each land-use are norms that regulate lot size, setbacks, and the height, mass and square footage of buildings. Conventional zoning focuses on the "micromanagement and segregation of land uses, and the control of development intensity through abstract and uncoordinated parameters (e.g., FAR, dwellings per acre, setbacks, parking ratios, traffic LOS), to the neglect of an integrated built form."[4]

"Zoning has also been associated as a primary driving factor in the rapidly accelerating unaffordability of housing in urban areas."[5] Urban Planning Professor Stuart Meck claims that "city planning, along with zoning, was a vehicle to control where African-Americans, the poor, and immigrants lived, and to keep them out of the areas where middle and upper class people resided. It is no coincidence that the initial efforts to adopt land use controls in the U.S. were aimed at enacting racial zoning - zoning that segregated cities by race. The first city to adopt racial zoning was Baltimore in 1910, and racial zoning spread to other eastern and southern cities (e.g., Atlanta, Louisville), even though the U.S. Supreme Court declared it unconstitutional in 1917, in a case titled Buchanan v. Warley."[6]

Nonetheless, with Conventional Zoning tools in hand, and in contempt of the place-making traditions of the past, that had with great efficacy often learned from and co-existed with the natural realm's 'living structures', late XX and XXI century city planners have prevalently rejected concepts and methods that historically guided the growth of cities. The zoning template, and it's even further diluted adaptations, fundamentally ignored local realities, neither placing value on historic structures, cultural heritage, nor the genetic material of historic urban tissues, instead exploding lot increments, and street sections while reducing the role of pedestrians in public life, and dilating the distances between uses - all rather unsympathetic interventions. Planners idolatrized modern engineering, laying the seeds of sprawl across the fertile, virgin soil of America's landscape, and ultimately pilfered public life from many existing cities as well. 'City Planning' became a servant to the automobile and in the ever more protracted, car-dependent society it generated, parent to urban blight and an incapacitating sub-urbanism.

"The Happy Motoring Economy"

In his book, *The City in Mind*, James Howard Kunstler traced the debacle of contemporary planning, evident in places such as Atlanta and Las Vegas - *"the place where America's spirit crawled off to die"* - and addressed the growing challenges of preserving, infilling, and expanding rich, historic urban fabrics. Kunstler delved into the intertwined destinies of a dwindling society, built forms and the natural realm. He outlined North America's urban development patterns and mapped some of the lesser-known reasons directing the unchecked growth of cities. These include the demise of the country's mass transit systems, the role of private interests (i.e. automobile, rubber, asphalt, steel, and oil companies), propaganda instruments, and the impaired characteristics of post-WWII sprawl that caters to the needs of vehicles above all other considerations.

The "Motor Age" began in the 1920's when the first automobiles were commercialized in the United States. At that time, pedestrians, police, downtown business associations and parents perceived automobiles as an intrusion onto the street and campaigned to eliminate or greatly reduce their presence in the urban realm and thus maintain the social and physical constructs of streets as they knew it. Within a decade, private interests in the automobile and insurance sectors paralleled others in related fields, including rubber, asphalt, steel, and oil industries, to launch similar assaults on any negative publicity the climbing number of automobile accidents were yielding, and to build a new social acceptance of the automobile.[7] The private sector propaganda machine began in earnest and found corresponding partners in academic circles, where in turn new visions for the city of the future were being embraced, along the lines described by leading architects such as Le Corbusier and Frank Lloyd Wright in "The Radiant City" (1935) and "Broadacre City" (1932).[8] Segregationists jumped onto the 'express-lane' as they searched for the means to create purified, utopian settings. Real-estate investors reveled at the idea of predicting exactly where to best invest and/or 'land-bank.' The emerging profession of urban planners would meld all these seemingly disparate agendas and facilitate the creation of a new type of place - the 'Land of Nowhere.' The introduction of Conventional (Euclidean) zoning, provided the legal armature to achieve multiple agendas, generally enabling the isolation of land uses into specified geographic districts and ensuring that cars would become an essential feature of daily life in new cities and suburbs.

The fact that existing cities were experiencing growing pains, grappling with population booms, public hygiene, congestion, a lack of housing, crime, class tensions, discrimination, and/or often poorly regulated building sectors made for fertile ground for the propaganda and experimental zoning tools to take root. Furthermore, the financial backing of large corporations, which made the constant flow of marketing saturate all forms of communication, was epitomized by the 1961 *Merrily We Roll Along*, TV show narrated by Groucho Marx, as part of the weekly *'DuPont Series of the Week'*, sponsored by Pierre DuPont, then majority stockholder of the General Motors Company. The print and media blitzes glorified the automobile, made it fashionable, and proclaimed "American's love affair with the automobile."

In the name of progress and innovation, at the intersection between shrewd and vast financial interests and romantic utopian visions - past and present - pedestrians lost their role in public life; the mix of uses, which had rendered cities vibrant, also disappeared, and in their place emerged the 'Automobile City.'

The Automobile City

The United States has more than 200 million cars traveling almost 4 million miles of road - nationwide roads and parking areas consume 39 million acres of paved surfaces.[9] Every second, these cars travel 60,000 miles, use 3,000 gallons of petroleum products, and add 60,000 pounds of carbon dioxide to the atmosphere - two thirds of the US carbon dioxide emissions.[10] Many of these cars are on the road precisely because 'office parks' are not located near residential 'developments' nor 'shopping malls', and, often in suburbia transportation networks between these mono-use destinations are unreliable and/or infrequent, making them implausible. The designs of these new cities or the expansions of existing ones, which follow current planning paradigms, are senseless and downright irresponsible. If one of the principal measures of a city's contribution to climate change is its reliance on the automobile, then America's current dependence on the automobile is to be singled-out and largely understood as an incidental product of 'conventional' zoning, which continues to perpetuate its use and result in overwhelming carbon emissions.

In cities like Houston and Miami, the 'car-cult' has begot strangling road networks, which in turn facilitates and exacerbates already hopeless mono-zoned terrains, while spawning suburbia, ravaging the natural realm, and dissecting existing communities - often through a city's poorest neighborhoods which can ill afford to weaken their social and cultural support networks. Furthermore, no longer are wider roads and highways constructed and traffic engineers declare them obsolete and in need of even further expansion. Social historians agree that these types of infrastructure investments represent a waste of resources and merely serve to further isolate and divide society and burden the environment, while purely furthering financial benefits to self-serving private sector industries.

Is that the "American way of life"?

The unrelenting application of obsolete planning tools, which segregate people and uses, increments automobile travel, which in turn, pollutes the environment, and also promotes fractured development patterns, which ironically resemble the artificial subdivisions of a zoo - manageable compartments, linked by a looped path - totally alien to its inhabitants.[11] In both of these contrived and synthetic systems, un-natural dependencies and shifts in behavior occur.

Sloppily compartmentalized expansions to cities and isolated land-uses have exalted the automobile, perpetuated sprawl and furthermore, have segregated and disconnected inhabitants from their natural and cultural contexts, consequently failing - morally. As a result *"the tragic 'sprawl-scape' of cartoon architecture, junked cities, and ravaged countryside where we live and work... created a landscape of scary places, and we became a nation of scary people."*[12] Compare that commentary on the state of contemporary American cities by social historian James Howard Kunstler to the one by turn of the twentieth century Cuban scholar and poet Jose Marti: *"The objective of life is the pursuit of ideal beauty; because just as acts of virtue result in beautiful places, so too beautiful places act upon our virtue."* Both Kunstler and Marti clearly denote that our human spirit, behavior, expectations, and potential are linked to the quality of our man-made and natural environments - for better or worse, we are inextricably linked, and choices made in the 'genetic' coding and design of cities impact the physical, environmental, psychological and spiritual realms of a human's existence.

THE AMERICAN CITY AND ITS COMING OF AGE - ACT III

The Relationship between Cities and Sustainability

At the core of the relationship between climate change and sustainable development is the planning of human settlements and their buildings. Sociologists, urban designers and environmentalists have exhaustively pointed out that in the twentieth and twenty-first centuries, city planning has largely served to deteriorate the natural realm as well as existing cities, moving industrialized countries farther away from the goals of the United Nation's World Commission on the Environment and Development. In 1983, that Commission defined sustainable development as the preservation and creation of *"livable, inspiring, enduring, and equitable places, where the quality of life and the long-term quality of human existence will be enhanced rather than depleted."*[13] This implies a triangulation and inter-dependence between environmental conservation, economic development, and social equity. Cities thus lie at the crux of both the problem and the solution.

The Resurrection of the Sustainable City

For over half a century, few questioned the constructs of modern city planning or its seemingly auspicious instruments. Reaping lessons from the past was in fact unthinkable, much until 1961 when Jane Jacobs wrote *The Death and Life of Great American Cities*. In it, Jacobs analyzed the complexities of cities, identifying four essential characteristics for the life and survival of a settlement: (1) high densities of population and intensity of activities; (2) mixed uses; (3) a compact urban fabric with pedestrian friendly streets; and (4) the conservation of existing buildings and urban fabrics, partnered by 'sympathetic' new contributions. These principles directly contrasted with the fundamental presumptions of Conventional Zoning employed by city planners, which more often than not, effectively subdivide the city into zones or districts of singular uses, favoring its dispersion, subordinating public spaces to the needs of traffic, while ignoring or razing the existing context.

Jacobs criticism of these planning tools and precepts, and their relation to 'urban renewal' instigated polemics and much needed debate, and because it redirected attention towards the inherently valuable principals and traits of traditional place-making, to date the publication remains as an influential reference regarding the study, preservation and planning of American cities.

Within a few years, architect Robert Venturi questioned the autocratic and fractured nature of modern architecture and planning in the 1966 book *Complexity and Contradiction in Architecture*, and later followed up with *Learning from Las Vegas.*[14] Venturi's revolutionary statement: *"Main-street is almost alright"* placed in doubt the principles of modern planning and laid another foundational layer for later movements that would propose viable alternatives. In 1977, historian Vincent Scully noted that Venturi's first book *"provided both architects and critics alike with more realistic and effective weapons, so that the breadth and relevance which the architectural dialogue has since achieved were largely initiated by it."*

The conversation between the environment and cities was dusted off and re-popularized during the counter-culture movement of the 1960's, led by Stewart Brandt and others. Brandt's 1968, first edition of *The Whole Earth Catalog* had an insightful sub-title, "access to tools." The catalog stated that anything, including books, maps and the prospects of personal computers were potentially useful tools for individuals to promote social and environmental progress. At the core of his philosophies, were the concepts of decentralization, personal empowerment, and technological freedom. It was his mandate for change and responsibility - a well-received message in the communes then sprouting around the country, and in academic circles debating social and cultural reformation.

In 1977, architect Christopher Alexander wrote *A Pattern Language: Towns, Buildings, Construction.* Rooted in his appreciation for and analysis of the harmonious evolution and characteristics of medieval settlements, he circumscribed, in user-friendly terms, an organization for contemporary cities and buildings. Alexander argued that the innate logic of cities stems from local regulations that require place-specific features, but that permit builders to adapt them to particular situations within the urban environment. Alexander's position was counter to the prevailing mass-production mind-set of the modern era that had led to the proliferation of generic models and responses. In a *Back to the Future* parallelism, he suggested that customization and localized responses, more typical of yesteryear, were preferable to the importation of homogenizing "international" ones. He described his theory of 'patterns' in terms that a theoretical mathematician or computer scientist would refer to as a 'generative grammar.'[15] At every scale, from entire regions, to neighborhoods, buildings, and their increments, Alexander provided for exact methods and instruments; all hitched onto a specific, local vocabulary, grammar, and syntax, evolving into a web of inter-dependent relationships between the macro and micro scales. The significance of character and the quality of human settlements was underlined, as was the charter guiding their making. Alexander presented his theory in terms that could be grasped by all, including the very engineers that were *driving* the planning of new cities and suburbs, while folding in aspects from formal and informal precedents.

Around this same period, theorist, urban designer and prolific essayist, Leon Krier, in alignment with the position and teachings of the renowned and influential turn of the century architect Heinrich Tessenow, pointed to the exacting correlations between the economic and cultural health of cities and their scale, composition and the relatedness of parts. Krier argued that a city's 'building blocks' are not accidental nor necessarily economically driven, but rather are the children of collective inheritances, including architectural, legal and moral ordering systems. Krier's own 'rational' un-built plan for his native Luxembourg campaigned for the reconstruction of the traditional compact city model. With his subsequent insightful writings and digestible cartoon-like sketches, he shed further light onto the ills of modern planning, consumerism, and capitalism, emphasizing that each contributes to the dissection of cities into sterile environments, leading to social, economic, and cultural dysfunction.

The timbre of these overlapping concepts by Jacobs, Venturi, Alexander, and Krier, among those of many others, were inseminated at a number of American universities, and served as a catalyst for change within academia and the profession, promoting healthy conversations related to the design of cities that led to the foundation of new movements and theories. In 1992, godfathered by Krier, a collective of scholars and practitioners from across the United States founded the New Urbanism; a movement that has since strived to create equitable, self-sustaining, and predictable settlements based on the lessons of traditional mixed-use pedestrian-friendly models. The early design of the town of Seaside embodies various *new urbanist* values and its development proved financially feasible. Seaside heralded a new era for sustainably minded development and town planning, and even if it fell well short of meeting the movement's socially pluralistic goals, it re-awakened an interest in spatial and formal planning models that had historically prioritized the role of pedestrians, accommodated a mix of uses, which in turn reduced automobile reliance.

An American Revolution: from Counter-culture to Institutional Reformation

Whereas Brandt and the counter-culture movements of the time focused on the individual, in his more recent and self-critical publications, he again stirs the environmentalist debate, stating that compact, dense "cities are green." He underlines that environmentalist and urban designers should not be at odds, but rather team up, to achieve common goals towards sustainability, arguing that urbanization is a significant 'tool' towards combating climate change, and inferring a need for aligned visions and tactics. The 'conventional' planning strategies that perpetuate America's simultaneous consumption of fossil fuels and land, and the physical segregation of uses that leads to social disparities stall such goals. Institutional obsolescence coupled with the unrealistic protraction of western society's *"Happy Motoring"* mindset, along with the absence of a significant number of political leaders in possession of longer-reaching outlooks and stiffer backbones to reject the self-serving interests of energy and development lobbies, and it is little wonder that many U.S. cities are struggling. Sadly, Euclidean Zoning's cancerous conventions continue gnawing on American land, and spreading to other countries. The resulting diseases of sprawl and segregation are equally unconscionable, devastating both US landscapes and those abroad. As these ills spread, sprawl's 'conventional energy' *drip-line* is all the while trickling away. Those wishing to punt the issues forward to the next generation are hoping unconventional options will save their contrived and selfish interpretations of the 'American way of life' and moreover have the capacity to steer attention and efforts away from proactive mitigation and mindful stewardship of the planet, because that would entail taking responsibility in the present.

"Designing with Nature"

By zooming out in scale and placing the topics of urban design, suburban sprawl and mindless consumerism within a larger, global context, reveals the interconnected consequences of car-oriented planning models, fossil-fuel addictions, and climate change, evidencing that civilization's well-being also hinges on the equitable, rational, and sustainable design of cities, in addition to the conservation of natural resources worldwide. To curb the adverse impact of twentieth century planning strategies on the environment and society, the outdated zoning instruments that facilitated their unbridled growth need to be over-hauled, allowing for more sustainable and socially nurturing patterns of development.

In 1969, Ian McHarg, author of *"Design with Nature,"* documented 'natural' system along a 'transect' as complementary, interconnected yet distinct parts of a whole, requiring differing intensities of human interaction, tools and adaptation.[16] So too the conception and construction of cities, towns, villages and hamlets have traditionally, and, in a few instances, start once again, to follow a corresponding and symbiotic reasoning. A fisherman in coastal regions is prepared with adequate tools and attire to interact with the environment, different from those that a hunter might employ in a forest. In like manner, the design of cities can possess logical, locally sensitized codes, with consequent urban and building elements and scales that are in accord with and cognizant of their location along a built 'transect', resulting in more sympathetic relationships with each other as well as with hosting natural contexts.

Sustainable developments can best be achieved through full implementation of evenhanded and coordinated legislation at the international, national, and state levels, facilitating leadership through environmentally conscientious cross-disciplinary programs and incentives across the board.

At municipal and regional levels, the core aspects of Conventional 'Euclidian' Zoning - specifically, those that promote segregation and car-dependence - should be re-worked and potentially partnered with or replaced by 'Form-Based' Codes (FBC) or other implements that promote predictable, compact, mixed-use development. FBC's can provide for contemporary building types, embrace an array of co-existing uses, guide contextually appropriate responses, reinforce urban agriculture, stress environmental considerations, underline the importance of preserving the historic urban fabric, and its increments, open spaces and culture, while addressing both contemporary realities and future growth. "The regulations and standards in *form-based codes*, presented in both diagrams and words, are keyed to a regulating plan that designates the appropriate form and scale (and therefore, character) of development rather than only distinctions in land-use types."[17 18] FBC's, such as those incorporated in a growing number of American cities, including Cincinnati, El Paso and Miami, can provide local governments with practical and empowering tools for change, creating the platform for residents and businesses to voice their needs, participate in and chaperone the 'envisioning' of their community. Thusly, FBC's can guide predictable growth, integrating priorities that result in sustainable developments - viable, equitable, desirable communities - that will weigh less on the shoulders of future generations, which a cookie-cutter formula simply cannot engender. Likewise, if the Industrial Revolution led humankind towards automation that in turn led to mass-production, and by consequence generic solutions to modern societal needs, including the design of automobiles, buildings and cities, all which greatly contributed to the climate crisis now being faced, then perhaps XXI century innovations will additionally facilitate the recuperation of 'customized' responses to place and society that can complement 'smarter' codes; together achieving sustainable design goals.

Certainly, present energy and environmental predicaments are instigating the long-awaited re-evaluation and re-structuring of current planning methods that partially brought them to bear. American planning institutions need a revolution - to be rattled to their core - to prompt strategies, tools, and public engagement that are more effective and lead to sustainable solutions.

As importantly, planning institutions across the globe should reconsider their importation of the unsuccessful Euclidian planning tools that have led to the swift degradation of American cities and towns, and their staggering contributions towards climate change, ideally reassessing the value of national cultures, innate place-based logic systems, including their own built heritage, traditions, and context. Examples of form-based codes are in fact appearing across the globe. Realizing that the capital of Havana is composed of neighborhoods with different constructs and the necessity for comprehensive tools to preserve the essence of each, local academics, preservation and planning institutions began the process of producing neighborhood specific codes for each of its 14 municipalities, commencing with those most vulnerable. The 2004 adoption (2006 publication) of the *Urban Regulations for El Vedado,* and the subsequent 2007 (2008 publication) *Urban Regulations for the Historic Center,*[19] divest themselves of nearly all the 'Euclidian' aspects of the *Ordenanzas*' 1963 revisions and replace them with a well-rounded approach to land use and urban planning as well as the preservation of the historic urban fabric of each neighborhood and the character of its streets and public spaces. Both codes make provisions for contemporary building types, underline the importance of preserving the historic urban fabric, providing for an array of uses to co-exist, the buttressing of urban agriculture, and environmental considerations. The codes' keystone elements address the preservation of historic structures, open spaces, sustainability, and culture, addressing both contemporary realities and future growth. In the development of an organizational structure, both new codes reconnect to the essence of the original form-based 1861 *"Ordenanzas de Construcción para la ciudad de la Habana y pueblos de su término municipal"* that had dexterously once guided the city's expansions, while marrying those inherited tools with an updated method and a graphic delivery of information. In addition, both codes are user-friendly because they are illustrated with comprehensible graphic summaries, based on updated form-based *Smart Code*[20] models and are downloadable from the internet.[21]

Clearing the Road to Sustainability and Livability

Across the globe, interconnecting environmental, social, and economic responses are at the crux of sustainable developments in the XXI century. A search for causational factors can lead to interdisciplinary, effective solutions capable of tackling the perpetrators steering climate change, (i.e. automobiles/ carbon related emissions) possibly begetting greater social interaction, cultural richness, economic independence thereby healing ailing cities. The wisdom of valuable and relevant local urban traditions, which tread more lightly on the environment, support social bonds and enable micro-economies are slowly being recuperated by practitioners and movements, and emergent interest groups across America and the globe, intent on resuscitating the material places of our civilization.

In the United States, "*Smart Growth, New Urbanism, and 'Transit Oriented Development' have all entered today's development lexicon, and all are considered sustainable options."*[22] To a greater or lesser degree, they each prescribe that new towns and the infill of existing cities should strive to create "walk-able neighborhoods; make development decisions predictable and fair; mix land uses; preserve: open space, farmland, natural beauty, critical environmental areas; provide transportation choices; develop existing communities first; provide for a range of housing, and encourage compact building design."[23] These three parallel movements, and more recent benchmarking systems, including LEED-ND by the USGBC[24] encourage the design of compact mixed use settlements so dwellers can reside closer to work, use public transportation or carpool, live in energy-efficient compact houses, which incrementally add to the character of 'place' while their footprint has a reduced impact on natural resources. Conscientious projects, generated by the private sector, can be augmented and best guided by integrated and more well-rounded, similarly spirited public sector planning tools, such as *Form-Based Codes.*

While the public sector plays catch-up, more recent private-sector driven methods have arisen. Following in the footsteps of "guerilla gardening" movements initiated in New York City in 1973, and in reaction to disingenuous community engagement processes that are often fractured or disconnected from communities and their actual needs, a more strategic, laser-like, nimble approach has emerged. *"Tactical urbanism,"* is a phased, line-of-attack, instigating change and offering local solutions for local planning challenges, often fostering short-term solutions and experiments that are capable of yielding high rewards at a lower initial capital investment cost, thereby improving the livability of towns and cities one block, street, or building at a time. In the "pursuit of resilient neighborhoods", one of the goals of *tactical urbanism* proponents is "to develop social capital between citizens, and the building of organizational capacity between public-private institutions, non-profits, and constituents...while creating a laboratory for experimentation and increased public awareness of pressing community issues."[25]

Cause and Effect: Human Settlement Patterns and the Acceleration of Climate Change

In a continual process of re-assessment, the discourse between the design of cities, sustainability and urban agriculture, underscore the direct relationship between human settlement patterns and the acceleration of climate change. Parallel to twentieth and twenty-first century enabling planning principles and methods, this progression can be tracked to the tangled and often dysfunctional evolution of America's physical, social, and political landscapes. This has led current urban designers to the conclusion that grave consequences are down the 'pike', if America is not weaned off its ineffectual fragmentation of cities, outdated infrastructure strategies, corrosive codes, and its addiction to the automobile and energy.

Late XX century theorists made 'learning from the past' once again credible and current thinkers and practitioners are moving towards sustainably minded solutions, realizing that often those two paths intersect.

Cities and suburbs serve as living classrooms, and learning from them as well as from allied disciplines and nature itself have all combined to allow for a clearer understanding of the physical realities of American cities and suburbs, as well as to their co-dependencies. This multi-pronged approach has revealed the overlapping roles of governmental, economic and design forces, both historic and present. The increasingly segregated and handicapped character of contemporary American cities has led to the apperception of their needed strategic retrofitting. To that end, the reconnection to their original compact, mixed-use, pedestrian friendly DNA and the greater protection of natural resources is pivotal. Local and state efforts must not only address the underlying causes accelerating emissions, but in addition, and in particular for dysfunctional cities in vulnerable locations, they must develop in-depth, place-specific impact and risk assessments, identifying mechanisms for adaptation and mitigation, addressing the needs of the disenfranchised as well as economic development; agile enough to modify as experience informs learning. According to a 2010 National Academy of Science report entitled *Limiting the Magnitude of Future Climate Change*, at federal levels, further policies related to greenhouse gas emissions, should include price trajectories adequate to incentivize investments in energy efficiency and low-carbon technologies, which run parallel to local and state efforts to design, retrofit, and/or adapt cities into healthier and more sustainable environments.[26]

Shaping Communities and Embracing a "New Order"[27]

Winston Churchill wisely stated, *"We shape our buildings; thereafter they shape us."*

Buildings come together to shape towns and cities, which in turn shape society. The "character of a society is the cumulative result of the countless small actions, day in and day out, of millions of people."[28] Kunstler and Jose Marti both noted the mirrored relationship between the design of cities, behavior, and social values. If buildings and towns embody sustainable design principles, they better model the quality of life of its users. There is a connection between urban and building forms, the environment, and the social condition - an important *moral* dimension. Moreover, understanding the relationship between urban patterns and an unregulated market leads to a political and social comprehension of the city. A city's buildings and public spaces represent and support its civic culture, rooting the urban identity of society to a decidedly articulated place and this too is an important element in the conformation of a sustainable environment.

As in Darwin's theory of 'survival of the fittest', tried and proven urban & building patterns are re-emerging as relevant, plausible, and desirable sustainable alternatives, capable of protecting natural resources and habitats, setting aside lands so that local agriculture/food production are feasible, reducing carbon emissions and waste, while strengthening social bonds and creating new economies based on 'sustainable development' goals.

The path to sustainability is one that some would prefer to avoid - the difficult and uncomfortable 'road' scientific truths forewarn of and conscionable private and public sector leaders are answering with a larger measure of responsibility.

A 'new order' in public policy and re-prioritized building and urban codes can result in logical human settlements, leading to economically competitive communities and vibrant eco-systems - a balance between the natural and the man-made realms - provided that private interests and public lethargy are kept in check.

Progressively, in the last century, urban planners and planning agencies chose to ignore precedents and time-proven strategies in favor of unbridled growth and land consumption, which certainly proved quite lucrative for developers and speculators. The resulting social, economic, and environmental precipice confronting the more recent and future generations of designers, government agencies, and the nation as a whole, are the unfortunate result. Therefore, future generations will inherit a world immensely different from that which industrialized societies enjoy for the time being if assertive action is not taken at present to tackle the impact of the built realm on the natural one.

In her final publication in 2004, *Dark Age Ahead*, the insightful Jane Jacobs pondered: *"At a given time it is hard to tell whether forces of cultural life or death are in the ascendancy. Is suburban sprawl, with its murders of communities and wastes of land, time, and energy, a sign of decay? Or is rising interest in means of overcoming sprawl a sign of vigor and adaptability in North American culture? Arguably, either could turn out to be true."*

Today's climate crisis calls for a comprehensive re-examination of the patterns of consumption, production, and living, which have led to it and in that re-assessment the design and regulation of human settlements, is undoubtedly a prominent factor. The path to environmental responsibility is thusly laid by sustainable architecture and urbanism practices, guided by 'transect' literate, cross-referenced urban, building and energy efficient codes that are respectful of natural, built and cultural inheritances. Furthermore, form-based codes can empower residents as well as regional and local governments, bringing about substantial, sympathetic, and predictable change to the built realm, so long as they are implemented with consistency. In parallel, tactical initiatives can adroitly respond to small-scale community needs, catalyzing change. In all instances, there should be an emphasis placed on context and a new appreciation for compact urban design patterns as well as nuanced vernacular building traditions, collectively capable of expediting learning curves and contemporary initiatives towards sustainable development goals. Maintaining languid attitudes towards climate change, and overlooking the social, physical, and economic pitfalls of fossil fuel reliance, energy consumption, as well as their facilitating 'conventional' planning strategies, is to remain on the current perilous course. Indeed, ignoring scientific and physical causational evidence, which reveal the correlations between the degradation of natural, built and social infrastructures, is a path that leads to nowhere - *a dead end* - one that only the truly reckless and *stupid* would continue to journey upon.

Endnotes

[1] John Nolen, Charles Warren, ed. *New Towns for Old*, Sheridan Books, Inc., pgs. 2-4, 2005 (Reprinted. Originally published in 1927, Boston Massachussetts, Marshall Jones Co.)
[2] Bruce Stephenson, *The Roots of New Urbanism: John Nolen's Garden City Vision for Florida*, http://www.cnuflorida.org/nu_florida/roots.htm (October, 2012)
[3] Ibid
[4] http://www.formbasedcodes.org/what-are-form-based-codes
[5] Edward L. Glaeser and Joseph Gyourko, *The Impact of Zoning on Housing Affordability*, 2002
[6] http://www.theatlanticcities.com/jobs-and-economy/2012/08/brief-history-birth-urban-planning/2365/
[7] Peter Norton, *Fighting Traffic: The Dawn of the Motor Age in the American City*, Massachusetts Institute of Technology, pg. 7, 2008
[8] Wright presented the idea of a "Broadacre City" in his 1932 book *The Disappearing City*
[9] 2006 Statistics, US. Department of Energy
[10] www.epa.gov
[11] Gustavo Sanchez-Hugalde, "The Preservation of Historic Design: The Smart Code," Lecture; *Under the Sun: Sustainable Innovations & Tradition* Symposium, 2007
[12] James Howard Kunstler, *The Geography of Nowhere: The Rise and Decline of America's Man-Made Landscape*, Simon & Schuster, New York, 1994
[13] *United Nations Brunkhart Commission Report*, 1997
[14] Denise Scott Brown and Steve Izenour were Venturi's co-authors in *Learning From Las Vegas*
[15] A linguistic theory that attempts to describe the tacit knowledge a native speaker has of a language by establishing a set of formal rules that generate all the possible grammatical sentences of a language, while excluding all unacceptable sentences, *Webster's Dictionary*
[16] Ian McHarg, *Design with Nature*, Natural History Press, 1969
[17] Form-based Codes website. www.formbasedcodes.org, September, 2011
[18] See: http://www.formbasedcodes.org/index.html and http://en.wikipedia.org/wiki/Form-based_codes
[19] *Regulaciones Urbanísticas Ciudad de La Habana: El Vedado* and *Regulaciones Urbanísticas Cuidad de La Habana: Centro Histórico*: http://www.planmaestro.ohc.cu/index.php/instrumentos/regulaciones
[20] www.smartcodecentral.org
[21] See: http://www.planmaestro.ohc.cu/index.php/otros-aspectos/62-publicaciones
[22] Sustainable Development, Urban Land Institute, 2005
[23] Congress for the Urbanism: www.cnu.org
[24] US Green Building Council: www.usgbc.org
[25] Tactical Urbanism Beta-Short-Term Action/Long-Term Change: http://www.ctdatahaven.org/know/index.php/File:Tactical_Urbanism_Guide_2011_sml.pdf
[26] See: http://dels.nas.edu/resources/static-assets/materials-based-on-reports/reports-in-brief/Limiting_Report_Brief_final.pdf
[27] Niccolo Machiavelli in *The Prince* proclaimed: *"There is nothing more difficult to carry out, nor more doubtful of success, nor more dangerous to handle, than to initiate a new order of things."*
[28] Quote by Duane Elgin. Discussion Course for 'Choices for Sustainable Living,' North West Earth Institute, 2000

CITY OF HABITATS

Gustavo Sánchez-Hugalde

Figure 1. Master plan of the 'Alturas de Manoguayabo' in Santo Domingo

Zoo City

Recently, while watching a program on the Animal Planet Channel, I observed a lion pacing its cage. Visitors walking by, stopped, stood, and watched him. The cage seemed far too small for an animal of such magnitude. Indeed, the lion appeared anxious, stressed, and depressed. It was a very sad scene, as you couldn't tell who was more miserable, the lion or the on-lookers who were expecting him to behave characteristically. At that moment, I asked myself what a lion (or by default any other species can do) within the confines of a cage. Without having to hunt or lead the horde, the poor creature was clearly not in its natural habitat, thus he could not behave naturally.

Ten minutes later, a magnificent lion freely roaming a Kenyan landscape appeared on the screen, moving with the self-confidence of a 'King,' immersed in his own kingdom, asserting his innate dominance with every step.

Humans continue to cordon off nature; be it in a zoo setting or on an animal reserve, separating animals into small, individual habitats.

Figure 3. Lion in a zoo cage
Figure 4. Lion in its own habitat

In many ways, the zoo is reminiscent of how humans construct their own habitat today. Separated land uses and stratification of socio-economic classes are like those cages, where connections are highly limited both physically and socially. Such places are now the reality of most North Americans, as described by Andres Duany, Elizabeth Plater-Zyberk and Jeff Speck in the book Suburban Nation.[2]

These "Zoo-Cities" are comprised of residential developments, the so called "gated communities" with their boring and identical houses, with little to do other than eat, sleep, watch TV; or if you feel social, jump in a car and go shopping. Of course, minimal if any public transportation can be supported in these dispersed areas; vehicles govern the open space, and pedestrians are held prisoners at the edges. Indeed, the sidewalks have no trees, and crossing the street requires negotiating a six-lane highway just to access convenience retail. Once in the shopping district, you park and "walk" in an amazing environment, one where the parking lots are twice, if not three times larger than the actual area designated for people. In many instances, one's place of employment or residence might be close by, perhaps a few blocks away. However, in most cases the pattern of development and the physical segregation of uses necessitates jumping into a car - the ultimate human cage. In ecology, a community is a group of interdependent organisms inhabiting the same region and interacting with each other.[3] For humans, our streets and civic spaces are the places destined for social exchange. As our current cities prove, this can't be done effectively from behind the wheel of an automobile.

The Role of Codes and Urban Designers

Figure 2. Interstate I-95 and 395 Intersection, Overtown, Downtown Miami

When flying over these fractured and car-dependent places, which are particularly common in the United States, it becomes apparent that this growth model is ubiquitous, implemented on a truly gigantic scale. Sure, there are a lot of visibly green areas, even where people live, work and shop. Yet, somehow nothing looks natural, and you can't survive without a car. These are all by-products of twentieth century conventional zoning.

This pattern of growth not only affects the edges of cities, but assaults its urban core. Highways have torn once viable neighborhoods apart, fragmenting them with large districts of disconnected single uses similar to those now pre-dominating the edge.

These places, whether urban or suburban, are designed and built by specialists, such as the developers who only build retail "plazas," office "parks," or residential "communities." Traffic engineers are in charge of thoroughfares that connect these pods; and the environmental analysts, well, they are only worried about the natural areas. At this point, not even statistics are helping these placeless burgs, because eighty percent of everything built in USA is imbued with these unfortunate characteristics.[4] These environments are the result of conventional land use codes, which rigidly use statistics to administer technocratic, artificial, restrictive, single-use zones that don't allow the diversity and evolution of the human habitat. Everybody looks closely at the statistical performance of their own specialties - how much land has been preserved, or how many cars are moved per hour - but whose taking a wholistic approach focused on the big picture?

Interestingly, conventional codes are visualized through zoning plans that resemble Zoo-Parks, where each area is subdivided by an unrelated monoculture, each with a specific specimen and with only one connection or controlled access point. While in the zoning plans we find large dedicated zones to office, retail or residential, in a modern zoo we find areas dedicated to the elephants, panthers, or pigs. Perhaps this explains why today's conventional codes consequently create 'mono-tone' environments. While these socially, physically and economically segregating conditions are most common in North America, the same development patterns can be found in a growing number of cities around the world. Urban planners and related disciplines have the responsibility to counteract the resulting maladies associated with the "zoo-city" model, in an effort to progress towards physically and socially sustainable objectives that can in turn also address global concerns.

By studying urban history, it becomes clear that numerous precedents can be applied in the repair of these dysfunctional cities. To be sure, that analysis would reveal that the constant physical evolution of place keeps them habitable, systematically teaching us how cities reflect the way humans continue to evolve and learn.

CITY OF HABITATS
Towards a Unified Theory

When we observe cities, we don't normally ask ourselves how the site once looked in its natural state, before the first settlers arrived.

In Figure 9, the left side of the rendering depicts the once wild and pristine island of Manhattan and the right side features an urbanized Manhattan, where the street intensity continues to fascinate millions of people.

A question arises: which stage of evolution or setting is more sustainable?

Environmentalists, many of whom fight to protect such lands will likely choose the left side of the image while urban planners, who dedicate themselves to making the

Figure 5. The landscape of income segregation: gated homogeneous housing pods
Figure 6. Suburban retail, offices, and residences

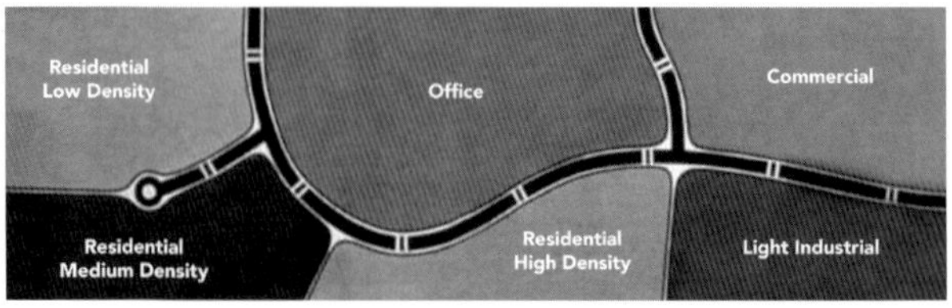

Figure 7. A modern zoning plan with its strict separations of land uses, a few big roads, and little else

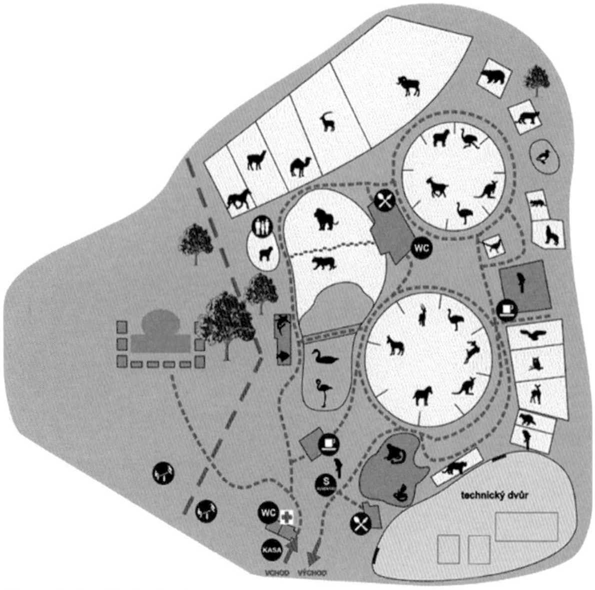

Figure 8. Zoo Hodonin plan

Figure 9. Mannahatta/Manhattan Exhibition.

Figure 10. Left: Aerial view of suburban office and retail parks with surface and undergrund parking, and a ten lane highway in Dallas.

Figure 11. Right: Aerial view of Avenida 9 de Julio in Buenos Aires, boulevard surrounded by a very intense mixed-use fabric.

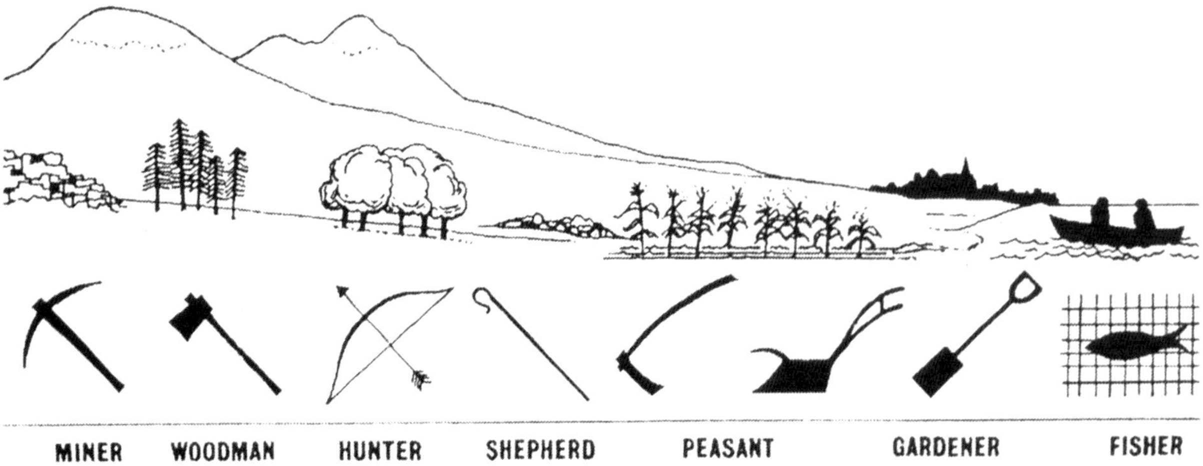

Figure 12. Sir Patrick Geddes' Valley Section.

Figure 13. Natural Transect of the Volcano Chimborazo.

built environment more livable, might choose the one on the right. A clear dichotomy arises between natural and human habitats because they are perceived as two exclusive realities.

In the 1800s, Naturalists Alexander von Humboldt and Charles Darwin made history while traveling around the world to observe and analyze the inherent similarities and differences of the planet's bioclimatic zones. In doing so, they were trying to understand how humans fit into the picture.

In 1807, von Humboldt published in his Essay on "Geography of Plants"[5] an illustrative cross-section of the Volcano Chimborazo (see Figure 13), showing an altitude mapping, an analysis of the topography, strata of the soil, and the changing flora related to its context. It required a great effort to understand the complexity, and the inherent interconnectivity of the variables associated with the transition between habitats.

At the beginning of the 20th century, Sir Patrick Geddes, biologist and town planner, made one of the earliest attempts to bridge Biology and the Social Science in his book "Cities in Evolution."[6] Figure 12 shows Patrick Geddes' "Valley Section," which from ridgeline to shoreline demonstrates the 8 dominant human occupations associated with natural resource extraction.

The geographer Otto Schluter is credited with having first formally used "cultural landscape" as an academic term

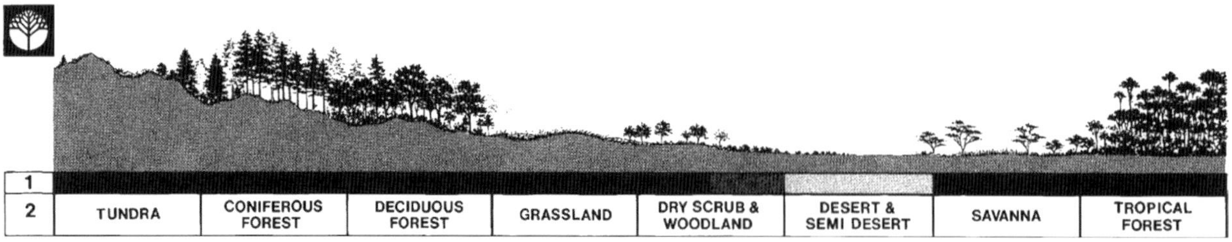

Figure 14. Pardisan Nature Park

in the early 20th century[23] In 1908, Schluter argued that by defining geography as a *Landschaftskunde* (landscape science) this would give geography a logical subject matter shared by no other discipline.[24][23]

He defined two forms of landscape: the *Urlandschaft* (transl. 'original landscape') or landscape that existed before major human-induced changes and the *Kulturlandschaft* (transl. 'cultural landscape') a landscape created by human culture. The major task of geography was to trace the changes in these two landscapes.

The concept of 'cultural landscapes' finds its origins in the European tradition of landscape painting.[25] From the 16th century onwards, many European artists painted landscapes in favor of people, diminishing the people in their paintings to figures subsumed within broader, regionally specific landscapes.[26]

The word "landscape" itself combines 'land' with a verb of Germanic origin, "*scapjan/schaffen*" to mean, literally, 'shaped lands.'[27] Lands were then regarded to have been shaped by natural forces, and the unique details of such *landshaffen* (shaped lands) became the subject of 'landscape' paintings.[26]

It was Carl O. Sauer, a human geographer, who was probably the most influential in promoting and developing the idea of cultural landscapes[28]. Sauer was determined to stress the agency of culture as a force in shaping the visible features of the Earth's surface in delimited areas. Within his definition, the physical environment retains a central significance, as the medium with and through which human cultures act.[29] His classic definition of a 'cultural landscape' reads as follows:

"The cultural landscape is fashioned from a natural landscape by a cultural group. Culture is the agent, the natural are the medium, the cultural landscape is the result."

In 1969, Ian McHarg - a Scottish landscape architect, planner and teacher whose passion for meshing communities and ecology inspired scores of successors - published the celebrated book, "Design with Nature."[7]

Among all the important methods of analysis, it was his capacity to study the diversity and complexity of the habitats through matrix tables, layers of plans, sections and pictures that sticks with so many planners to this day.

In what may be his most famous project, Pardisan Nature Park, an environmental theme park for the Shah of Iran in Tehran, he developed a program for vegetation exhibits. It relied upon an illustrated cross section to organize a continuum of bioclimatic zones, which corresponded to water demand, plant community characteristics, and the relationships between plants, animals, and human communities.[8]

But while there had been several, albeit unsatisfactory, attempts to consider humans as an essential part of nature, working a theory that could unify the two sides remained missing.

It is of particular importance to understand efforts to conceptually conciliate natural and human environments in the work of Christopher Alexander, from *A Pattern Language: Towns, Buildings, Construction* (1977), *The Nature of Order: An Essay on the Art of Building and the Nature of the Universe* (2003-4), which includes *The Phenomenon of Life, The Process of Creating Life, A Vision of a Living World* and *The Luminous Ground*, his latest, most comprehensive and elaborate work. In it, he puts forth a new theory about the nature of space and describes how this theory influences thinking about architecture, building, planning, and the way in which we view the world in general. The mostly static patterns from *A Pattern Language* have been amended by more dynamic sequences, which describe how to work towards patterns (which can roughly be seen as the end result of sequences). Sequences, like patterns, promise to be tools of wider scope than building (just as his theory of space goes beyond architecture).[22]

From Nature to Urban Transect

Today, natural scientists are still debating the terms and definitions of various concepts.[9] Nevertheless; the information available to the general public converges to recognize three distinct scales of analysis represented by biomes, ecosystems and natural habitats.

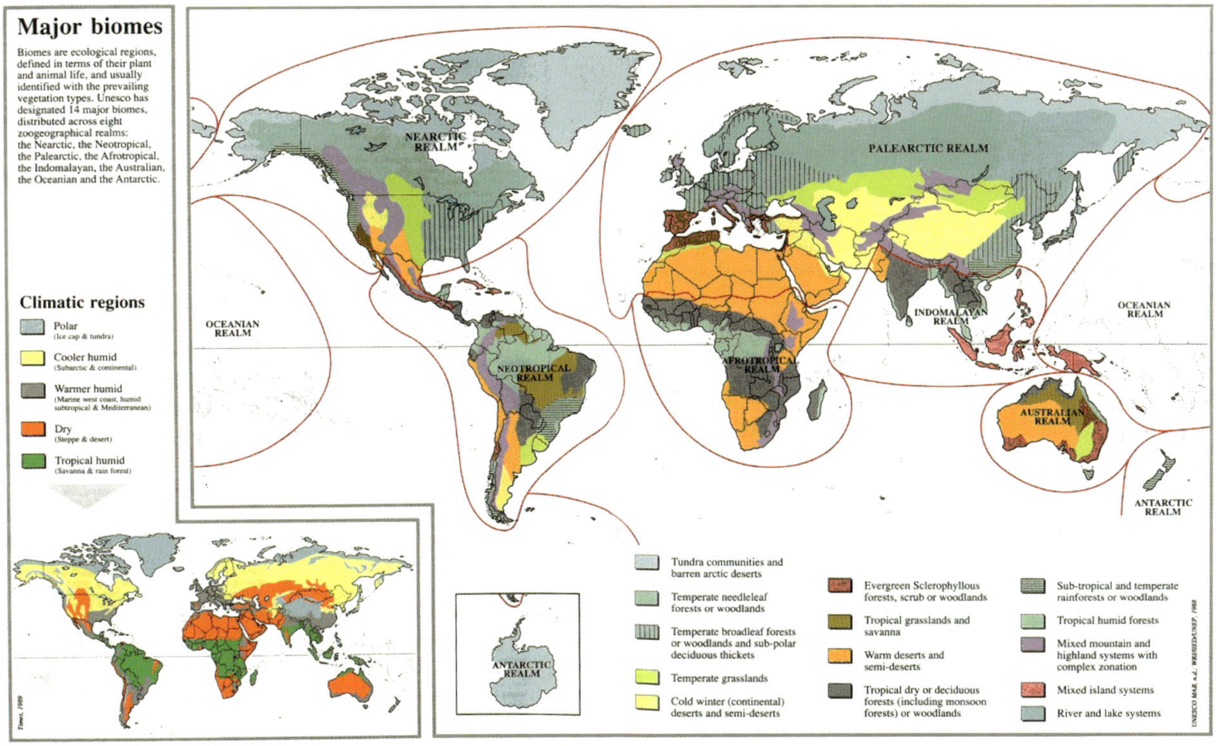

Figure 15. Major Biomes.

Biomes (bioclimatic zones) are used to organize the natural world. It is a large geographical region with plants and animals that are able to live in that location, given its particular climate. [11, 12]

An *Ecosystem*, however, is much smaller than a biome. Conversely, a biome can include many similar ecosystems found throughout the world. Ecosystems are comprised of dynamic interactions between plants, animals, microorganisms, and their environment, which help form a functional unit. Ecosystems fail if they do not remain

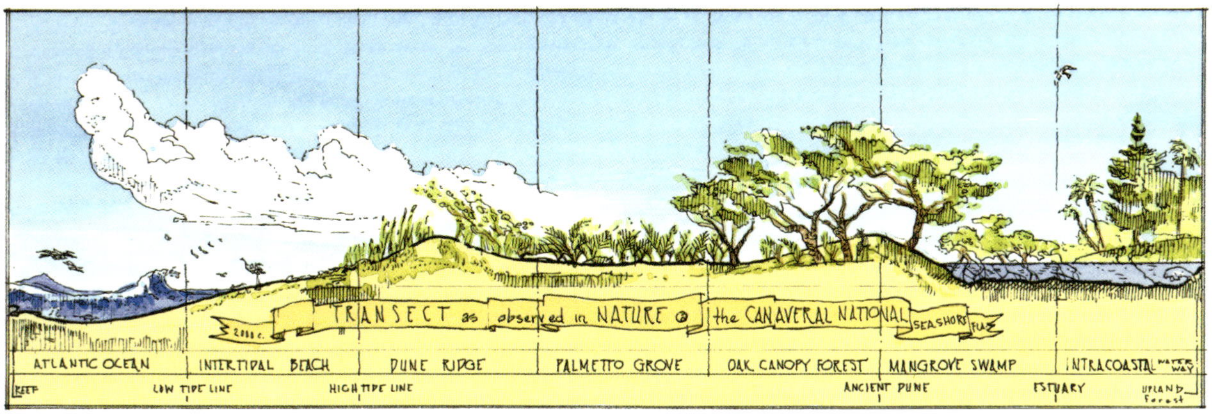

Figure 16. Example of a Natural Transect through an Ecosystem

Figure 17. Furnarius rufus building its nest

in balance. No community can carry more organisms than its food, water, and shelter can accommodate. For example, in the forests there is the rotting tree stump ecosystem, the forest floor ecosystem, the canopy ecosystem, etc. They are all a part of one biome - the deciduous forest biome.[13]

Ecosystem diversity can be measured by the richness of genetic diversity within individual species, by the number of different species present, and the variety of habitats. Diverse ecosystems are believed to be more stable and productive.[14]

The special place in which a plant or animal live is called *habitat*. The ecosystem can be considered the zone where an animal lives, and the habitat would be its address in that zone.[15]

If we look more closely at nature, we can observe a series of concatenated biomes, ecosystems, and habitats. For instance, we can analyze the Marine biome transitioning to the Rainforest biome, the ocean ecosystem with its coral reefs, sharks, fish, among other habitats; followed by the beach ecosystem with its specific fauna and flora habitats, followed by the dunes and wetland ecosystems with their respective habitats; all transitioning in a continuum that make sense not only because they are different, but also because they support each other. The absence, or even a fundamental change within the habitat will, in a chain reaction, definitively affect all of the others.

The Transect Theory

At the turn of the 21st century, with an understanding of the research and propositions of Geddes, Schluter, McHarg and others, New Urbanists Douglas Duany, Andres Duany and Elizabeth Plater-Zyberk developed the Transect theory; a geographical cross section that introduced humans habitats into the larger scheme of nature (see Figure 11).[10] Philosophically, the Transect theory is a natural law that can be observed anywhere and everywhere because it emerged organically in human settlements, preceding its explicit conceptual formulation. The concept of the transect is illustrated in Chinese scroll paintings dated from the 9th century (Figure 18) - in them it's very easy to identify the "human ecosystems" that transition in a continuum from natural, rural, to the urban center. The Transect is a tool that unifies the natural and human environments addressing the three scales of analysis for the study of nature. In the regional scale, we can analyze the "human biome," which is defined by the relationship and interaction among the urban settlements, working rural areas, and uncompromised nature.

Urban settlements can be categorized by size, intensity and diversity: Hamlets, Villages, Towns, Cities and Megalopolis. Each type is conformed by "human ecosystems" called transect zones, which are at the same time conformed by "human habitats" at the smallest scale increment: individual buildings.

It is important to clarify that the Transect diagram represents an ideal continuum amongst the individual Transect-zones; not all "T-zones" can be found in a specific order, nor are they found in every urban settlement. In traditional settlements you will typically find three to four T-zones -- the size of the settlement, determining the T-zones that are likely to occur.

Figure 18. Chinese scroll painting of 9th century with basic human activities related to different urban conditions

The Context

Like ecosystems, each transect zone has its own context. The Transect diagram shown below includes six different context zones: T1-Nature Preserve, T2-Rural Reserve, T3-Sub-urban, T4-General Urban, T5-Urban Center, and T6-Urban Core.

T1- The Natural Context includes all lands that are in pristine condition and permanently protected from development, either by purchase or by environmental law. In the Natural Context zone, the continuity of nature trumps roads and other man-made elements. The only buildings likely to be found are campground structures.

T2- The Rural Context includes lands that are not appropriate for development, but that have not been permanently protected as in the Natural Context. The Rural Context usually includes agricultural land uses and/or woodland. Typical buildings include farmhouses and cottages.

T3- The Sub-urban Context is similar to conventional suburban residential areas except that they are within a pedestrian shed. The pedestrian shed involves the area that a person is willing to walk for daily needs. The pedestrian shed radius has cultural variations and adaptations to nature of the place, but generally it is accepted as a quarter of mile distance. T3 should always be connected to a more diverse community. The buildings consist of single-family homes with large lots and setbacks from the street. Office and retail use is generally restricted. The character of its public space is still quasi-rural.

T4- The General Urban Context is where buildings and public space begin to coalesce into an identifiable urban fabric. This T-zone is within easy walking distance to a village, town or neighborhood center. A larger variety of building types exist, many of which allow mix-uses in small and medium size lots. Public spaces become more defined and more urban, with more activity along the street. While T3 is decisively sub-urban and T5 and T6 are uniformly urban, T4 allows characteristics of both to be present.

T5- The Urban Center Context features a wide mixture of land uses and building types. The Urban Center includes merchants, offices, live work-units, townhouses, and wide selection of apartment types that attract young and old to vibrant streets, squares and Plazas. T-5 is perhaps best embodied by the Main or High Street.

T6- The Urban Core Context only occurs in regional centers. It has the tallest buildings, and the busiest and most diverse street life. T-6 is where one-of-a-kind functions with regional relevance, like cultural and government buildings are located. The Urban Core is where many people willingly trade more space for less so that they can enjoy all the benefits of a highly urban lifestyle.

SD- District designations are assigned to sites and structures that by virtue of their intrinsic function, disposition or configuration, cannot be incorporated into one of the regular Transect Zone Community Types. Typical Districts are entertainment and tourist districts, college campuses, capitol districts, hospitals, large scale transportation or manufacturing facilities, such as airports, container terminals, refineries etc.

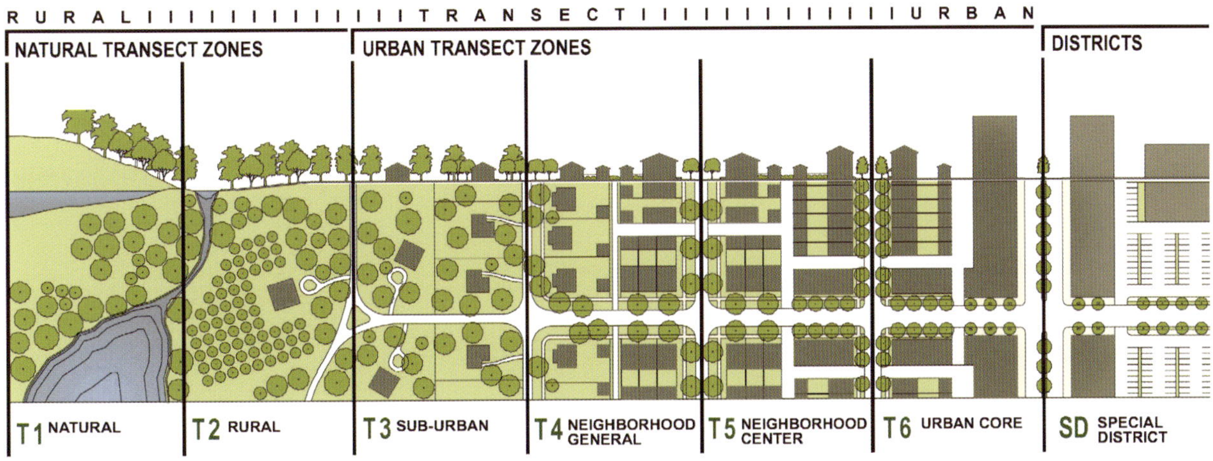

Figure 19. From Nature to Urban Transect

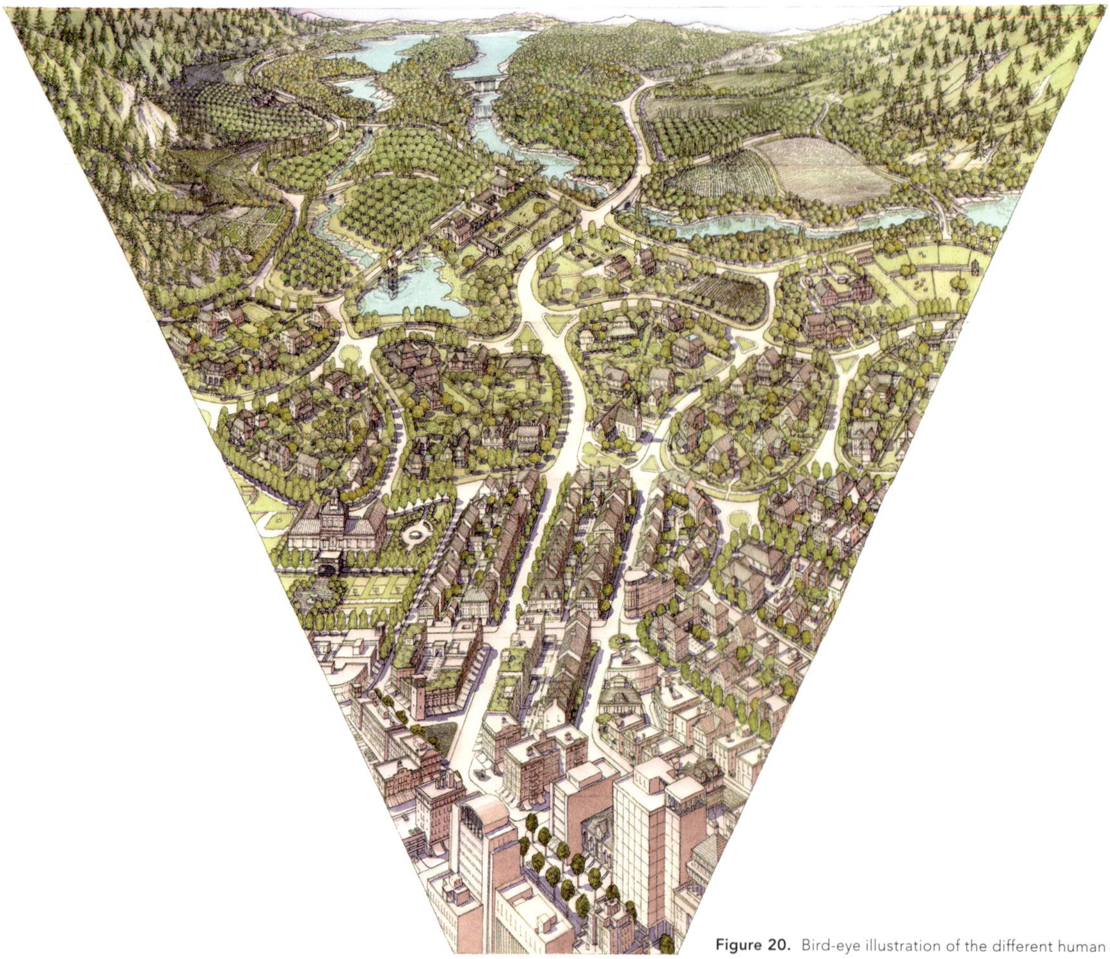

Figure 20. Bird-eye illustration of the different human ecosystems

Thus, like a sequence of biomes or ecosystems, the distribution, geographic area, and relationships among T-zones vary. In most Hamlets, for example, the most rural T-zones are common (T1-T2-T3 and T4), whereas the presence of the T-5 zone distinguishes towns from hamlets. Similarly, a "downtown" core rarely contains any vestiges of real nature as found in the most rural T1-T2 zones.

As in the study of Nature, the study of urban settlements through the lens of the Transect helps differentiate appropriate scales by which to organize the human habitat and its relationship to nature.

In Nature, the basic elements for each category of study possess common conditions but at the same time specific adaptations to the place. When you walk through different tropical forests, there are certain features that at first glance look similar everywhere, like the presence of some very large trees, or the general shape of the trees. However, if you look closer you will find different adaptations to the soil, vegetation, and the relationship between the components (overall diversity), and to natural disasters such as hurricanes, earthquakes, tsunamis, etc; that in conjunction create the unique characteristics inherent to that place.

Trees range from spindly under story shrubs to enormous buttress-rooted rainforest trees festooned with vines and peppered with orchids, ferns and bromeliads. Tropical trees depend on animals for pollination and seed dispersal and are constantly assaulted by insects, fungi, maelstrom and machete. Furthermore, soil types, rainfall, the frequency of disruption (hurricanes, fires, etc.) and the various assemblages of plants and animals vary widely from one tropical forest to another.[16]

Just as unique characteristics distinguish individual biomes, ecosystems, or habitats, so do they distinguish the human habitat, as supported by the Transect. The so-called "cultural differences" of different urban settlements is

Figure 21. Tropical Forest Ecosystem

Figure 22. Rambla of Barcelona

Figure 23. Aerial view of T6 in Paris

Figure 24. T6 in New York by night

no more than a variety in adaptation made by humans at all scales, as each human settlement is comprised of the same basic natural and built elements.

Context zones or T-zones are not to be defined by various degrees of density; low, mid or high density areas can all provide a setting for the natural social exchange inherent to urbanism. Rather, it is the public realm as best defined by the street that reveals the various intensities associated with human settlement patterns.

While civic spaces such as Plazas and Parks can make a city memorable, streets are the single most important urban structuring element in human ecosystems. Interconnected, they are by far the biggest spaces in size in an urban settlement, even though they are not the main theme of discussion among urban planners. Parks and Plazas seem to be more important these days. In many cities like Bogota, there is a compulsive need to count square meters of green area per habitant as indicator of a healthy environment. So you have big plans of re-forestation and new parks without placing an emphasis on street trees and their ecological advantages. Streets play diverse roles, structuring the city with a hierarchy of connections to different points through a network. They define not only the character of the concatenated elements - such as sidewalks, planters and trees, lighting and street furniture, curbs or swales, vehicular lanes and parking, but also the transitions between the private and public space (such as setbacks, arcades, etc) in a pedestrian environment, all subject to evolution and succession through time. Streets are in constant change because of the intensity and ebb and flows of its uses both daily and overtime. They have character and create dynamic rhythms. Indeed, no one street is exactly like another, except seemingly in some suburban tract developments.

The Rambla of Barcelona is a great example. It does not have a constant right of away; its spatial form is a direct consequence of its ecological condition as a natural drainage stream area. Today, that ecological condition is controlled, connects two very important places of the city with a unique atmosphere, creating one of the most vibrant, memorable and recognizable streets in the world. Besides, it is more visited than any other famous park or plazas in Barcelona.

The Calibration

While the six Transect Zones are normative, countless adaptations may be studied around the world. Paris, for example, has a different transect than Mumbai. Thus, it is essential to study both the sociocultural and natural place characteristics before calibrating and assigning the transect to a given context.

One method for doing so is the 'synoptic survey,' which is how environmental scientists study habitats. This survey is a systematic visual inspection that identifies the typical characteristics of each habitat. After the 'synoptic survey' is complete, the paradigms can be assumed, and aberrations identified for further study. The most representative paradigms can be understood through studying the *dissect* and *quadrat* within a given area.

The Quadrat selects a portion of the land - let's say 100 x 100 ft. - where the component elements of flora and fauna are itemized and counted.

The Dissect is a cross section where you recognize the different composition and strata of the soil, the health of the roots, trunk, leaves, water table, etc.

While these techniques are most often employed in the natural sciences, they can also be applied to the study of Transect zones. It is from the Urban Quadrat and Dissect that planners and designers can extract the genetic material for regulatory codes adapted to highly specific human environments.[17]

Once this information is gathered, analyzed, and verified, the calibration of the coding process may begin to standardize the local physical and cultural characteristics.

Figure 25. The Natural Quadrat and Dissect

T4

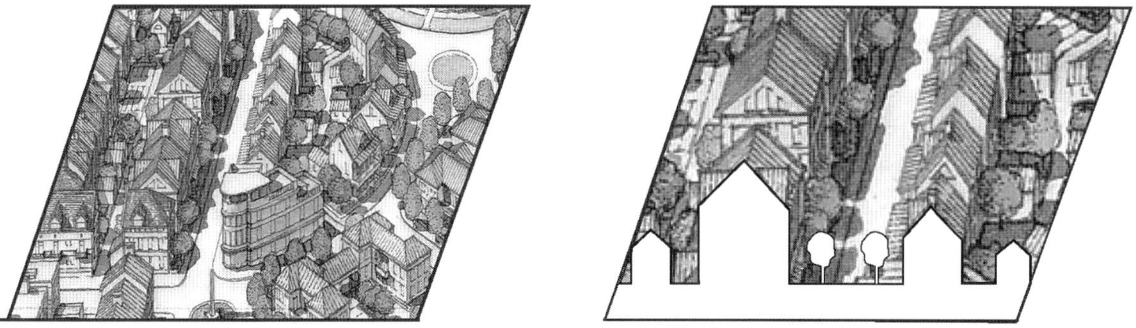

Figure 26. The Urban Quadrat and Dissect

The Succession and Climax

Over long periods of time, ecosystems change in appearance and composition. Succession is the regular replacement of populations in a habitat. Some communities may follow a recognizable sequence of change ending in a relatively stable community referred to as a climax community.[18]

For instance, in Ohio, a simple description of a sere - the series of stages in an ecological succession - that would develop on an abandoned field might be:
grass → shrubs → trees → oak-hickory forest

In this sere, the grass is the *pioneer community* and the oak-hickory forest is the *climax community*. Each step in the sere (grass, shrubs, trees, oak-hickory forest) is individually known as a *seral stage*.[19] There are two main types of *succession*:

1. Primary succession
- begins with bare rock exposed by geologic activity
- example sere: rock → lichen → moss → grass → shrub → trees → oak hickory forest

2. Secondary succession
- begins on soil from which previous community has been removed (by fire, agriculture, etc.)
- old field succession
- example sere: grass → shrub → trees → oak hickory forest
- secondary succession can proceed much faster because the soil has been prepared by the previous community

Early seral stages are highly productive but require large inputs of nutrients, as they tend to lose nutrients. Biomass increases, but there is low productivity and fluctuations in biomass becomes common.[20]

Primary Succession Following Glacial Retreat

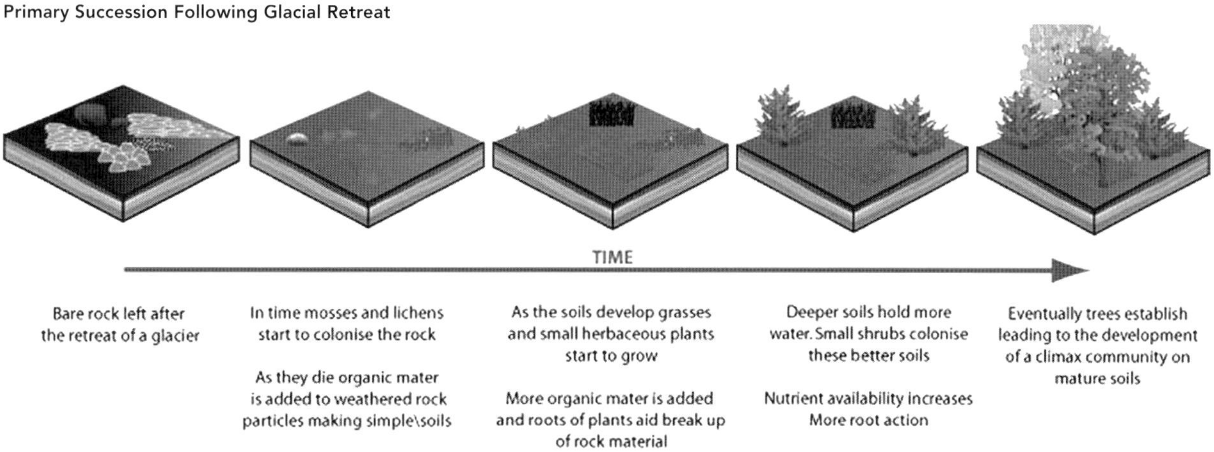

Figure 27. The Succession in Nature

Figure 28. Oak-Hickory Forest Climax

Climax seral stages are very complex. They create a favorable environment for many species. However, the biomass does not fluctuate, and decomposition rates are stable - roughly equivalent to new production. Nutrients are cycled efficiently, and rarely leave the ecosystem. Individual organisms live longer, since they invest more resources in themselves and less in producing offspring.[21]

Successional Stages
Urban Climax & Intensity of Interventions

In the built environment we can also study the sequence of growth and succession from the pioneer to the climax community. The Transect can be also understood as a sequence of successional stages of the same place or case of study, as shown in Figure 29.

Before the industrial revolution, succession in urban settlements was very slow compared to present rates. After the industrial revolution, migration to the cities forced urban centers to evolve, in many cases unnaturally so. To better control growth, the Transect may be used to allocate each urban element within defined parameters. This helps achieve maximum efficiency through the successional stages of growth in the built environment.

In many towns or historical urban centers, we can observe where morphological conditions have stayed static for a long period of time. This can be attributed either to the slowing of economic activity, or that a given population declares its "urban climax" with an end to morphological succession through regulatory growth controls - historic preservation laws being but one example. In such cases, there are lessons to be learned for integrating preservation techniques and the ability of a historic fabric to adapt its uses to the needs of modernity.

This can also be accommodated by Transect "intensity of interventions" context zones across a historic fabric. The use of low, medium and high intensity of interventions tools is very sustainable because it only utilizes and renovates the existing resources, but also identifies the type of interventions needed in specific areas of the city.

Figure 29. The Succession in Human Settlements

Conclusion

Returning to the question of whether natural Manhattan would be more sustainable than built Manhattan, it is best to understand that succession in both the natural and built landscapes are two forces belonging to just one phenomena, as a Natural and Cultural Ecological Unit.

Integrated Ecological Analysis		
Regional Scale	Biome	Settlement Type
Community Scale	Ecosystem	Context Type (T-zones)
Dwell Scale	Habitat	Building Type
Natural & Cultural Ecological Unit		

The island of Mexcaltitan, Nayarit, Mexico, is a simple and great example of a Natural & Cultural Ecological Unit; a place to re-discover the basic human needs in communion with nature, to understand how little we need to affect the natural land to survive and the little amount of urbanism we need to make a complete community with a decent economic standard and more attuned quality of life.

Legend tells it was the Aztlan of the Aztecs, their home city and birthplace from where they set out on their pilgrimage in 1091 that led them to the founding of Tenochtitlan.

Later, it was further developed by the Spanish, culture which is imprinted on their architecture and urbanism. This 200m radius almost circular island can be accessed only by boat. In its center and highest point, a squared Plaza -with grown trees, handsome gazebo and buildings with public arcades - holds the main activities of 1,000 habitants. A beautiful Catholic Church with one tower and campanile, a museum, a "Casa Ejidal" or Municipal Hall, the police station and a bar with pool, cards and domino players surround the Plaza. In the afternoons, men meet at the bar and kids play soccer while women meet at the Plaza to chat and make sure the men and kids don't get into trouble. The island also has a school and high school (the latter functions in the afternoons, with classes taught through Satellite TV), a Health Center; and every street terminates with a view of the water or piers. Improvised altars along the streets, worship San Juan in the east and San Pablo in the west. Processions on boats take place on Easter.

People still make their living fishing at night until sunrise. It has always been like this. Siestas are long and time seems to stretch. Every high tide the island gets flooded and people move around in canoes. That explains why buildings are elevated from the street 1 to 3 ft. - depending on their location. Surprisingly, its demography is diverse, not only European and Native Americans descendants but there is also a Chinese colony that arrived at the end of the 19th Century.

The cultural and natural transect is perfectly obvious. The unity is astonishing. Of course, it is not perfect, but compared to "zoo cities," this one actually makes sense because it is scaled perfectly to a day's worth of human activity. Thus, as a self-sustaining habitat, one could guess that their low-tech environmental performance is supreme. Indeed, the carbon footprint for each individual is probably close to zero.

This also make us think Mexcaltitan might serve as an inspiration for more "down to earth" projects that can serve as an alternative to much more provocative new projects like Masdar, in Abu Dhabi, designed by Foster + Partners, which trusts enormously upon an expensive high tech cost-prohibitive infrastructure, architecture and urbanism.

Nevertheless, because of its geometrical configuration, both Mexcaltitan and Masdar seem to share the inability to expand and grow. Then, settlements should be designed in a way that they are not only capable of achieving natural and cultural climax, but also to adapting easily to succession and future growth demands. Indeed, demography shows us that human population will continue to expand and we need to accommodate this growth as sustainably as we can.

We know that a healthy ecosystem needs a diversity of species so that it is less likely to be seriously damaged by natural disasters and climate change. Every species has a niche in its ecosystem that helps keep the system healthy. We are learning about new species every day, and we are just figuring out the roles they play in the natural world. By studying and maintaining biodiversity, we help keep our planet healthy, and further apply those lessons to place-making strategies.

I believe that this new way of understanding urban settlements and human behavior, in congress with the natural phenomena - at every scale and cross referenced with the natural sciences - has opened a field of discussion and study related to the complex variables that define a place, with the aim of achieving a realistic and sustainable understanding of the potential for a 'city of habitats.'

Figure 30. St. Emilion, Bordeaux, France. The Climax in Human Settlements.

Figure 31. Mexcaltitan Island

Figure 32. Mexcaltitan Island, Nayarit, Mexico

Endnotes

[1] Italo Calvino, *Invisible Cities* (Harcourt Brace Jovanovich [first English edition], 1974).
[2] James Howard Kunstler, *The Geography of Nowhere* (New York: Simon & Shuster, 1993).
[3] Modern Language Association (MLA):"community." WordNet® 3.0. Princeton University. 03 Nov. 2007. <Dictionary.com http://dictionary.reference.com/browse/community>.
[4] Andres Duany, Elizabeth Plater-Zyberk and Jeff Speck, *Suburban Nation* (New York: North Point Press, 2000).
[5] Alexander Von Humboldt, *Essays on the Geography of Plants* (History of Ecology Series) (1978).
[6] Patrick Geddes, *Cities in evolution* (Williams & Norgate, 1915) (Routledge – 1997).
[7] Ian McHarg, *Design with Nature* (Garden City, New York: Natural History Press,1969).
[8] Anne Whiston Spirn, Ian McHarg, *Landscape Architecture, and Environmentalism.* This is an extract of *Environmentalism in Landscape Architecture* edited by Michel Conan (Washington, D.C., Dumbarton Oaks, Trustees for Harvard University, 2000).
[9] See, for example, literature about Biomes at: http://www.tarleton.edu/~range/Literature%20Review/biome.htm.
[10] Andres Duany, *Introduction to the Special Issue: The Transect, Journal of Urban Design*, Vol. 7, No.3 (2002), pp.221-60.
[11] Dennis Paulsen, *World Biomes: Rationale for Hierarchical Organization of the World's Environments* (University of Puget Sound, 2007) http://www.ups.edu/x5680.xml.
[12, 13, 14, 15] Definitions found at:
http://www.scor-int.org/Publications/Biogeography.doc.
http://library.thinkquest.org/CR0210360/biomes.html
http://www.abheritage.ca/abnature/Ecosystems/intro.htm
http://www.nhptv.org/NatureWorks/nwepecosystems.htm
Christian Lévêque, *Ecology from Ecosystem to Biosphere* – (Science Publishers, 2003).
[16] Helene Muller-Landau , Diverse tropical forests defy metabolic ecology models. The complex patterns of tropical forest structure demand more complex explanations (Smithsonian Tropical Research Institute, 2006). http://www.stri.org/english/about_stri/media/press_releases/PDFs/Muller_Landau_for_release_2006.pdf.
[17] Andres Duany et al., *Smartcode & Manual* (Miami: New Urban Publications, Inc., 2005).
[18] Deanne Erdmann, *Interdependence of Life: Introduction to Ecosystems* http://www.bioedonline.org/slides/slide01.cfm?q=%22abiotic%22&dpg=2.
[19, 20, 21] Marietta College Department of Biology and Environmental Science's http://www.marietta.edu/~biol/biomes/succession.htm.
[22] Chirstopher Alexander, http://en.wikipedia.org/wiki/Christopher_Alexander.
[23] James, P.E & Martin, G (1981) *All Possible Worlds: A History of Geographical Ideas. John Wiley & Sons.* New York. Page 177.
[24] Elkins, T.H (1989) "Human and Regional Geography in the German-Speaking Lands in the First Forty Years of the Twentieth Century." Entriken, J. Nicholas & Brunn, Stanley D. (Eds) *Reflections on Richard Hartshorne's The nature of geography.* Occasional publications of the Association of the American Geographers, Washington DC. Page 27.
[25] Pannell, S (2006) *Reconciling Nature and Culture in a Global Context: Lessons form the World Heritage List.* James Cook University. Cairns, Australia. Page 62 .
[26] Gibson, W.S (1989) *Mirror of the Earth: The World Landscape in Sixteenth-Century Flemish Painting.* Princeton University Press, Princeton, New Jersey .
[27] Haber, W (1995) *Concept, Origin, and Meaning of Landscape.* UNESCO's Cultural Landscapes of Universal Value: Components of a Global Strategy. UNESCO, New York. Pages 38-42.
[28] James, P.E & Martin, G (1981) *All Possible Worlds: A History of Geographical Ideas.* John Wiley & Sons. New York. Page 321-324.
[29] Sauer, C (1925) *The Morphology of Landscape.* University of California Publications in Geography. Number 22. Pages 19-53.

Image Sources

Figure 1. Plan of Manoguayabo courtesy of University of Miami School of Architecture Center for Urban & Community Design, http://arc.miami.edu/community/center-for-urban-community-design
Figure 2. Google map of Interstate I-95 and 395 Intersection in Overtown, Downtown Miami
Figure 3. Information & Computer Sciences, University of California – Irvine www.ics.uci.edu/~eppstein/pix/sfzoo/LionCage.html
Figure 4. Roger Beau, http://outdoors.webshots.com/photo/1040321087035204585YXIswL
Figure 5 & 6. SkyscraperCity, USA Sprawl Festival: January 1 to December http://www.skyscrapercity.com/showthread.php?t=383911
Figure 7. Source: Andres Duany, Elizabeth Plater-Zyberk and Jeff Speck, *Suburban Nation* (New York: North Point Press, 2000).
Figure 8. Zoo Honodin. http://www.zoo-hodonin.cz/en/
Figure 9. Manhatta/Manhattan Exhibition, Museum of the City of New York http://www.mcny.org/exhibitions/past/mannahatta-manhattan-a-natural-history-of-new-york-city.html
Figure 10. SkyscraperCity, Best Highways (EU vs USA) http://www.skyscrapercity.com/showthread.php?t=338024&page=3
Figure 11. SkyscraperCity, http://www.skyscrapercity.com/showthread.php?t=987693&page=2
Figure 12. Patrick Geddes Trust. http://www.patrickgeddestrust.co.uk/valleysection.htm
Figure 13. Alexander von Humboldt, http://www.geographicus.com/blog/
Figure 14. Anne Whiston Spirn, Ian McHarg, Landscape Architecture, and Environmentalism. This is an extract of Environmentalism in Landscape Architecture edited by Michel Conan (Washington, D.C., Dumbarton Oaks, Trustees for Harvard University, 2000). http://www.doaks.org/publications/doaks_online_publications/Environmentalism/env4.pdf
Figure 15. Major Biomes. United States Department of Agriculture, Natural Resources Conservation Services. http://soils.usda.gov/use/worldsoils/mapindex/biomes.html
Figure 16. James Wassell, Duany Plater-Zyberk and Company
Figure 17. JOÃO-DE-BARRO (Furnarius rufus) Dario Sanches http://commons.wikimedia.org/wiki/File:Furnarius_rufus_building_nest.jpg
Figure 18. Chinese scroll painting of 9th century. Source: Museum of Tapei, Duany Plater-Zyberk & Company
Figure 19. Nature to Urban Transect, Duany Plater-Zyberk & Company
Figure 20. Bird-eye illustration of the Transect. Eusebio Azcue, Duany Plater-Zyberk & Co.
Figure 21. Tropical Forest. http://treebankingllc.com/images/stories/cr rainforest.jpg
Figure 22. Cinthia Windblown. http://www.baldheretic.com/2007/10/18/barcelona-buskers-of-la-rambla
Figure 23. http://br.olhares.com/vista_aerea_de_paris_foto3129527.html
Figure 24. KuShAsH's Profile http://s285.photobucket.com/albums/ll75/KuShAsH/?action=view&current=800px-New_York_City_at_night_HDR-1.jpg&newest=1
Figure 25 & 26. Quadrat and Dissect. Duany Plater-Zyberk & Company
Figure 27. Succession. Mr G's Environmental Systems. http://sciencebitz.com/?page_id=41
Figure 28. Oak-Hickory Forest. Tarleton State University. http://www.tarleton.edu/Departments/range/Woodlands%20and%20Forest/Oak-Hickory%20Forest/oakhickoryforest.html
Figure 29. *Succession in Human Settlements.* Duany Plater-Zyberk & Company
Figure 30. St. Emilion. http://www.tunliweb.no/Bilder_SM/_album_bordeaux/g1.JPG
Figure 31. Mexcaltitan. Revista Buen Viaje http://www.revistabuenviaje.com/conocemexico/destinos/nayarit/mexcaltitan/mexcaltitan00.jpg
Figure 32. Mexcaltitan. http://lh4.ggpht.com/_L4j1yux2sWU/RpFlcgSIH4I/AAAAAAAACR4/uLXx262ex-c/Alrededores+de+isla+Mexcaltit%C3%A1n.jpg

Cocoon House (Healy Guest House), Siesta Key, Florida, Paul Rudolph, Architect, Library of Congress, Prints & Photographs Division

SUSTAINABLE ARCHITECTURE:
under the sun at mid-century

ARCHITECTURE UNDER THE SUN:
a lifelong conversation between Florida and Cuba reaches its zenith at mid-century with a Sub-Tropical Modern Regionalism

Sonia R. Cháo

Figure 1. Beeber Residence, Miami, 1968, Peter Augustus Jefferson

Figure 2. Bacardi Advertisement

A "lifelong conversation between Florida and Cuba"[1] has existed since Taino Indians first traversed the narrow body of water between them, establishing settlements in both locations. Centuries later, Spanish colonizers ruled over the region, followed by waves of pirates, merchants, and entrepreneurs. The relationship across the Florida Straits intensified in 1898 when the US intervened in Cuba's war for independence, exerting influence, political control, and facilitating American investments. Spurred by new forms of communication, transportation, tourism, and situated at arm's length from strict prohibition laws, construction booms ensue in both Miami and Havana just as the XX century dawns. An ebb and flow of ideas and professional exchanges increases between architects and planners over time. Those ties reaching their zenith at mid-century, when analogous, explorations for an authentic, tropically anchored architecture strongly influences the constructs for a sub-tropical Modern Regionalism in the northern Caribbean Basin.

To lay the foundation for those readings and to understand the circumstances which eventually lead to their similarities in architectural thought and aligned pursuits requires identifying the divergent realities of these two locations, the underpinning objectives, and the cross-pollination that at times feed a convergence of interest between architects. To do so, it is fundamental to rewind to the onset of the 20th century, when the cultural, physical, and economic asymmetry of Florida and Cuba could not have been more striking.

ASSYMETRIES AND COMMON DENOMINATORS

Florida

The development of South Florida, calibrated by natural disasters, economic decline, and wars, echoes the characteristic cyclical rhythms of expansion and contraction of 20th century America.[2] At the end of the nineteenth century, Florida's half-million population is concentrated in the northeastern quadrant of the peninsula with only 5 percent of residents (approximately 25,000) sprinkled across the southern tip of the state.[3] As early as the mid 1700's, Cuban fishermen established temporary settlements along Tampa's bay. Between 1868 and 1878 many prominent Cubans fled the island due to civil wars. In general, along the southeast coast, together with the vestiges of Spanish colonial forts and isolated Native American settlements, the region's earliest buildings, constructed by Northeasterners and Bahamian pioneers, were utilitarian wood frame vernacular derivatives that adapted imported constructive traditions to local climate and materials, in turn, providing models for residential and commercial development. Porches for living and sleeping, verandas, loggias, walled patios, terraces, balconies, habitable roof decks, and exterior stairways are characteristic elements of the acclimatized wood vernacular that arises.[4]

Figure 3. The Barnacle, Coconut Grove, 1948, Commodore Monroe

In Key West and Tampa, Cuban immigrants establish enclaves with a strong sense of identity, in each instance, making proud reference to their island's Spanish colonial architecture. In 1885, when Henry Plant's railroad was extended into Central Florida, Vicente Martinez Ybor moved his cigar manufacturing operations from Key West northward. Proximity by sea to the island facilitated the importation of tobacco and the railroad made transporting finished cigars easy by land to major American cities. Tampa's economy boomed and Ybor constructed housing and civic structures for his growing number of employees. Ybor City was developed employing architectural types and morphological rhythms typical of Cuban towns. These cultural references represent another trickle of influence from Cuba onto the peninsula, following the indigenous Taino settlements and common Spanish colonizers.

Figure 4. The first building constructed by the Círculo Cubana, Ybor City, Tampa, 1907

[Miami] Dade County's first significant growth spurt occurred in 1895 when Julia Tuttle and William Brickell offered half of their land holdings around the mouth of the Miami River to the entrepreneurial Henry Flagler in exchange for his agreement to extend a railroad line to Miami and to build the grand Royal Palm Hotel.[5] The seeds of Miami's tourism industry are thusly laid, fueling

Figure 5. The Royal Palm Hotel, Miami, Henry Flagler

Figure 6. Villa Vizcaya under construction, employing clay barrel tiles taken from historic Cuban structures.

Figure 7. Miami-Biltmore Hotel, Coral Gables, 1931

Figure 8. Coral Gables Advertisement, 1925

Figure 9. Collins Avenue, Miami Beach

a fledgling economy and igniting interest in local real estate investments, which until this point were dormant. By the early 1920's, new roads connecting Florida towns are linked to new highways stretching to northern cities.[6] These umbilical cords nurtured population growth, tourism, and land booms.

In Miami, widely available pattern books facilitated the quick construction of modestly priced bungalow homes (pictured on page 82). Mediterranean and Spanish colonial traditions soon substitute vernacular ones with a new and at times, commanding scale, offering "an urban architecture where the whole adds up to more than the sum of its parts," while giving "definition and character to a quickly developing boom-time city - where whole towns seem to appear almost overnight."[7]

During this budding period, South Florida's economy depends on the expansion of its tourism base, which to some measure entailed attracting winter-birds away from the closest competitor: Havana. Carl Fisher and George Merrick were astute developers armed with talented architects eager to introduce fashionable Mediterranean Revival style to the blank slates of Coral Gables, Miami Shores, and Miami Beach. Fisher, and in particular Merrick, who was enamored by Spanish architecture and had also traveled to Havana, sets out on a commercially driven quest for identity.

The Panama-California Exposition held in San Diego between 1915 and 1917, and organized by architects including Bertram Goodhue, who had traveled to and designed in 1905 a building for Havana, thus steering the expositions focus toward Spanish Colonial and Baroque architecture, serves to crystalize the intentions of Merrick and Fisher. In sliding degrees, they deliberately choose to emulate other 'exotic' Mediterranean destinations,[8] as well as, the colonial old world charm of the Cuban capital. South Florida begins to "rise above the swamplands and emerge as a 'synthetic' tropical paradise."[9] Responding to the same alluring 'foreign' call, everything from town layouts and street names, to the artisans and re-constituted building materials (removed from historic structures) were imported from the neighboring island nation or were otherwise sources of inspiration. From this period forward, the "vogue of Havana insinuates itself into the vision of Miami"[10] and an architectural dialogue subtlety re-emerges yet again across the Straits.

Divested of traditional precepts and ornamentation, buildings were soon draped in elegant Art Deco attire. Clean, machine-like volumes were appended with window 'eyebrows' and porches–elements that adapted the style to the requirements of the sub-tropical climate. Frequently, designs employed the courtyard type and present an uninhibited playful exploration of form and decoration; the latter repeatedly inspired by the local flora and fauna (pictured on page 83), sculpted into readily available stones quarried nearby or highlighted in striking murals (pictured on pages 84 and 85). Art Deco marks a distancing from traditional precedents, staging the set and shifting attention towards the more austere Modern Architecture that will follow it.

Figure 10. Cottage

Figure 11. Cottage

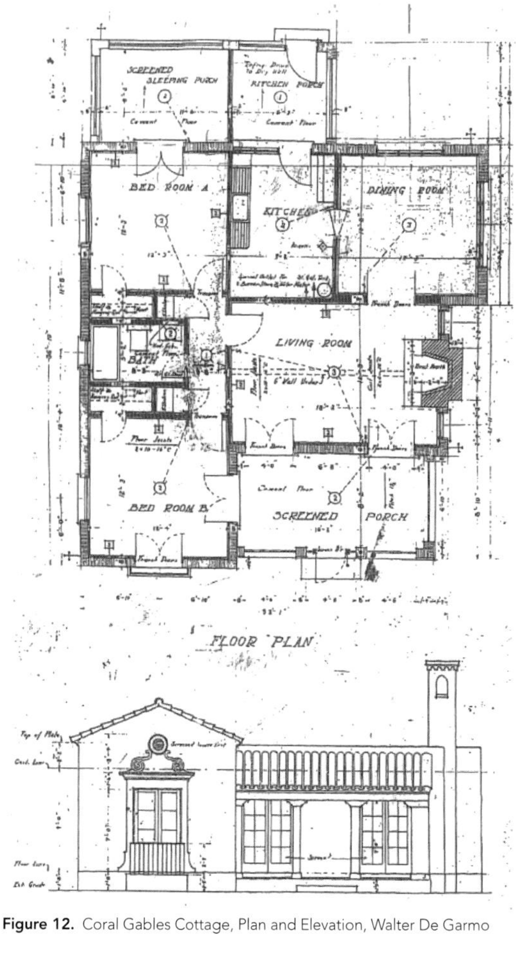

Figure 12. Coral Gables Cottage, Plan and Elevation, Walter De Garmo

Figure 13. Cardozo Hotel, Miami Beach, 1939, Henry Hohauser

Figure 15. Detail of Art Deco relief above fountain, Jefferson Avenue, Miami Beach

Figure 14. Century Hotel, Miami Beach, 1939, Henry Hohauser

Figure 16. Mural in the lobby of Plymouth Hotel, Miami Beach, 1939, R. Chatov

Figure 17. Mudéjar inspired pivoting wood screened panels along a portico that in turn surrounds a courtyard. Diego Velázquez House, Santiago de Cuba, XVI Century

Havana

Evolving over a span of nearly four centuries under the tutelage of Spain, the island nation's villages, towns and cities unfold against the backdrop of the lush landscape, conformed by found and imported architectural expressions and regulated town planning principles of Afro-European roots. Due to its privileged position straddling the Gulf Stream, since shortly after its founding, Havana serves as the transfer point of wealth between the new Spanish colonies and the Iberian Peninsula. Hence, it is the consequent depository of cultural and architectural waves of influences.[11] Havana's initial settlement developed into a polycentric city. It's mercantile and agriculturally based economies gradually prospered thanks to its abundance of fertile lands just beyond the city limits, with pronounced wealth amassed around the sugar cane, tobacco, and coffee industries. Because the city is initially confined between the harbor and fortified walls, the "compact" courtyard type is adopted pervasively and a dense urban fabric results over time. Along with the Roman pedigreed courtyard 'patio' type - of Southern Iberian inheritance, Spaniards import a chorus of architectural elements often grafted from Moorish and naval architecture.[12] Over the centuries, the patio house is adapted to the tropics, incorporating extended eaves and additional tempering elements that soften the harsh light while serving to mitigate the blankets of humidity and rain. By the Late-colonial period, these acclimatizing elements included the light-filtering stained-glass 'medio-puntos' (lunettes), set above doorways, windows, and along courtyard arcades; exceptionally high 'puntales' (ceiling heights), often coffered in wood that wick away the dense air, and deep 'porticos' (galleries) to protect interior spaces from the unforgiving sun yet welcome cooling breezes into interior spaces while offering an alternative 'outdoor' living room.

Under Spain's umbrella, across the centuries, Colonial, Baroque and Neo-classical architecture prevail, accompanying the early fortifications of Italian design while supplanting indigenous settlements. Havana's urban patchwork responds to a progression of form-based urban guidelines (decrees) and later codes (1861 *Ordenanzas de Construcción para la ciudad de La Habana y pueblos de su término municipal* - Construction Ordinances of Havana and Towns within its Municipal Jurisdiction). By the end of the nineteenth century, an extended, compact urban realm results, colonial neighborhoods consolidate, and new suburbs such as El Vedado emerge along with new building typologies, such as the sideyard house.

Figure 18. Early XX travel advertisement

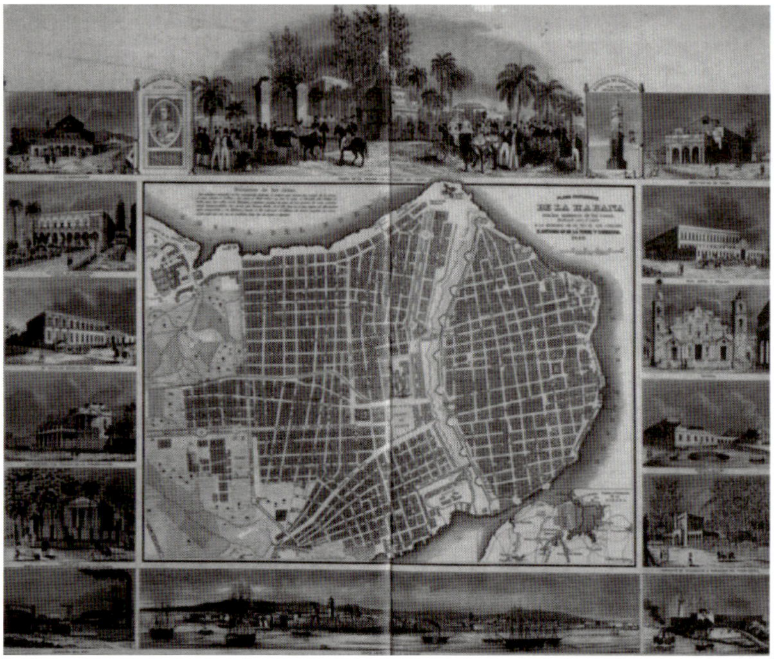

Figure 19. Plano Pintoresco de la Habana, 1849

Then, after three and a half centuries of Spanish dominance, in 1898, Havana's quarter-million population reveled in her newfound political independence.[13] Without fear of reprisals, initial collective celebrations perpetuated and in no time became a way of life. Alongside customary religious and cultural activities, new forms of entertainment and recreation nourished urban life. In response, the tempo of construction increased exponentially. New and grander public spaces would be constructed, including boulevards, parks, plazas, and promenades, accompanied by a chorus of new uses and building types including cinemas, nightclubs, casinos, racetracks, stadiums, seaside establishments, lavish hotels, along with more traditional civic institutions, and social clubs; collectively, "transforming" the city over the coming five decades.[14]

Figure 20. Exemplifies the courtyard type surrounded by deep 'porticos'

Between 1895 and 1927, US investments on the island grew from 50 million dollars to 1,500 million.[15] During this period, US interests on the island propagated at a phenomenal rate; marshaled by the US military's intervention governors and followed closely by American banking, communication, institutions, construction firms, businesses, investors and professionals. "The American interventions of generals Leonard Wood (1898-1902) and Chad Magoon (1906-1909) are dedicated basically to infrastructure improvements... to improve the educational system and to the construction of schools and hospitals; besides undertaking works of urban beautification, the construction of the School of Arts and Crafts and the rehabilitation of the Academy of Medical Services."[16] During Magoon's autocratic tenure, "the head architect of the interventionist government's Civil Construction Department, Mr. Thomas M. Newton, resuscitates Classicism, teaches the academic styles, and trains excellent Cuban disciples, such as Francisco Centurion and Felix Cabarrocas. Newton introduces to Cuba an austere Classicism of which the later constructed Havana Institute of Secondary Learning by Mario Romañach Sr. (1928) stands witness as an excellent example."[17]

Figure 21. Elements of colonial architecture included - stained glass lunettes and louvered windows and doors

With the objective to grow mutual commerce, industry, trade, and tourism, partnerships with Americans catalyzed the expansion and modernization of public works projects, including improvements to the aqueduct, the initial construction of the waterfront boulevard - El Malecón, early projects to reconstruct and improve the Paseo de Marti (today Paseo del Prado), and eventually the construction of a national transportation network. The Paseo's beautification and the construction of the Malecón, extending to Lealtad Street, further sustain urban life, representing transcendental accomplishments, which ultimately redefined the image of the city.

Figure 22. Church of La Santísima Trinidad, 1905, Bertram Goodhue

The building panorama changes in 1909 with the second and final departure of the US intervention government. A building frenzy ensues and opens the path towards prominent commissions for recent graduates of the nascent University of Havana School of Architecture and Cuban professionals trained abroad, such as Leonardo Morales and Luis Bay Sevilla. Contracts were also seized by US professionals, commencing with Bertram Grosvenor Goodhue (Santísima Trinidad Church, 1905) and continuing with architect Kenneth Murchison (Central Railway Station, 1912), and Barclay, Parsons & Klapp (Custom's Building, 1914).[18] Versed in Beaux-Arts traditions, New York's A-list architectural firms of Schultz and Weaver (Hotel Sevilla Addition, 1923; La Concha Baths, 1929 & Gran Casino remodel), Walker & Gillette (The National Bank of New York, 1925), and Carrère and Hastings (Narciso Gelats Bank) were involved in significant undertakings in the private sector that further transform the city's Spanish colonial image. The well-connected American construction firm of Purdy and Henderson built numerous civic buildings over a period of several

Figure 23. Central Railway Station, Havana, 1912, Kenneth Murchison

Figure 24. Havana's Capitol Building, period postcard, designed by Govantes & Cabarrocas Architects, built by Purdy and Henderson

decades, including banks, hotels, and social clubs as well as the nation's Capitol building.[19]

During the twenties and thirties, eclecticism became the predominant trend. The prospect of political independence and the [first] 'vacas gordas' economic boom era were paralleled by a potpourri of architectural expressions, ranging from an eclectic palette to a Catalan inspired '*Modernismo*' version of *Art Nouveau*. The added importation of the Mediterranean Revival movements popular in Texas, California, and South Florida also influences several architects in Cuba during this period, coupled by an even greater acceptance of the style among the burgeoning middle and upper income populations seeking to emulate US design trends.[20]

As of 1925, fashionable Beaux-Arts planning, spearheaded by Jean-Claude Nicolas Forestier's *'Enlargement and Re-beautification Master Plan'* team, linked to a late-eighteenth century Neo-Classical Revival Style, was favored for grand civic projects as well as residential buildings located in the hygienist-inspired El Vedado suburb.[21 22] In parallel, Cuban architects acquired Beaux-Arts training either in the US, Paris or in Havana, and were eager to exercise their knowledge as well. They catered to an affluent clientele equally enamored with established Parisian precedents and the implied social correlations.[23] Not surprisingly, period tourism slogans promote Havana as the 'Paris of the Western Hemisphere', 'Paris of the Caribbean' and as others had before him, dictator Geraldo Machado defined it as the 'Nice of the Caribbean'.[24] By all definitions, Havana is already a consolidated, sophisticated, cosmopolitan metropolis albeit with compromised infrastructure networks, increasingly challenged by the logarithmic eruption of its population.

Figure 25. Example of Beaux Art Planning, aerial view of La Murallas Neighborhood, 1935

Figures 26 a-g. Examples of Art Deco details.

In 1927, within two years of the Decorative-Art Exposition in Paris, the now termed 'Art Deco' style was imported by local architects and fluently spoken in a tropical voice. Initially, the style passes through a French sieve and later derivations move towards a North American Streamline.

Art Deco catapults the capital's image into the 20th century, with a plethora of samples eventually strewn across its fabric, including the city's first 'skyscrapers' and cinemas. The Bacardi headquarters, by Esteban Rodriguez Castells,[25] is a regal French-inspired example. Art Deco was more ornate in its earlier iterations, but over time partially due to economic challenges, it evolved into pure volumes, incorporating limited decorative subjects in low relief with motifs ranging from simple geometric configurations to anthropomorphic or landscape inspired scenes. Eventually, compositions were dominated by horizontal instead of vertical striations, probably inspired by the leaner, minimal *Streamline* versions that were proliferating across Miami and Miami Beach. Construction materials likewise migrate from the initially expensive and exotic lacquers, inlaid woods, and natural stones toward industrial materials such as aluminum and stainless steel. This tendency is soon after further distilled, as exemplified in Pedro Martinez Inclán's

Figure 27. Bacardi Headquarters, Havana, 1930, Esteban Rodriguez Castells

Figure 28. Solimar Apartments, Havana, 1944, Manuel Copado

Figure 29. Commercial and residential building, Pedro Martinez Inclan

1932 apartment building in El Vedado, a hybrid solution bridging between Art Deco and an avant-garde's rationalist ideology. In fact, Art Deco serves as the perfect conduit between the traditions of the past and the even further 'purified' architecture of the International Style that shortly trails.

Parallel Lives

Whereas the trajectory of each city to date had been quite different, as of the 1920's parallel endeavors become more commonplace, marking the beginning of a new age of engagement. The faces of both Miami and Havana were altered dramatically in a short period of time, as each became a notable repository of Art Deco buildings, respectively boasting several thousand examples.[26] The predominant Art Deco palette had responded effectively to pre-war economic constraints and material limitations – its sober characteristics a prelude to Modernism. In both locations, it seamlessly morphs into the International Style. The fledgling International Style indeed re-emerges with renewed vigor and clarity in the postwar era and in addition to its ideological and functionalist attributes, its minimalism is preferred as an indicator of optimism, technological advancements, and innovation. In time, a prioritization or a recuperation of climatically synchronized building types and elements surfaces as well.

Coinciding with mounting local appropriations of Modern architecture, postwar transformations in the built environment commence in both Cuba and Florida, as effervescent economies and development opportunities escalated; catalyzed by swelling population numbers. The explosion of their respective housing markets has a trickledown effect, further feeding their prosperity. A speculative, commercially driven architecture takes hold in both cities.

Havana's economic engines, already revved up during the war, lead to a significant rush in construction as of 1945. Projects significantly increased in scale due to the 1952 adoption of the "Horizontal Property" legislation, which permits the subdivision of one lot into multiple owners, resulting in condominiums and cooperatives. Taking advantage of the economic bonanza and the new law, skyscrapers proliferate shortly thereafter, in particular along the fashionable waterfront Malecón Boulevard and in its downtown area along Calle 23 in the El Vedado neighborhood. The city's next wave of expansion will revolve primarily around the construction of skyscrapers,[27] apartment buildings, and mansions.[28]

Florida's post-war building boom paralleled the one in Havana. As new jobs were created, Miami's downtown was

Figure 30. La Ley de Propiedad Horizontal, Havana

Figure 31. Lincoln Road, Miami Beach, Florida, 1942

further consolidated. The city's skyline changed drastically with the addition of taller skyscrapers. Industrial areas expanded. Tourists returned. The hotel industry exploded. Developers flocked back to the region, eager to build housing for newly settled veterans leaving behind their depression era losses. Overnight, new suburbs emerged, and the city began to sprawl.

Architects in both locations address housing shortages with contemporary solutions, expressing post-war confidence and experimenting with material and/or structural advances. Although these innovations allowed professionals and builders to expedite the process, housing initiatives fell well short of meeting the unprecedented need for lower and middle-income dwellings. Even so, a wide array of scales and types, from individual mansions, middle-income villas, and suburban track developments to affordable housing initiatives surface during this period. Expressions of Modernity became increasingly de rigueur and some of the most noteworthy realizations in the region's architectural history will occur precisely during this brief period in Havana, Central and South Florida.

EXTERNAL INFLUENCES

The International Style

During the initial post-war 'transformative' period, Florida and Cuba experienced waves of influence from different shores. Fundamental CIAM canons set 'international' standards. Le Corbusier's seminal book *Towards a New Architecture*, distributed in Florida and Cuba, outlined the modalities for creating a modern architectural aesthetic in the new century based upon science and reason, while utilizing technology and industry. Le Corbusier espoused harnessing the potential of new materials, learning from industrialized fields, such as shipbuilding and liberating the spirit of the times with new solutions and forms of expression. He upheld that by severing ties with tradition; architects aspired to a new social order with a focus on the construction of much needed housing for the masses.

These principles presented compatible propositions to architects addressing on the one hand Florida's essentially blank canvas and on the other a Cuba searching to break away from its political colonial harness, while offering a practical solution to the dire housing shortage in both locations. Of Corbu's 'five points,' several are in tune with tropical living and are readily assimilated, including the column/piloti system, the free plan, roof gardens, and the horizontal banding of windows; the first two finding precedents in regional vernaculars.

Between 1929 and 1962, Le Corbusier traveled 8 times to Latin America. "In September 1950, Le Corbusier made a short stop in Miami during a layover from his flight between Bogotá, Colombia and New York City. After drawing a small sketch in his book, he wrote the names of six architects, including 'Polevitzky' and stated - "*all great guys, ardent, ideal, professional qualities. Very much artists, consider me to be the leader of modern architecture. Build very honestly but eccentricities for rich people. Social relevance is not at stake here.*"[29] Le Corbusier's varied visits south influenced his own vision while they enriched the architects he met and/or collaborated with,[30] including Oscar Niemeyer. In this manner, his ideologies permeate, albeit through a different prism, to other practitioners in the hemisphere, including those in Florida and Cuba. Consequently, early modern buildings designed by architects in the region are often an embodiment of rationalist principles.[31]

Figure 32. Bauhaus, 1919, Walter Gropius

Figure 33. Villa Stein, 1927, Le Corbusier

Figure 34. Brazilian Pavillion at the New York's World Fair, 1939, Lucio Costa and Oscar Neimeyer

Latin American Regionalism

Regionalist movements began to appear precisely as the standardizing formulas of the International Style seem to reach universal authority. Latin American architecture during this period inflects the path of Modernism, including its trails through the peninsula and island. In the Americas, wealthy patrons, lax regulatory laws, readily available construction materials and cheap labor converge, liberating architectural exploration, resulting in spectacular forms and vibrant color palettes in tune with cultural values. As leading architectural historian, Henry Russell Hitchcock evidences in his later MOMA exhibit entitled *Latin American Architecture Since 1945* and underlines in the accompanying publication, "in most Latin American countries today there is both quantity and quality in architecture."[32] Not surprisingly, in short-term, Latin American 'translations' of the International Style by Lucio Costas, Oscar Neimeyer, Lina Bo Bardi, Vilanova Artigas, Affonso Eduardo Reidy, Carlos Raul Villanueva and others offered viable and exciting socially charged and locally responsive 'dialects'; alternatives rooted in the particularities and heritage of place. Latin American Regionalism's tenor and connectedness to place is expressed with sculptural bravura, charged color palettes, the marriage between industrial and natural materials and a cultural specificity, which in turn had a marked influence on architectural thought in Florida and Cuba.

Case Study Houses

Another source of external reference was the California *Case Study House* initiative for the experimental explorations of materials, methods, and structural systems, which pushed envelops- literally and figuratively. Sponsored by *Arts & Architecture Magazine*, and running intermittently between 1945 and 1960, *Case Study Houses* proposed an American residential architecture aimed at addressing the housing shortage following the end of the war. Conceived as "prototypes for low-cost housing, using standardized mass-produced components," they were a "romanticized reflection of an emerging pragmatism."[33] Buildings were constructed of concrete masonry units, steel beams, and/or industrial steel framing. The earlier houses evidenced a high degree of "bold experimentation of a non-commercial kind;" in many cases, their designs informed by the technological innovations developed for wartime purposes. Modular building systems, pre-fabricated components, glass expanses, and Japanese-inspired floating partitions were characteristic. Designs experimented with arrangements of expansive sliding glass doors, jalousie windows with extruded aluminum frames, asbestos boards, and various combinations of interior finishes. They were functional - often balancing sterile innovative building materials with warm traditional ones. Major architects of the day were commissioned, including: Richard Neutra, Raphael Soriano, Craig Ellwood, Charles and Ray Eames, Pierre Koenig, and Eero Saarinen. Neutra forged professional affiliations or asserted influence directly upon Floridian and Cuban architects, including Paul Rudolph, Raul Alvarez, and Mario Romañach.

Figure 35. Case Study House, 1946, Richard Neutra

Figure 36. Richard Neutra, Eugenio Batista with emerging Cuban architects in Havana, 1954

International Journals & Direct Interaction

Readily accessible professional magazines such as *Architectural Record, Arts & Architecture, Home & House,* and *House Beautiful* introduced avant-garde precedents, publishing projects by International groundbreaking architects such as Marcel Breuer, Ludwig Mies van der Rohe, Walter Gropius, Richard Neutra, Eliel Saarinen, Josep Lluís Sert, and Frank Lloyd Wright.

Figure 37. Walter Gropius meeting with Havana's Planning Board

Figure 38. Cursillo de Josef Albers at the Colegio de Arquitectos

Figure 39. Florida Southern College, Lakeland, 1938, Frank Lloyd Wright

Due to their frequent visits and consequent direct contact with professionals in the region, several of these architects exerted a discernible influence over the Caribbean's Modern architecture over the coming decades. The at times nurturing presence and/or interest of Modern Masters in the region, included but was not limited to Frank Lloyd Wright, Mies van der Rohe, Josef Albers, Richard Neutra, Walter Gropius, Franco Albini, and Josep Luis Sert. These leading architects openly impacted architectural quests through formal and/or informal encounters and in other instances, via their commissions in the region.

Walter Gropius traveled to Havana on several occasions and enthusiastically cultivates and applauds the pioneering architecture. His visits to Havana cemented local commitments towards a rationalist architecture in young architects such as Mario Romañach, Frank Martinez and Nicolas Quintana as does his mentoring of recent Harvard graduates, such as Paul Rudolph in Florida. Later, Gropius will also instigate the regional exchange of ideas.

Frank Lloyd Wright's organic architecture also attracted followers, as it was deemed well suited to the tropics. The deep overhangs, the less formal compositions, and the resulting play of light, textures, and materials were likewise more palatable to the general public than the ascetic Corbusian 'machines for living,' at least initially, according to Cuban scholar Mario Coyula Crowley.[34] Projects by FLW in Lakeland and later Neutra in Havana swayed the design currents of key architects in the region. For example, the plastic qualities of Alfred Browning Parker's work can be directly attributed to FLW. In a similar manner, although less clear, but with some measure of probability, Mario Romañach's fascination with Japanese traditions, was informed by scholarly writings on Asian vernaculars by FLW, Gropius, Neutra, and others during this period.[35]

Eventually, on the island, Josep Lluis Sert also exerted significant influence on a large number of practitioners with his organized visits and later important contract to formulate a masterplan for the entire city of Havana, in collaboration with local architects, including Romañach.

The architecture of both Havana and Florida learned from global tendencies. Cuba's insatiable appetite for 'modernity,' initially dermal and later more conceptually anchored, welcomed innovations; a craving that is largely fueled by converged pursuits-a desired alignment with progressive industrialized nations and broader distancing from Spanish roots. Likewise, in Florida, a desire to project a carefree frontier spirit coupled with pragmatism conducted designers towards a sub-tropic modernity.

EMERGING MODERN REGIONALIST CONSIDERATIONS IN FLORIDA

Precedents

"Modern architecture, understood in a non-stylistic, environmental definition, first arrived in Florida with the young Bernard Maybeck- famous for his later work in California - [he] was the construction architect for Carrère and Hastings's Ponce de Leon and Alcazar Hotels in St. Augustine in 1885-86."[36] It was the innovative construction, including the deployment of cast concrete incorporating local coral stone as aggregate and the use of iron railroad rails as a kind of primitive reinforcement over openings and not the design of the buildings, that marked these works as modern. From this moment forward, the most significant constant through the works of succeeding generations of Florida modern regionalist architects was the adaptation of new construction techniques to regional traditions of building and locally available materials.[37]

Transitional Figures

As early as 1901, after the Great Fire of Jacksonville, Henry John Klutho was credited with introducing to the state the 'Prairie School' Style,' "which discarded traditional European standards."[38] Nearly three decades later, Ralph Twitchell in Sarasota, Marion Manley, Wahl Snyder, Igor Polevitzky, Russell Pancoast, Robert Law Weed, and Robert Little in Miami, were all leading transitional figures that bridged between the traditions of the past and a modern present, although with diverse tools and ideological underpinnings.

Figure 40. Showboat House, Sarasota, 1937, Ralph Twitchell

Ralph Twitchell graduated from Columbia University in 1921 and remained in New York City to also work with the prominent firm of Carrère and Hastings, architects of Henry Flagler's two St. Augustine hotels. Twitchell may well have been aware of the projects' early use of architectural concrete, the utilization of indigenous materials such as coquina shells, along with its sophisticated awareness of the larger cultural context.[39] After a two-year stretch in France, Twitchell settled in Sarasota Florida in 1925, establishing a full service firm that can design and build projects- an unusual arrangement at the time, but certainly a combination which offers Twitchell complete control over the entire process and in later years proves pivotal in the success of his partnership with Paul Rudolph. "*Typical of all his work, Twitchell utilized the current [Art Deco/Moderne] stylistic language as a means to express ideas about climate and context. One striking example of this is his 1937 Showboat House on Lake Louise, a composition of planes, entire walls of glass and extended horizontal rooflines, built at the edge of, and partially in, the lake, as though a boat moored along the bank … and based on Le Corbusier's inspiration in ship design… literally, immersing it in the natural landscape.*"[40] Henceforth, Twitchell became more cognizant of the vastness as well as the fragility of the landscape, sublimating his contributions by sympathetically introducing an architecture intent on celebrating and framing views of nature while reducing physical disruptions. His early practice was quickly associated with subtropical modernity and in years to come, continues to propose the tropical house in a modern idiom with unprecedented open plans and connections to the landscape. Once Paul Rudolph was employed by Twitchell, the firm's projects increasingly emulated vernacular architecture's honest expression of both function and construction methods, but in a clearly modern palette.

Further south, in Miami, inventive modernists like Igor Polevitzky, Robert Law Weed, and Robert Little "sought to adapt the austerity and other signature elements of Mies van der Rohe's International Style to the local environment in a loosely-federated school of "Subtropical Modernism"… The door to "Subtropical Modernism" is opened by Robert Law Weed."[41] As a pioneer of Miami's architectural establishment, he bridged between established trends in architecture and a progressive modernist agenda. After working for the renowned architect Richard Kiehnel for three years, the young architect initiated his own practice in 1922. Over time, the firm "serves as a springboard for many of Miami's leaders in modern design."[42] Commissions, including the 1933 Art Deco Streamline 'General Electric' house in Morningside, cement his rising reputation. As a result, the State of Florida hires Weed to design the "*Florida Tropical House*" for the 1933-34 Chicago Century of Progress Exposition,[43] expecting the design to evidence the region's positive characteristics and carefree lifestyle- architecture as a promotional tool for the Sub-Tropics.

Figure 41. The Florida Tropical House, *A Century of Progress Exhibition*, Chicago, 1933, Robert Law Weed

In an event related publication, Weed describes the project as follows: "*The major considerations in the design of the "Florida House" are the unusual climatic conditions of Southern Florida…The "Florida House," in so far as is possible, is built of Florida materials… (i.e. Portland cement, limestone, concrete, stucco, clay flooring, and roofing.) The absence of quick changes in temperature and freezes makes reinforced concrete and concrete building tile practical materials for substantial construction in this climate… Projections from the face of the building, about four feet, serve as a protection to windows and doors from the rain and sun…The roof area of the house is usable…divided into three parts: a covered area as a second floor loggia, a part as a deck for sun baths, and another portion as a recreation deck… Windows are plentiful and are so placed that trade winds of southern Florida may reach all parts of the house… The rooms themselves become part of the out-of-doors… In the*

Figure 42. General Electric Model Home, Morningside Neighborhood, Miami Beach, 1933, Robert Law Weed

"Florida House" the problems peculiar to Florida in the construction of residential buildings have been controlling factors. The first requisite being substantial, permanent, and waterproof materials; and second, the plan being as open as possible, consistent with storm proof construction. These two major considerations are reflected in the construction and planning." Clearly, practical matters, not only theoretical ones, drove Weed's project objectives, resulting in a modernist house that explored responses to South Florida's climate while successfully marketing an alternative, relaxed lifestyle 'under the sun'. His utilitarian approach follows vernacular traditions, which other 'modernist' colleagues, at this time, in particular Marion Manley and Alfred Browning Parker, are intrigued by as well.

"Environmental Fitness"

In a 1949 issue of *Florida Architecture Magazine*, editor Lee Childress analyses postwar building to that date and writes:"*... The architects of Florida acknowledge a responsibility to bring design for the individual needs to the greatest number of people... [they] invented a new tradition based on 'environmental fitness'...The warm climate dictates control of the prevailing breezes and of the intense sunlight, the maximum coolness and scenic beauty of the outdoors, therefore, is integrated with the architecture... The term 'indoor-outdoor' thus has become a popular descriptive phrase for the openness and the informality embodied in planning for the way of living and working in this tropical region... A close integration with natural surroundings is almost always felt, and a positive trend towards an Architecture, essentially regional in character is frank in its treatment of the problems of the tropics."*

THE 'MIAMI SCHOOL'

Shared interests, goals, and sources of influence became progressively evident in the works of Robert Bradford Browne, Robert Hansen, Alfred Browning Parker, Wahl Snyder, and George Reed in the 'Wrightian' and 'Neo-vernacular' camps. In the 'International Style' group, regionalist pursuits were legible in the works of Robert Law Weed, Robert Little, Marion Manley, Rufus Nims, Russell Pancoast and Igor Polevitzky. The body of work of these architects pre-dated and outnumbered the works of the renowned *Sarasota School*.[44] Their innovation and execution were of equal caliber, as was their characteristic harmonizing with the environment, topography, and climate of South Florida. Several of these architects also tackled the challenge of designing prototypes for affordable and middle-income housing. Nonetheless, this valuable regionalist movement is not recognized as such, much less as a school, as it should be, perhaps in some measure due to their division into 'sub-camps,' according to architectural historian Jan Hochstim, who more recently baptized them as the '*Miami School*'.

However, overwhelmingly, this generation of Miami architects evidenced a dexterous ability to reinterpret vernacular heritage, further develop lessons of 'passive design,' marry a new language with local building materials, address project economy, and experiment with innovative methods of construction. For their deftness and design fusion as well as their practical inventive usage of materials to resolve problems related to tropical living,[45] they independently received awards and are defined as regional innovators; their architecture recognized by peers, journals, and the general public as a celebration of life in the tropics. The '*Miami School*' provided alternatives to universal formulas and their buildings embody an entirely fresh, pragmatic, ecologically-tuned vision that bridges between traditions and modernity. Their body of work related architecture to place, climate, and landscape as well as to the free spirit and aspired tropical lifestyle of Miami's multiplying residents.

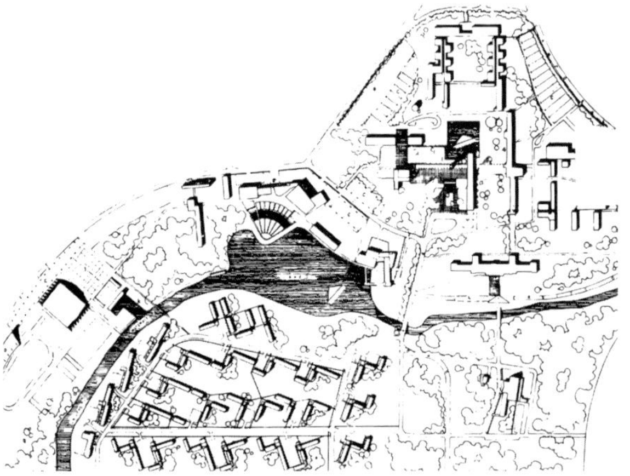

Figure 43. University of Miami Master Plan, 1947, Robert Law Weed and Marion Manley

Robert Law Weed, Marion Manley & Robert Little

Marion Manley had a career filled with accomplishments. In 1917, she graduated with a degree in architecture and by the next year she was the first woman architect registered in South Florida. Early on, she worked for both Walter de Garmo and later Phineas Paist, gurus of South Florida's Mediterranean Revival imaging era. By 1931, she established her own practice where she initially designs modestly sized Mediterranean Style houses. During the Depression era, Manley worked on Miami's U.S. Post Office and the Federal Building. In later projects, her interests in technological innovation, vernacular heritage, and environmental concerns became self-evident. Two smaller scaled, yet excellent examples of how these interests were interwoven are the *Wylie Residence* of 1948 in South

Figure 44. Proposed dormitory, aerial renderings, schematic designs, University of Miami, 1945, Robert Law Weed and Marion Manley

Miami and her design for a two-story house in Coconut Grove for the Bell family, in which she employed a courtyard scheme set on pilotis.

Robert Little opened his practice in South Florida in 1933, after a circuitous path taking him from the University of Pennsylvania to a protracted apprenticeship with Florida architect Robert Taylor. Little designed some of South Florida's finest residences of this period, but he is best known for his multiple contributions to the University of Miami campus, including the redesign of the Merrick building, the Alfred Pick Music School Library, The Ring Theater (in collaboration with Manley) (pictured on page 99), and Eaton Hall, a multi-storied dormitory.

In the wake of WWII, Marion Manley,[46] Robert Law Weed, and Robert Little, experienced architects each in their own right, came together to collaborate on multiple occasions for the fledging University of Miami, beginning with its internationally acclaimed Campus Masterplan. The 1927 hurricane pummeled a campus building under construction causing classes to be held in an off campus location in Coral Gables. By the end of the war, the overwhelming influx of new students, many of them veterans, and the outpouring of federal coffers allowed the new university president to charter a different course for the abandoned site and hire the trio of architects to plan its renaissance.[47 48] The previous campus masterplan was scrapped and completely redesigned by Weed, Manley, and Little with a renewed approach in its place.

Envisioned between 1944 and 1947, the design was advertised as "*the first modern college campus in the United States.*"[49] The composition broke from the typical quadrangle model and the masterplan called for buildings to be set as objects within the landscape in a Corbusian manner, sited to capitalize on northeasterly breezes and to reduce sun exposure. "*Fresh, clean planning, with every building designed to serve its particular function is the rule by which we are being guided as we proceed with our work,*" Manley is quoted as saying to a local paper in 1946.[50] The masterplan soon received nationwide publicity, followed by international accolades and awards, setting the

Figure 45. Florida Southern College, Lakeland, 1938, Frank Lloyd Wright

standard for contemporary academic architecture in the United States. Of note, the UM masterplan was relatively concurrent with Frank Lloyd Wright's designs for Florida Southern College campus in Lakeland. Begun in the late 1930's, the FSC campus experienced a constructive boom immediately following the war.[51] "Under construction during and after the war, this largest grouping of Wright's buildings on a single site brought the focus of modernism into the heart of Florida."[52] Undoubtedly and directly influencing several generations of regional designers that followed, it perhaps partially inspired the UM campus and building designers for its break with traditional typologies, organic disposition, extensive use of concrete, inclusion of covered walkways, outdoor rooms, and mindful tempering of sunlight.

In concert with its progressive masterplan, the University of Miami commissioned the design of several needed facilities over a brief period. As a result, the campus becomes a depository of mid-century regionalist buildings, at times echoing the informal and sensual character of the local landscape and the adventurous spirit of its pioneering leaders. In general, the buildings share common characteristics, often including, extruded porches, brise soliel, and natural ventilation made possible by expansive "Miami"[53] awning windows, complimenting the extended eaves, walkways, and breezeways, that in congress protect students and faculty from the harsh sun and torrential downpours. The sum of these 'accommodating' responses results in comfortable interior and exterior spaces for learning and interaction across the campus, instigating a visual and tactile relationship with the landscape.

Continuing to take advantage of the "GI Bill," the University again hired Manley and Weed in 1947 to design 27 two- and three-story apartment buildings on the south end of the campus, intended to house the great influx of married war-veteran students. Manley is the lead designer. Floating across the tabula rasa terrain, building placements do little to engender a sense of community or to activate campus life. Their siting is instead primarily driven by the direction of prevailing breezes and contemporary urban planning trends. Their language clearly informed by Bauhaus canons. The elongated buildings, tailored in a taut and efficient skin, are illustrative of an adapted International Style.[54] Spaces within the slender buildings are flooded with natural light and made comfortable by cross-ventilation as windows are placed in large banks across from each other in main rooms. Extended eaves, known as 'eyebrows', often protect window bands on south and west facing elevations and staircases pulled outside read independently. Buildings are distinguished for their "scarcity of ornamentation, mixture of stucco and brick surfaces, flat roofs, metal framed windows, and pipe railings."

Modern pioneering architects Robert Little[55] and Wahl Snyder[56] also made significant contributions to the campus, including administrative, classroom, library, and theater buildings. However, at the time, the most celebrated building of this period was the Oscar Dooley Memorial Building, designed by Marion Manley, Robert Little, and Robert Law Weed in 1948. The outstretched structure is situated on the northeast end of the campus, placed to minimize heat gain, frame views, and to define the intended outer limit of the campus. The generously proportioned, continuous single-loaded exterior corridor is the spine of the composition, linking all the narrow classrooms and a centrally located theater. Midway along the corridor a shift occurs at an intersecting breezeway found by the outdoor seating area that flanks the theater. A double height space and an ample porch above it, both providing areas for congregating comfortably in a protected environment, mark the intersection. The design of the upper floor corridor handrail slips below the floor line, strategically doubling as a compact *'brise-soleil'* (pictured on pages 100 - 103) for the level below it. This element is replicated at the roofline as well. The north-east facing elevation of classrooms, sheathed in 'Miami' awning windows, capture the breezes and provide abundant natural day-lighting while tall ceiling heights accommodate operable transom windows, located on the opposite walls, allowing hot and humid air to rise and escape. Building ornamentation is limited to local Oolite in a rubble pattern, a running bond Tennessee limestone veneer and sparse geometrically designed decorative metal panels. The Memorial Building[57] project is extensively published in *Progressive Architecture, Architectural*

Figure 46. Veterans' housing project, aerial photograph, University of Miami, 1946, Marion Manley

Figure 47. Ring Theater, University of Miami, 1951, Robert Little

Figure 48. Memorial Classroom Building, University of Miami, 1948, Robert Law Weed, Marion Manley, and Robert Little

Figure 49. Cafeteria and Recreational Center, University of Miami, 1948-49, Robert Law Weed and Marion Manley

Forum, L'architecture d'aujourd hui, and also in the Cuban journal *Arquitectura.* In 1950, its novel design is awarded a Silver Medal at the Pan-American Congress of Architects held in Havana.

The University of Miami Cafeteria and Recreational Center project presented Manley and Weed with yet another opportunity to collaborate in 1948-49. The courtyard design features continuous banks of windows and deep overhangs in two perpendicularly set buildings, connected by covered walkways. Partially perched over Lake Osceola, added walkways frame picturesque views, house a corner stage, and accommodate additional outdoor dining areas. This project likewise drew national and international attention, receiving praise from Progressive Architecture jurors during its annual awards issue noting, "The architect[s] uses concrete with great content and facility. He [They] uses the site unusually well, making architecture thorough acceptance of the climate."

Due to the scale of the project and the quality of the progressive designs, the masterplan for the University campus and its accompanying ensemble of buildings placed South Florida's pioneering modern architects on international radars.

Figure 50. View of completed Solomon G. Merrick Building, University of Miami, 1949, Robert Little

Figure 51. Memorial Classroom Building, University of Miami, 1947, Robert Law Weed and Marion Manley

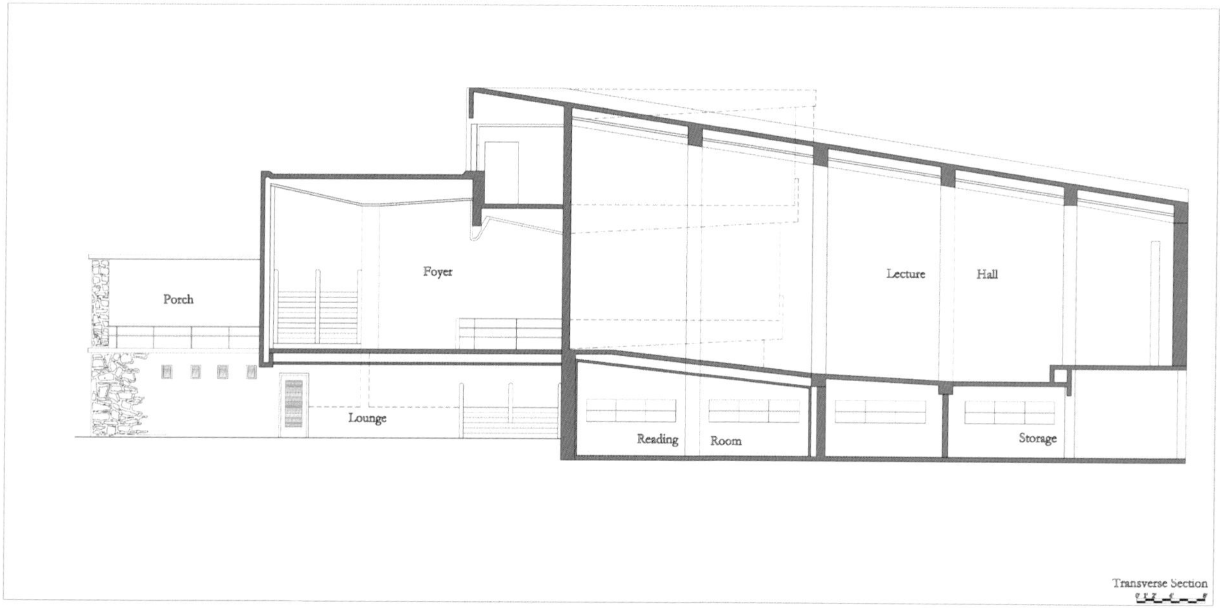

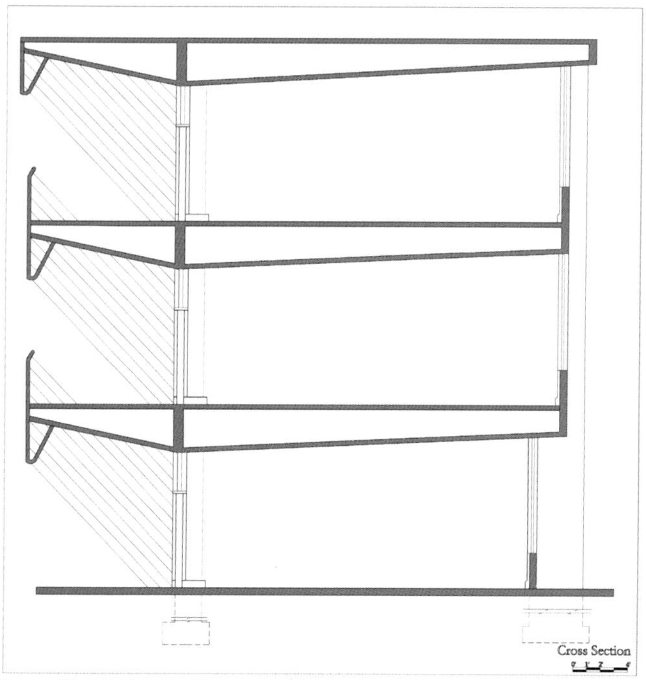

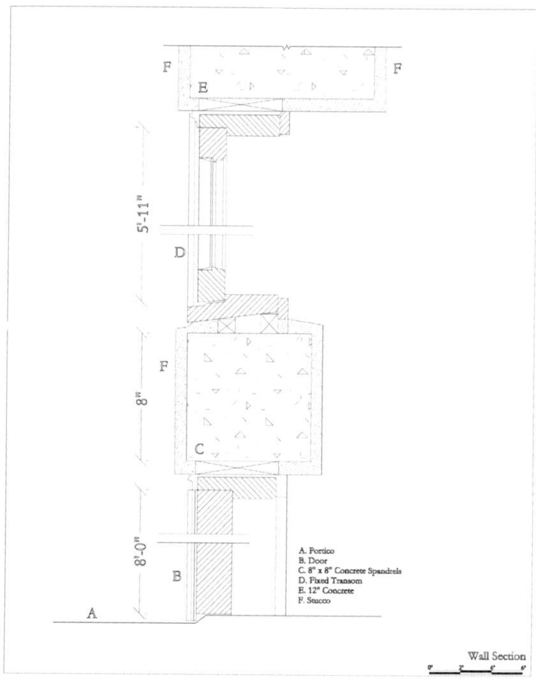

Figures 52 - 55. Memorial Classroom Building, University of Miami, 1948, Marion Manley and Robert Law Weed

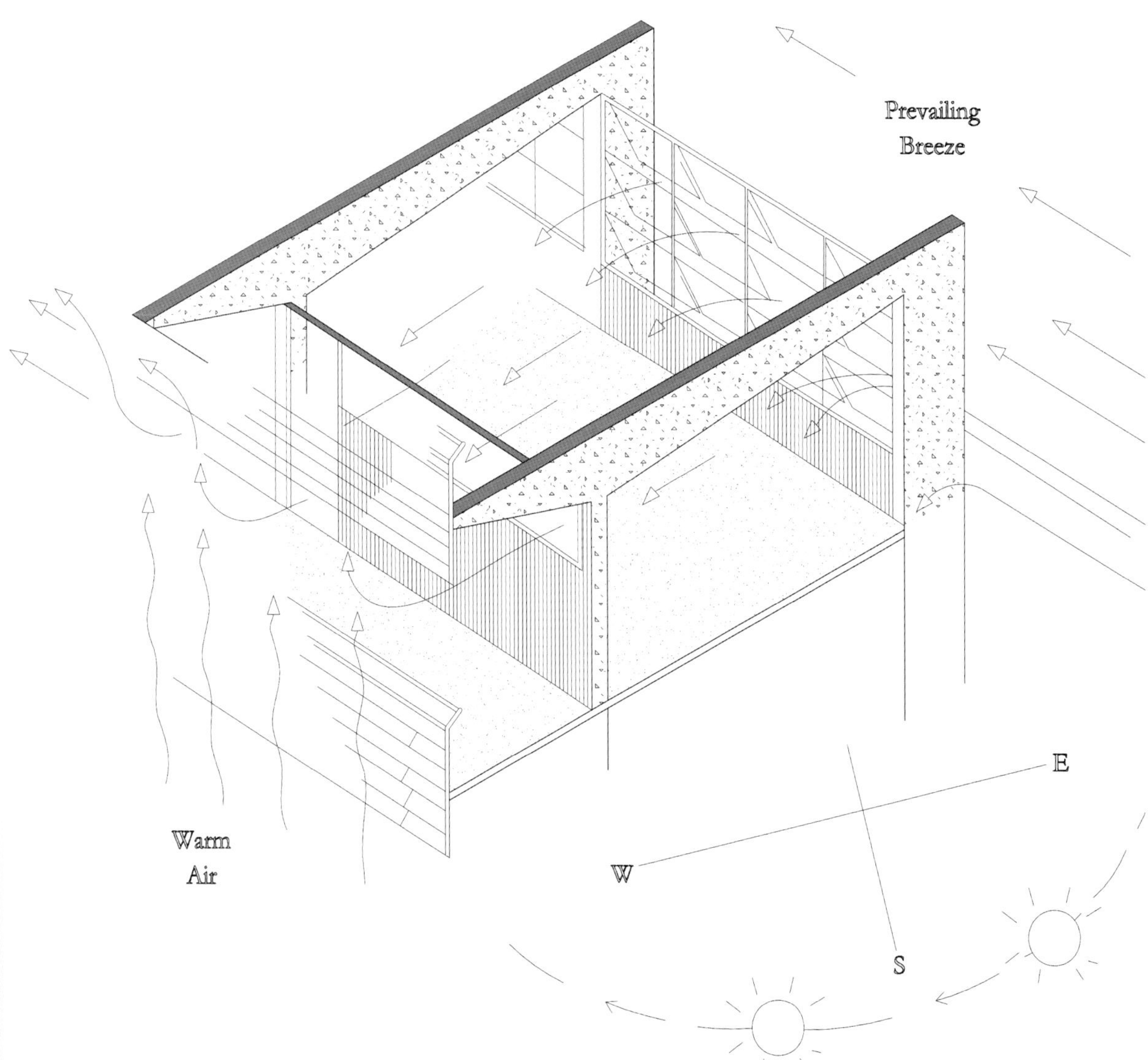

Ventilation Diagram
Through Classroom

Figure 56. Chandler and Hopwood Residences (in a rockpit), Coconut Grove, 1950-51, Alfred Browning Parker

Alfred Browning Parker

Alfred Browning Parker pioneered Modern Regionalism in South Florida from a distinct optic, defined by fundamental modern ordering systems, yet removed from stylistic currents in the early years of his career, drawing primary inspiration from regional cues and graduating towards a more plastic and geometrically complex architecture inspired by the works of Frank Lloyd Wright. Parker's prolific career spanned over five decades and encompassed more than 6,400 projects.[58] He studied at the University of Florida under his initial mentor, Rudolph Weaver, graduating in 1939, but not before traveling to the Royal Academy of Stockholm on a one-year exchange scholarship that exposed him to local nationalist movements and vernacular building traditions. Nazi occupation in the region caused the trip to be cut short. One year later while teaching at UF, Parker received a traveling fellowship, allowing him to spend two weeks in Cuba and several others in Mexico. Lessons garnered through these trips nourished Parker's interests in the region's architecture. During this period, he also learned of research by a pioneering ecologist at the University of Miami, Dr. John Gifford, and he decides to audit his class. Their meeting altered the path of Parker's destiny in two ways: one professional and the other personal; he married Gifford's daughter two years later, and the young couple end up settling in Coconut Grove, Florida.

Parker's first project in the region was the remodeling of a gas station into his house and architectural studio; it is the first of his many projects to receive national press coverage. Every aspect of the project was considered and designed, its disposition straightforward and compact, with construction materials locally harvested and rustic in their finish. Parker and his wife built the dwelling together. Across the coming decades, after serving in the US Navy, Parker acted as architect, builder, and client on another seven occasions, as he does in this initial Coconut Grove project, a process Parker later admits allows him to better understand and evolve the craft of his trade. Parker states, *"I know of nothing I like better than to build with my own hands. The strongest training for the architect is to build - to have knowledge of how things are put together. Otherwise, he tends to become less of a realist and more of a dreamer."*[59] Parker regularly designed every aspect of a project, from the macro to the micro scale, including the furniture. When he was not directly building, he was commonly involved in project management at each project site.

Architecture, until and largely through this era incorporated 'passive' methods of design to mitigate climate. Yet in Parker's case, he goes beyond those standards. He celebrates the relationship between building and context and sees the rapport as an opportunity for architectural exploration and expression, always treading lightly on the terrain. This duality sets him apart and exemplifies that architecture need not depend on technology to achieve environmentalist goals. Years later, when asked to define his views on the relationship between nature and the built form he states, *"It's like two hands in a meaningful grip. What you call nature is a lot of things around us. It's the air, water, rain, wind, trees and soil. All of these things in our environment are necessary for our well-being. Having said that, I can also add that they are essential to architectural design, architectural planning, and construction."*[60]

Enamored by Florida's sub-tropical environment, Alfred Browning Parker was drawn to reinterpreting indigenous responses to the setting. His early designs are a degree of separation from 'cracker' or local vernaculars;[61] simply composed and detailed, they embody a modernity ingrained in context. His utilitarian approach was typified by his frequent use of locally harvested 'oolite' stone and cypress, striated plywood with a natural finish, and exposed concrete blocks, viable thanks to an abundance of sand. Parker experimented with these and other materials and methods of construction in an attempt to strike a balance between his interventions and their setting, tackling the climate's inherent nuisances along the way.

Repeatedly, in keeping with early wood frame precedents, Parker lifts buildings off the ground to cool them naturally and to shield structures from insidious termites. On occasion, buildings are placed on stilts, in particular whenever on a storm-surge prone waterfront site or in challenging rock-pit topography. Existing trees are removed sparingly from jobsites; rather, their presence generate design compositions. Examples of his respectful attitude towards the landscape are illustrated in several projects, including: the Parker Residence, Gainesville (1949), "Two Residences in a Rock Pit"- Hopwood & Chandler, Coconut Grove (1949 and 1951), Gayer Residence, Coconut Grove (1953), Ewing Residence,

Figure 57. Marko Residence, Coconut Grove, 1958, Alfred Browning Parker

Figure 58. The Pacesetter House, Coconut Grove, 1954, Alfred Browning Parker

Figure 59. The Pacesetter House, Coconut Grove, 1954, Alfred Browning Parker

Figure 60. The Pacesetter House, Coconut Grove, 1954, Alfred Browning Parker, axonometric view of roof garden

Coconut Grove (1955), Marko Residence, Coconut Grove (1955) and, "A Jewel in the Treetops" Parker Residence, Coconut Grove (1957).

In 1948, Parker summarizes many of his design objectives in the "*Tropex-pansible Home*" design, a prototype for modest residential projects in the tropics. The open plan design is compact and intended for owners to self-build with locally available materials and an uncomplicated construction system. The rectangular footprint is covered by an exposed wood beam shed roof, which, in turn, allows hot air to rise and escape through a row of clearstory windows. The frugal interior extends outside through a bank of doors into a screened porch, underlining the indoor-outdoor relationship.

That same year of 1948, Parker attends the Pan American Congress of Architects held in Havana Cuba. In an interview with this author,[62] Parker recounts that during his early trips to Havana he is "*...impressed by the colonial and the modern projects that I visited. I also went to a job-site. I fell in love with the magnificent wooden louver doors and windows that I saw at projects by the Cubans as well as at the Hotel [Nacional]. I wanted them for my projects, so I requested to meet the carpenter of one of the projects we had visited.*" From that moment forward, solid wood 'persiana' doors and windows were a mainstay of Parker's designs. He further remarked, "*I had them custom-built in Havana for my Florida projects... until I eventually had to find a local artisan that could match their quality.*"[63] Clearly, Parker admires the work of his contemporaries and understands the '*persianas*' as a perfect arbiter to humidity and bright light, wasting no time to expand his reference base 'regionally.' In so doing, Parker once again demonstrates an uncanny ability to assimilate and reinterpret sources of inspiration and then combine them in both creative and practical ways.

Over the years, four of Parker's residential projects are recognized as a *Pacesetter House* by *House Beautiful Magazine*. He is the only architect to achieve the distinction more than once, consequently, his career skyrockets. Curiously, Frank Lloyd Wright learned of the initial winning house while visiting the magazine editor and he volunteers to contribute to the issue writing, "*This Florida house aims at the highest goal to which architecture may aspire: organic architecture. Along this new but ancient way a home where the enlightened mind can flower, where people can develop their fullest potentials, is still a possibility.*"[64] For years, Parker had corresponded with FLW, even as a student as far back as 1939;[65] thus one can only imagine the distinct honor Parker experienced when his (second) mentor praised his work. *House Beautiful* editor, Elizabeth Gordon, adds her accolades of the house in the same issue stating: "*I have seen many good houses. I have seen some great houses. And, we have been showing them regularly, but this is the first time I have wanted to say to you, this is it! This is the House Beautiful.*"[66]

Figure 61. The Pacesetter House, Alfred Browning Parker

Figure 62. The Pacesetter House, Alfred Browning Parker

Figure 63. Friedman Residence, Alfred Browning Parker

Figure 64. Mass Residence, cross section, Palm Beach, 1954, Alfred Browning Parker

Figure 65. Mass Residence, interior view, Palm Beach, 1954, Alfred Browning Parker

Known as the "*1954 Pacesetter House*",[67] the home was designed for his family in 1953 on Royal Road in Coconut Grove. The design embodies organic principles espoused by FLW, exemplified in its engagement of the terrain, structural logic, open floor plan, and orientation of rooms - down to the handsome attention to details in the geometrically arranged limestone walls, floating planters, and decorative cornice. FLW's stream of influence is clearly enunciated at multiple levels. Concrete slabs hover freely over porches, protecting the building from Florida's pounding rain and deflecting its glaring light. The expansive roof deck can accommodate large gatherings, where pleasant breezes and views of the landscape are afforded.

In this house, as in so many of Parker's projects, wood persiana doors dominate, spanning from floor to ceiling and funneling air. Parker employed the Cuban handmade version, akin to their colonial ancestors and banks them together across entire rooms. Parker refers to them as "*breathable walls.*" Persianas are a predominant feature in his Streate Residence, Miami (1950); Bal Harbour Club (1952); Litsey Residence, South Miami (1952); Freidman Residence, Coconut Grove (1953); Mass Residence in Palm Beach (1954); and Marko Residence, (1955).

In 1955, Parker designed a $22,000.00 compact home for Mr. and Mrs. Marko in Coconut Grove, Florida. Joseph Barry, author of *The House Beautiful Treasury of Contemporary American Homes* at the time noted:

""Theirs is not a typical house but it is a profoundly significant one. It means, to believe, that no man need be common, no life need be ordinary, and no man can ever know the joys of it unless he tries uncommonness for himself. The Marko house suggests this. Certainly it has meaning for its owners, who say, "Now we tell everybody who says we live like a king and queen, instead of a hard-working couple, 'We do, indeed!'... It's so beautiful, it's so wonderful, we think we're dreaming, but we're not. We're just living, really, really living!""

In a 1957 article featuring the Mass Residence, *Florida Architecture Magazine* described Parker's sensibilities and the breath of his talents as follows:

"This home is built on an exciting and wonderful site of several acres located on the southeast tip of an island in Lake Worth bordering Palm Beach. It is constructed of enduring and basic materials that weather gracefully and actually improve in appearance with age. For example, the great weeping roof clad in copper sheets will eventually glow with a soft blue green patina against the blue water of the lake. The other materials are Florida quarry keystone, Florida cypress, steel, glass, concrete and tile. The owners of this home placed an unusual confidence in their architect. In addition to customary services they requested him to help them in the selection of a building site, design of all of the furniture, and laying out the landscaping. This home demonstrates a unity in all of its parts... furnishings and landscapings because of this single design responsibility. Details such as lighting sources were all designed by the architect."

In a much later publication entitled *You & Architecture: A Practical Guide to the Best in Building*, Alfred Browning Parker identified the five principles of building that guided his practice:

- *Build strongly.*
- *Build as directly as possible with no complications.*
- *Use the materials at hand and keep these as few as you can.*
- *Let your building love its site and glorify its climate.*
- *Design for use, make it beautiful.*

"With the progression of each home Parker's skill set also grew, which improved the quality of his buildings and gave him an understanding of how the materials weathered in the local environment and he expanded his relationships with local builders and craftsmen." Certainly, Parker's distinctive style of modernism, *"embedded into the local vernacular created unique buildings that embraced their local environment, blurring the boundaries between building and landscape,"*[68] and that plainly defines him as a pioneering 'green' architect.

In 1959, Frank Lloyd Wright recommended Parker as an American Institute of Architects (AIA) Fellow. *"An AIA Fellowship recognizes architects who have made a significant contribution to both architecture and the greater society, achieving a standard of excellence in architecture at both a local and national level. Parker was the only architect Wright ever recommended for the Fellowship."*[69]

Igor Polevitzky

Igor Polevitzky was a principal transitional figure in early twentieth century Florida architecture. Trained in Beaux-Arts traditions at the University of Pennsylvania under Paul Cret, he arrived in South Florida upon graduation in 1934 and shortly thereafter began collaborations with Robert Law Weed and a partnership with architect Trip Russell. Polevitzky's prolific career originated with important Miami Beach hotel commissions, most executed in a handsome Art Deco style, including the Shelborne Hotel (1940) and the earlier and more streamlined Albion Hotel (1939).

Figure 66. Shelborne Hotel, Miami Beach, 1940, Igor Polevitzky

Figure 67. Albion Hotel, Miami Beach, 1939, Igor Polevitzky

In the years following WWII, Miami shifted from a seasonal destination to a year-round home to new waves of permanent residents. Coinciding with modernist thought, a functionalist approach emerged to achieve accommodating environments for continual users and to meet new life-style related design challenges.[70] Around this period, Polevitzky veered his attention towards an 'annealed' modern architecture. During this second phase of his career, Polevitzky's design of houses, civic, and commercial buildings in Florida and eventually including a key commission in Havana, Cuba expanded on regional notions, eventually making him a leader in sub-tropical regionalism in the northern Caribbean.

Figure 68. Sailing Baruch Residence, Miami, 1938, Igor Polevitzky

In 1938, his regionalist trajectory began in earnest with the Sailing Baruch Residence, his first '*Tropotype*' House. Polevitzky is cognizant of the value of vernacular precedents and the dominant role of their weather tempering features. He dedicated his career to re-interpreting, filtering, and repurposing those characteristics, altering their relationships and spatial qualities, and assigning them new uses while exploring the potential of the latest materials and methods of construction. His investigations resulted in permeable building envelops, open-planned designs that transition users from interior to exterior living spaces, progressing from living room to screened porch in a manner that acknowledged both the evolving role of women in contemporary households, and also the informal nature of Florida living.[71]

In 1949, *Florida Architecture and Allied Arts* magazine highlighted samples of "*good regional character*" and illustrated the range of outwardly focused architecture under production with a 'patio' house by Rufus Nims on Indian Creek, a mixed-use, live-work building by Alfred Browning Parker on Biscayne Boulevard, followed by an article featuring a Miami Beach commercial project by Igor Polevitzky - the Arthur Murray Studio. The project exemplifies his innovative approach to architecture. Located at the intersection between a busy main street and a canal in Miami Beach, the composition is anchored at the corner by a monumental pylon with equally oversized signage. The main street façade is lower, but still a story and a half high. Its over-scaled aluminum "*Thermashade*"

Figure 69. Arthur Murray Dance Studio, Miami Beach, 1948, Igor Polevitzky

Figure 70. Arthur Murray Dance Studio, Miami Beach, 1948, Igor Polevitzky

Figure 71. Arthur Murray Dance Studio, Miami Beach, 1948, Igor Polevitzky, interior view

wall shields the glass plane behind it, grafting from traditional architectural elements. A single story high tongue and grove wooden screen bisects the façade, sinuously curving across the reception area, reading like a screen or 'mampara.' The wall is accompanied by tropical landscaping, which flows into the interior. Meanwhile, the main dance hall's retractable roof structure, consents dancers to "sway under the stars during balmy nights," in a "patio" space, underlining the role of innovation, the re-interpretation of building types and connectivity to place. The magazine describes the dance hall as follows: "*The native understands this to be a Miami Beach building, specialized though it is, while the vacationer realizes he could not receive dance instructions in a building like this other than in Florida.*"[72] This architecture is a reflection of the jovial and casual characteristics of its sub-tropical locale as well as of the designer's capacity to fuse the past with the present in a novel manner.

The last and best of Igor Polevitzky's '*Tropo-type*' home series, developed between 1936 and 1949, is the second Heller Residence or more commonly termed '*Birdcage House*,' (pictured on page 82) a notable example of regionally inspired design. In a 1949 lecture, the architect described the house as "*...architecture as a volume rather than a mass.*" As its nickname alludes, these prototypes are specifically designed for the tropics. Tropo-types present ambiguous relationships between indoor and outdoor spaces and rely on passive cooling and lighting features.

The house opens onto a "*diaphanous*" double height screened room, which wraps the outdoor pool area. The main room of the house is not inside, but rather is precisely this outside space. Polevitzky often "*experimented with the theme of the building envelope, which he progressively distort[s] and reduces from the white planar masses of the Bauhaus until the envelope itself becomes little more than a frame.*"[73] As in other of his designs, here too there are novel spatial relationships. The sequential transformation underlines the procession from inside to outside. The *Birdcage House* exemplifies tropical living where the distinction between indoor and outdoor is intentionally ambiguous. Designed for an appliance salesperson, the wood and concrete '*Birdcage House*' integrates an ample array of innovatively employed building materials, including open-web steel trusses, a first in residential design.[74] The split-level plan presents an original program, true to tropical living and to Miami's rising laid back and exotic iconography.[75] An exterior stair connects the deck with the upper floor terrace, an extension of the interior's main living spaces. In another twist, the drum shaped pool is expressed, emerging from within an artificial pond/beach, that in turn is a microcosmic representation of an idyllic South Florida setting.[76]

Figure 72. Birdcage House, Biscayne Island, 1949, Igor Polevitzky

Figure 73. Birdcage House, Biscayne Island, 1949, Igor Polevitzky, outdoor room

Figure 74. Birdcage House, Biscayne Island, 1949, Igor Polevitzky, outdoor room

Featured alongside projects by Richard Neutra, Walter Gropius, and Marcel Breuer in a 1952 book *"82 Distinctive Houses of Architectural Record,"* Polevitzky's was featured in an article entitled *House Designed for the Sub-Tropics.* Here again, the unusual character of South Florida's climate generated an interesting solution whereby the architect develops a large but inexpensive, semi protected living space, specifically suited to the area's heat and humidity. *"A considerable amount of the living area is constructed of wood frame, partial roofing, and baffle walls for privacy. The screened-in 'atmospheric envelop' can reportedly be used for 95% of the weather conditions."* The article points out that few spaces are completely enclosed and are only esteemed necessary *"during the few really cold days in the area,"* and concludes by stating that the structure's Douglas fir frame was designed to withstand hurricane winds of 150 miles per hour and is anchored in reinforced concrete footings.[77] Once again, Polevitzky demonstrates great regional sensibilities and pragmatism.

Less than a decade later, Racketeer Meyer Lansky approached Los Angeles architect Wayne McAllister, designer of several lavish Las Vegas hotels. Both he and subsequently the renowned Phillip Johnson decline Lansky's hotel commission for a prime location in Havana, according to historians siting the client's hurried timeline as the supposed deterrent. Next in line, Igor Polevitzky took on this career defining challenge: merging his mastery of hotel design with his regionalist objectives; and he thankfully meets the imposing deadline with a striking result. The Havana Riviera opened in 1957, six months after its design was completed.

The 21-story building is situated on a prime, wedge-shaped waterfront site along the celebrated Malecón Boulevard and its canted Y-shape, affords dramatic views to each of the 443 rooms. Visitors are greeted by a visual orgy. A tapered masonry screen flows into the porte-cochere entrance, sliding below an equally striking cantilever as it skirts a vibrantly tiled custom greenish-blue[78] dome. The floating plane rests upon a dark granite clad wall, punctuated by a striking sculpture of an intertwined mermaid and swordfish by Cuban artist Florencio Gelabert. The lobby, conceived as a promenade of alternating levels and bridges, is an outdoor room, leading from the cavernous casino, past murals by Rolando Lopez Dirube and Cundo Bermudez, towards open reception areas. Restaurants and bars follow, ending in the pool area beyond that in turn is flanked by luxuriously appointed cabanas and a covered terrace, which play double duty and shield pool-goers from the often-fastidious winds and the wafting sea mist generated by the pounding waves one level down. Below the terrace, and less successfully thought out, the building turns its back onto the Malecón, presenting a long 'inactive' façade at street level.

As the hotel tower rises, a staccato of thin horizontal projecting fins score its façade, protecting the floor to ceiling windows, transoms, and doors from direct sunlight, while splaying out to accommodate balconies at corner suites. A massive ship-like stack, housing the hotel's iconic signage, pierces the building mass as it caps the composition. Ironically, the Riviera was the first Cuban hotel to offer air-conditioned rooms and would be one of the last hotels designed by a US architect in the city.[79]

Figure 75. Hotel Havana Riviera, Havana, 1957, Igor Polevitzky

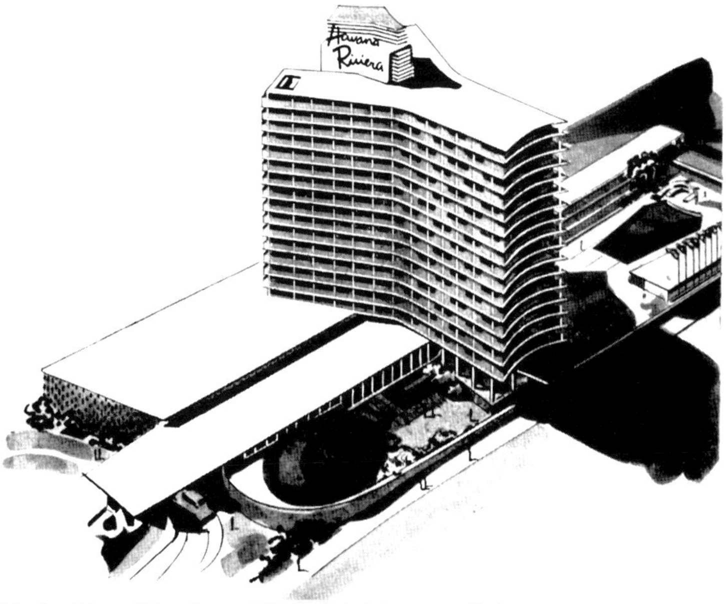

Figure 76. Hotel Havana Riviera, Havana, 1957, Igor Polevitzky, axonometric view

Figure 77. Hotel Havana Riviera, Havana, 1957, Igor Polevitzky

Riviera

Figure 77. Hotel Havana Riviera, Havana, 1957, Igor Polevitzky

Figure 78. (Opposite Page) Hotel Havana Riviera, Havana, 1957, Igor Polevitzky
Figure 79. Hotel Havana Riviera, Havana, 1957, Igor Polevitzky

Figure 80. Hotel Havana Riviera, Havana, 1957, Igor Polevitzky, interior view

Paul Rudolph

Further north, catching everyone's attention was internationally recognized Paul Rudolph, principal pioneer of the renowned post-war modern regionalist movement known as the *Sarasota School of Architecture*.[80] With a focus on architecture harmonizing with its surroundings, *Sarasota School* projects featured "clean, open contemporary floor plans, filled with light and cool terrazzo floors, wide overhangs, and flat roofs."[81]

Notions of regional adaptation played a fundamental role in the early career of Paul Rudolph. His sensibilities are the natural by-product of three currents of influence: Frank Lloyd Wright's explorations into the interconnection between building and landscape; Richard Neutra charting the importance of subtropical climates in the development of Western Architecture and his embrace of cross-cultural connections;[82] and finally, Rudolph's own apprenticeship in Central Florida with Ralph Twitchell. After a brief initial stint with Twitchell in Sarasota, Paul Rudolph attended Harvard University, where he meets his mentor, Bauhaus founder, Walter Gropius. During WWII, Rudolph interrupted his education to serve in the military at the Brooklyn Naval Yard where he learns of innovative materials and first imagines their architectural applications. "*As an officer in the U.S. Naval Reserve, he worked on the design and building of merchant ships.*"[83]

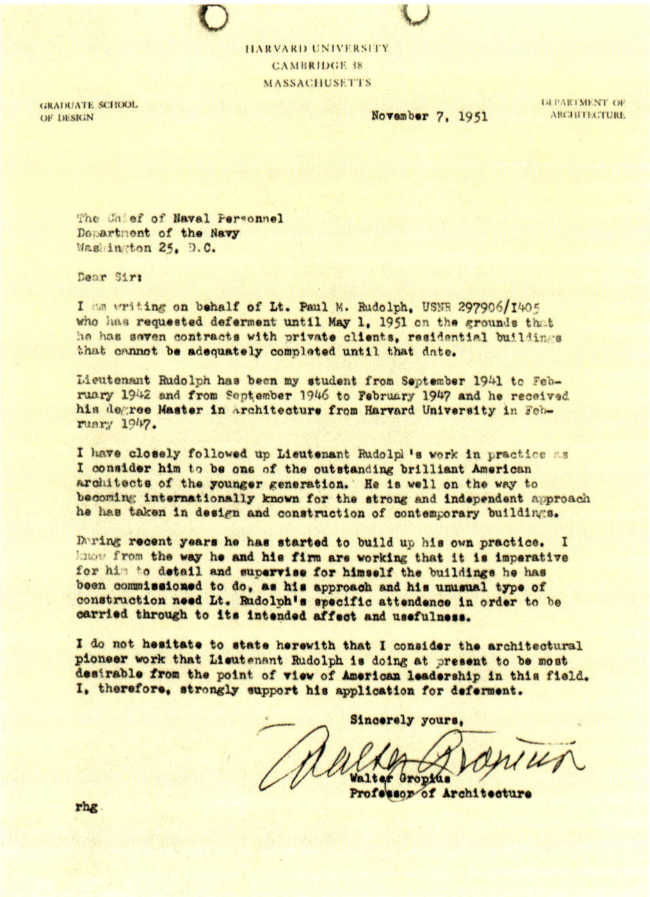

HARVARD UNIVERSITY
CAMBRIDGE 38
MASSACHUSETTS

GRADUATE SCHOOL OF DESIGN

DEPARTMENT OF ARCHITECTURE

November 7, 1951

The Chief of Naval Personnel
Department of the Navy
Washington 25, D.C.

Dear Sir:

I am writing on behalf of Lt. Paul M. Rudolph, USNR 297906/1405 who has requested deferment until May 1, 1951 on the grounds that he has seven contracts with private clients, residential buildings that cannot be adequately completed until that date.

Lieutenant Rudolph has been my student from September 1941 to February 1942 and from September 1946 to February 1947 and he received his degree Master in Architecture from Harvard University in February 1947.

I have closely followed up Lieutenant Rudolph's work in practice as I consider him to be one of the outstanding brilliant American architects of the younger generation. He is well on the way to becoming internationally known for the strong and independent approach he has taken in design and construction of contemporary buildings.

During recent years he has started to build up his own practice. I know from the way he and his firm are working that it is imperative for him to detail and supervise for himself the buildings he has been commissioned to do, as his approach and his unusual type of construction need Lt. Rudolph's specific attendence in order to be carried through to its intended affect and usefulness.

I do not hesitate to state herewith that I consider the architectural pioneer work that Lieutenant Rudolph is doing at present to be most desirable from the point of view of American leadership in this field. I, therefore, strongly support his application for deferment.

Sincerely yours,

Walter Gropius
Professor of Architecture

rhg

Figure 81. Letter to the Chief of Naval Personnel, 1951, Walter Gropius

After the war, Rudolph and Twitchell became partners and together they "*developed a series of striking original modern buildings whose character were derived in no small part from the unique characteristics of the place... and, they were seen as ... making the new architecture a meaningful contemporary expression of the cultures and climates in which they were designed.*"[84] Rudolph chose to return to Florida because according to him, "*there was something about Modern Architecture which makes it more sympathetic to warm climates than cool climates.*"[85] "*Regional characteristics are a part of all good architecture,*" he said, "*and should be accepted without either resistance or overemphasis.*"[86]

As partners, Rudolph & Twitchell's initial project was the 1950 Healy Guest House, known more popularly as the "*Cocoon House.*" It is novel at many levels; from the constructive means and applied technologies, down to the assemblage of elements and the re-interpretation of precedents. Steel straps span between sidewalls to support the bowed roof and form its silhouette. Insulating panels are sprayed with the trademarked '*Cocoon method,*' which is composed of a waterproofing and flexible saran-vinyl plastic, a technique introduced by the U.S. military to sheathe vessel components and protect them from the elements. The catenary roofing system sits on a wood post and lintel frame with additional steel ties. This allows the building to cantilever well over the edge of the water and whereby the architects resolves the apparent collision between a rational floor plan, conceptually derived from Bauhaus teachings, and the romantic influences of a Frank Lloyd Wright, by which the building engages the landscape.[87] But perhaps even more interestingly, Rudolph and Twitchell handsomely fused innovative structural systems with re-interpreted traditional building elements, resolving the ostensible tension between traditional and modern design strategies. The building is lifted off the ground, suggestive of the light-weight structures of early Native-American dwellings in Florida. Southern Colonial louvers or perhaps Caribbean Colonial wooden "persianas" were re-interpreted, becoming expansive, permeable walls. The resulting chiaroscuro effect achieved in the interiors mimics the quality of light found in neighboring mangroves. While, these innovative yet traditional operable walls model light they simultaneously harness the prevailing breezes, permitting not only a visual connection to the exterior, but also a sensorial one. Clearly, a tropical house, the building was designed for a specific site, a hot and humid

Figure 82. Healy Guest House ("Cocoon House"), 1950, Paul Rudolph, axonometric view

Figure 83. Healy Guest House ("Cocoon House"), 1950, Paul Rudolph, interior view

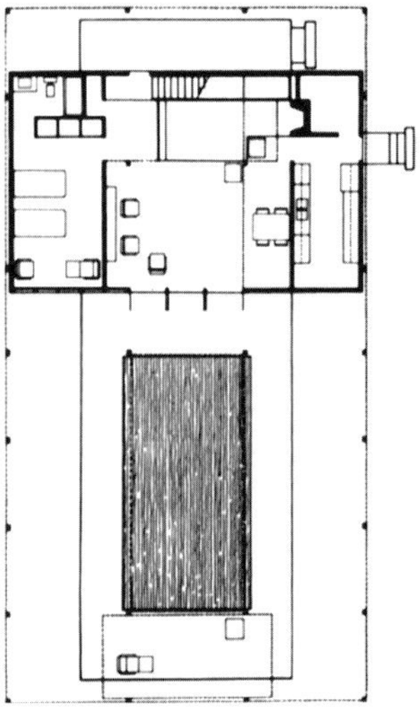

Figure 84. Umbrella House, Lido Shores, 1953-54, Paul Rudolph

Figure 85. Umbrella House, Lido Shores, 1953-54, Paul Rudolph, east view

climate, well versed in both technological innovations and historical precedents, and due to its scale and method of construction, it was intended as a candidate for pre-fabrication. For all its virtuosity and inventiveness, the *Cocoon House* continues to serve as a model for architects across the tropical belt.

The year 1954 was pivotal in Rudolph's career; his partnership with Twitchell dissolves and he travels extensively, also attending two decisive conferences. At the first, held in Mississippi, he meets Richard Neutra, which further channels his interests in regionalism. At a second international event, held in Brazil, he had the opportunity to become more familiar with Oscar Niemeyer's locally rooted work and to increase his awareness of Lucio Costa's collaboration with Le Corbusier. These experiences and his travels to the Middle East guided his evolving design principles over the coming years.[88] Now practicing independently and eager to exploit the international attention he had garnered thus far to further establish himself as a leader of his generation, Rudolph once again explores the integration of tectonics and form while reinterpreting regional precedents, and the 1954 *Umbrella House* design exemplifies the attuned direction of his forthcoming work.

A two-story speculative dwelling, the *Umbrella House* is positioned on its site to capitalize on view corridors and to embrace the prevailing breezes. The design suggests a seam-less indoor and outdoor living experience; the product of its orientation, overlapping volumes, and the freedom conceded by its lightweight structure. The overhead canopy structure, for which the building is nicknamed, is externally braced by diagonal steel members and built of stock lumber and hardware, topped by a filigree of thin wooden slats. The resulting filtered light evocative of the dappled light produced by Native American reed structures in the region or by the effects of typical reed mats hung across a Moorish 'patio' or street and coincidentally typical of Moorish-tinged Spanish Colonial settlements in the Caribbean, suggest Rudolph's embrace of cross-cultural reflections. The parasol extends from the east facing swimming pool courtyard and continues over the nestled volume of the house proper, promoting ventilation across the 17' high living space, while cooling the exterior's microclimate, occasioning comfortable indoor and outdoor rooms- a model mid-century Florida house.

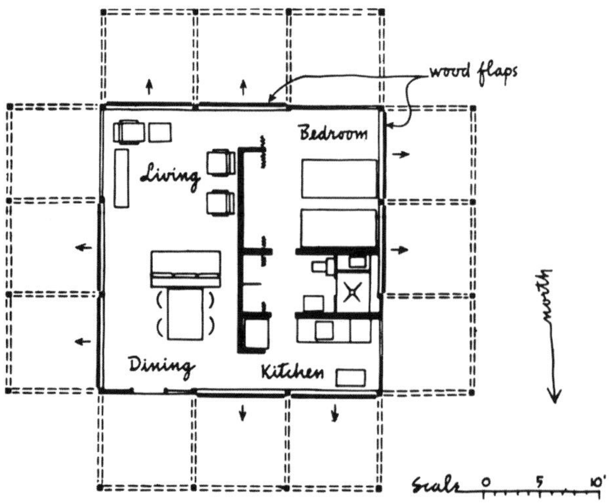

Figure 86. Walker Guest House, Sanibel Island, 1952, Paul Rudolph, plan

The Walker Guest House in Ft. Myers is perhaps the purest, most geometrically ordered Rudolph building. It is a Greek plan, with only the central 24' x 24' square enclosed by hinged panel doors that serve to secure the building from intruders and storms while shading and defining the four implied porches. Rudolph described the house as follows: *"Two bays on each side of this guest cottage are filled with pivoting panels which function as 1) the enclosing wall, 2) the ventilating element, 3) the shading device, and 4) the*

Figure 87. Umbrella House, Lido Shores, 1953-54, Paul Rudolph, interior view

hurricane shelter. The third bay is filled with glass, to admit light and splendid views. When the panels are closed, the pavilion is snug and cave-like - when open, the space psychologically changes and one is virtually in the landscape."[89] The stock lumber and plywood pivoting awnings can respond to the path of the sun and intensity of the wind or rain. Its unpretentious pulley system composed of rope and 77-pound counterweights, a nod to the site's marine location. The compact ship-like interior is divided into two sides: one public, the other essentially private. Astutely set back from the potentially menacing shore, and sited near the road, the lightweight structure gingerly floats above the landscape; a stalwart example of the principles of the *Sarasota School of Design* for its environmental responsiveness, spatial simplicity and its paired homage towards vernacular inheritance and modern tenets.

"The obvious precedent for the house is Mies's Farnsworth House, but it is just as much a progeny of Philip Johnson's Glass House (itself a child of the Farnsworth). Johnson and Rudolph were good friends, close since their days studying architecture at Harvard. Johnson visited Rudolph in Sarasota not long after this house was completed. Like the Glass House, it is classical in its symmetry, with the box-frame forming a kind of diagrammatic, low-end peristyle. The whole thing was built with off-the-rack parts on a tight budget. In this it is the antithesis of the very effete Glass House, but it shares the idea of creating a space open to nature in every direction."[90]

As modernism became the shared architectural expression throughout postwar America, a strong interest developed in regional interpretations of modern design and construction methods, and Twitchell and Rudolph, and later Rudolph on his own, caught the attention of architects and the press, with their minimalist regionalist approach being emulated both near and far.

"ARCHITECTURE UNDER THE SUN": *'a lo cubano'*

The search for Cuba's cultural identity has its origins in the late nineteenth century, when "the cultural debate concerning the nature of Cuban identity - *cubanidad* - had political resonance with the movement for independence from Spain.[91] Jose Marti, the most important intellectual figure in the struggle for independence, recognized the impact of the urban realm on society when he stated, "*The objective of life is the pursuit of ideal beauty; because just as acts of virtue result in beautiful places, so too beautiful places act upon our virtue.*" In other writings Marti iterated that establishing a clear sense of national identity is an essential ideological component to creating a unified patriotic movement to liberate the island from Spanish domination. "*The idea of regional specificity of Cuban culture, that is its otherness to Spanish culture, found some of its most coherent expressions in Marti's writings, though other intellectuals, such as Felix Varela had been examining this in the earlier part of the century.*"[92]

Following the 1901 Platt Amendment, stipulating that the United States could exercise the right to intervene in Cuban political, economic and military affairs as it deemed necessary, a majority of Cuban citizens experienced bitter resentment. Not surprisingly, early XX century intellectuals will draw parallel conclusions to Marti's earlier preoccupations regarding the correlations between identity and autonomy, but now in reaction to the omnipresence of North American interests on the island, in particular during and after the two periods of "intervention" following the War of Independence.[93]

During the coming decades, *Cubanidad* is continually debated and in a constant process of definition, finding reflections in musical, literary, fine art disciplines, and later architectural endeavors. Parallel and seemingly at juxtapostion to this

Figure 88. *Discovery of the Caribbean (Nacimiento de las Antillas)*, 1940, Mario Carreño

inward reflection on identity, cross-cultural referencing also becomes more frequent, manifested in various fields as commercial, trading, and political ties amplify between Cuba and new trading partners, including the United States. In the first instance, there is a reevaluation of intrinsic values and traits, and in the second, the assimilation of external streams of influence, each scenario generating contemporary interpretations of Cuban identity.

Great synergy exists between all the arts during this period as well. Artists, writers, and architects frequently socialized and debated issues, leading to a healthy crosspollination between them, as well as to some later collaborations. Early host to many of these soirees, was Don Fernando Ortiz Fernández, a Cuban essayist, ethnomusicologist and scholar of Afro-Cuban culture, dedicated to instigating explorations and a better understanding of all aspects of indigenous Cuban culture--later coining the term "transculturation," the notion of converging cultures.

According to Ortiz, Cuban identity is modeled by three external "forces." Two centuries of 'flotillas' hailing from different countries transiting through Havana's harbor, convey early wealth, and new settlers such as mariners, explorers and second tier nobility, settle in the area, introducing a variety of European cultures and customs. Slaves from NE Africa, including Egypt, were transported to Havana, bringing with them their traditions and rituals, and lastly, the physical proximity to the United States resulted in a constant flow of commercial activities and growing presence of business interests, transmitting a "protestant work ethic." Ortiz further expounded on these topics in journals he helped establish: *Revista Bimestre Cubana, Archivos del Folklore Cubano,* and *Estudios Afrocubanos*. For his writings and activism, he was later nominated for the Nobel Peace Prize in recognition of his love for culture and humankind.[94]

Cultural Ripples

The by-products of those conversations, investigations and yearnings by many lead to creative confluences appearing across the cultural spectrum, in some instances, reaching international acclaim and in other instances, vernacular annotations. For example, Spanish, African, and Haitian French-Creole cultures had fused during Cuba's extended colonial era. Over time, vernacular derivatives in music and dance, such as the Danzon, Guaracha, and later the Chachachá, Salsa, and Mambo emerged, largely contributing towards the birth and evolution of early jazz,[95] "providing what Jelly Roll Morton called the Latin tinge," according to Cuban historian Mario Coyula Crowley. The masterpieces of avant-gardist painters Wilfredo Lam, Amelia Pelaez, Rene Portocarrero, sculptors such as Rita Longa, the research of anthropologist Lydia Cabrera, the influential writings of Jose Lezama Lima, Alejo Carpentier and the graceful choreography of prima ballerina Alicia Alonso[96] also elevated inward reflections from whence came an outside appreciation and study of artistic expressions emanating from the island during this same period.[97][98] In turn, Cubans continue to assimilate external forces.[99]

Figure 89. Cha-cha-cha lessons at the Arthur Murray Dance Studio

Figure 90. Beny Moré

In the field of architecture, South Florida architects referred to Cuba's colonial architecture at the turn of the century as they simultaneously looked at Mediterranean sources for image-making purposes. However, a less dermal re-evaluation occurred on the island during the same period. Cuba's colonial architecture had developed over centuries through a vernacular process, evolving stylistically, eventually embracing Neo-classical and baroque detailing, far removed from its initial imported characteristics. That distancing from the original source, both from a climatic and stylistic perspective, distinguishes the Late Colonial as 'cubano,' facilitating a sense of ownership and its fluid assimilation as a 'nationalist' reference point in the XX century. This fact, coupled with period publications on the subject by leading architectural historians,[100] lead to a wider appreciation of colonial architecture's features, accelerating its adaption, or re-appropriation and gives way to a Neo-Colonial style that in turn serves as the precursor to further distilled investigations in subsequent years.

The initial expressions of 'lo cubano' in architecture responded to a need for conveying *"a national style for official buildings in foreign countries"* and the product was a Cuban colonial revival style. The first of such buildings is the San Carlos Institute, in Key West, Florida, by Francisco Centurion in 1924. The second is the Cuban Pavilion by Govantes and Cabarrocas in 1927 at the Iberian-American Exposition in Seville. A year later, in Havana, Leonardo Morales designed the first neo-colonial building in the city- the residence of the Countess of Buena Vista in the Miramar neighborhood.[101]

The writings of Pedro Martinez Inclán and the buildings by Eugenio Batista prior to WWII provided the road map for the convergence of a national colonial architecture with modernity that would be explored further by post-war architects. In fact, in parallel to the increasing waves of external forces, the next generation arose philosophically connected to the homegrown regionalist positions defined prior to the war by Leonardo Morales, Martinez Inclán, and Batista.

The Functionalist, the Traditionalists & the Expressionists

One objective of this generation of architects was to express '*lo cubano*' as a cultural construct, combining to a greater or lesser extent "the different myths that shape what may be labeled as the nature of Cuban-ness,"[102] drawing from lyrical, colonial, and/or Afro-Cuban sources of inspiration with the equally important aim of adapting to the harsh climate. Obtained from various trajectories across the island's history, these varied cultural myths nourished diverse positions, and for this reason the regionalist camp was not homogenous.

Historian Narciso Menocal termed the first of these mythical sub-sets as the '**lyrical**' group, drawing inspiration from the national landscape as an *"image of utopia."* The second myth is the '**colonial**', in particular as associated with the climatically attuned later architectural adaptations produced during the more sophisticated second half of the nineteenth century, and deemed culturally imbedded. Lastly, there is the 'Afro-Cuban' myth - "***lo criollo***"- based on the syncretism of the Spanish traditions "made rich with African rhythm, sensuality, color, laughter, insouciance, and outright sexuality."[103] Until combined with the other myths in the early XX century by Cuban avant-garde movements, the Afro-Cuban myth had garnered less cultural credence. When these three streams of influence converge in the 1920's, expressed in particular in music, art, graphic design and literature, the initial search for a national identity surfaces, shaping intellectual, and artistic pursuits. "A*rchitecture was the last of the arts to integrate itself with that cultural summa,"*[104] as embodied in the works of Eugenio Batista.

Figure 91. House and Studio of Nicolas Arroyo and Gabriela Menendez, 1942, Nicolas Arroyo & Gabriela Menendez, 'Functionalist' example

As a consequence, distinct regionalist camps developed in Cuba's postwar era. The '***functionalists***' rationalism understood from a climatological perspective, pragmatically predicated on dealing firstly with the tropical environment,[105] followed the earlier (1934) philosophical lines of Leonardo Morales, when he stated: "In our city of Havana, buildings that conform to the modern ideas of architects from France and Northern Europe have already been built. But in our architecture do we need to follow the creations of foreigners or use the fundamental principles that guided them? They solved their problems from the point of view of their climatic, economic and social conditions... We should not use as a basis for ourselves what they created for Germany and Scandinavia... We should not plagiarize, but create something appropriate to our conditions... The solution should owe more to the requirements of the Tropic of Cancer and our social Latin American context than to those of the temperate zone, of which we have already wrongly adopted prototypes valid for their climate and for their characteristics - so different from ours - but not for us."[106]

The second sub-group, the '***traditionalists***' camp, bridged between the colonial past and the modern present, seeking to define a Cuban identity through a distilled architectural incorporation of typologies, elements, and materials.

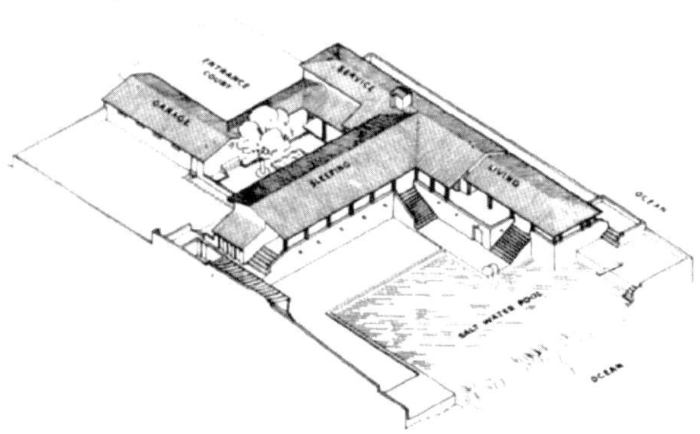

Figures 92 & 93. Casa Eutemio Falla Bonet, Miramar, 1937-39, Eugenio Batista, rear elevation and axonometric view, 'Traditionalist' example

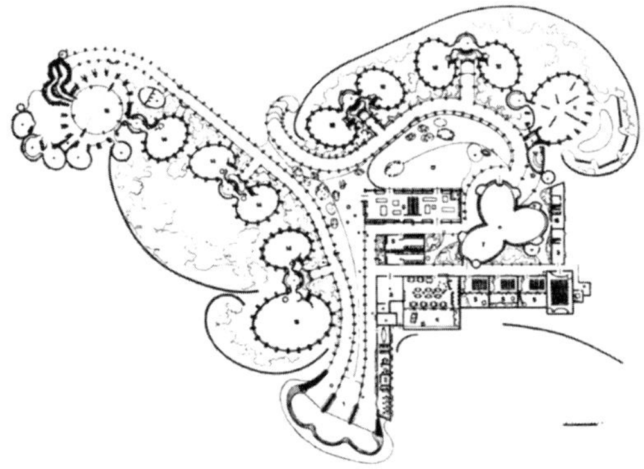

Figures 94 & 95. Escuelas Nacionales de Arte, 1961, Ricardo Porro, Roberto Gottardi, and Vittorio Garrati, elevation and plan, 'Expressionist' example

Vernacular tools re-appear, with some adjustments for morphological changes, building types and materials - which is to say from a compact to semi-compact urban form, from centralized courtyards typical of party-wall sites to side yards in suburban lots, and finally, from handcrafted materials to industrialized ones.

Unsentimental transformations occur but sources remain legible: the 'patio' courtyards, the 'persiana' jalousies, 'medio-punto' stained glass windows, the 'porticos' galleries, the 'mamparas' wooden room dividers, tall and elaborately modeled ceilings, and the bay windows are built in keeping with local traditions, using materials such as: wood, brick, and terra-cotta to contrast contemporary construction methods and finishes, including the smooth concrete surfaces and sleek glass elements.

Lastly, Afro-Cuban symbolism, its flowing rhythms, organic forms, and pulsating color palettes inspired the '***expressionists***.' Eugenio Batista defined the work out of this camp as "*arquitectura de planos movidos*" (architecture of dynamic motion) given the common utilization of highly sculptural and often fluid forms, including hyperbolic and parabolic shapes, butterfly and accordion roof planes, all visually denoting movement.

This sub-group's culminating project was the post-revolutionary National Art Schools (Escuelas Nacionales de Arte) complex, designed by Ricardo Porro and his Italian colleagues, Roberto Gottardi and Vittorio Garrati.[107] The two buildings designed by Porro are particularly synchronized with the 'criollo' spirit for several overlapping reasons, not the least of which is how the organic designs celebrate early Afro-Cuban vernacular models of place-making. The buildings incorporate an Afro-Cuban (religious) cultural narrative, including a sexually charged symbolism that lends further readings to the 'fecund' massing, 'coital' composition, and 'phallic' details.[108] Then there is the intricate play of light and forms, the studied relationships between buildings and the natural realm, and the handsome details and handcrafted construction, including Catalan vaults, which collectively distinguish these buildings as a masterpiece. Although several of the projects remain "unfinished,"[109] they are nonetheless a paradigmatic example of Cuba's modern regionalist era. Sadly, they are practically the closing chapter of that era.

In all sub-groups, a thought-provoking marriage between tradition, modernity, and climatic considerations consolidates, and thusly the search for '*lo cubano,*' became a formal pursuit. All these fundamental and compositional determinations, according to historians, incorporated the past in a manner, which did not aim for a picturesque or nostalgic effect so much as for the construction of a genuinely Cuban, yet contemporary atmosphere, using local materials and adapting itself to the local hot and humid climate.[110]

Point of Inflection

The trajectory of Cuban architecture was inflected in 1944 when University of Havana School of Architecture students and recent graduates assaulted academic standards. They irreverently burn copies of the *Canon of the Five Orders of Architecture* by Jacopo (Giacomo) Barozzi da Vignola (1507-1573), a formative reference until that time. Amongst the participants were Max Borges Jr., Frank Martinez, Ricardo Porro, Nicolas Quintana, and Mario Romañach; all soon to become second-generation trailblazers of Cuba's modern 'regionalist' movement. The "*quema de los Vignolas*" incident marked the break from established traditions and methodologies and is a call to a new order, one focused on innovation, technology, and social prioritization. According to Cuban architect and historian, Nicolas Quintana, the 'new order' gives way to a "Cuban Renaissance" period across the arts, which will parallel international vanguard movements and at times intertwine with them.

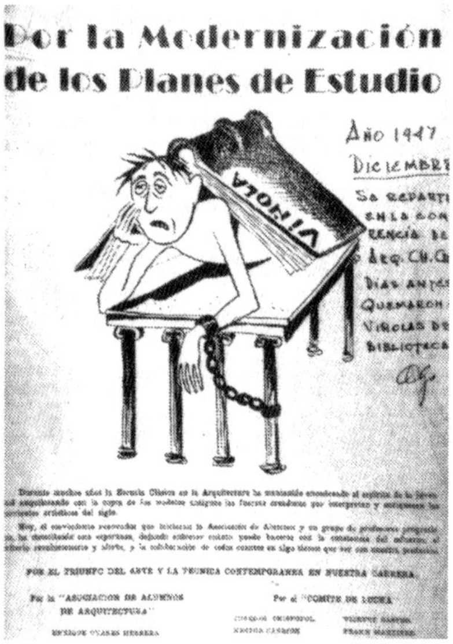

Figure 96. Pamphlet with 'Declaration of Principals'

Figure 97. Eugenio Batista, Nicolâs Quintana, Eduardo Montoulieu, Mario Romañach, Juan I. Guerra, Manuel Gutierrez, Frank Martinez, Alberto Beale, and Emilio de Junco

At this pivotal and symbolic moment, those in academic and architectural circles that had not already taken notice of Modernisms theoretical and constructive principles and its regional and nationalistic inroads surely do so. Academia responds, soon after altering its curriculum. Several of the students participating in the "*quema*" also advocate a search for the 'essence' of Cuban architecture. From this moment forward, Schools of thought re-emerged, in which national identity and modernity were partnered in varying degrees. Some in the fledgling group developed with a formidable nationalist resolve, attempting to reconcile previously incompatible categories: "modernity and tradition; the universal and the local; the international vanguards with national identity."[111] Moreover, thanks to these tendencies, over the coming two decades, Cuban architecture reclaimed the formal, compositional, and decorative richness cast-off by rationalist dogma.[112] In retrospect, the Cuban novelist Alejo Carpentier observed: "*You had, of course to be a nationalist, while trying one's best to be a vanguard at the same time…It was something of a tall order, since all nationalism is founded on the cult of tradition, whereas vangardism, by definition, implies a severance from tradition.*"[113] Toward the end of the 1940's, acclimatization or "aplatanamiento"[114] of modern architecture began in earnest. The 1947 Radiocentro-CMQ multiuse complex by Junco, Gastón, and Dominguez sent an initial shock wave through the city, heralding the second coming of Modern Regionalism to Havana, and "kicking off the development of La Rampa," over the coming two decades evolving into the "Paseo del Prado of modernity." Havana's building stock would nearly double, and a bumper-crop of young talented architects would forge a modern image for the city.[115]

Figure 98. Radiocentro - CMQ, Havana, 1947, Junco, Gastón, and Dominguez

Figure 99. Barrio Obrero Luyano, 1944, Mario Romañach

Mario Romañach

In 1944, Mario Romañach Paniagua collaborates with Pedro Martinez Inclán and Antonio Quintana on an important commission which catapults his career and places him in a leading role among the nascent modern regionalist generation. The trio designed a new suburb, the Barrio Obrero Luyano, just south of the capital. The project shares common traits with other large-scale international commissions of the time and informed by a Corbusian planning model, it proposed distended relationships between sober multi-storied buildings but with a mix of uses and types. The project includes 1,500 dwellings, eight apartment complexes in four-story buildings, and several ancillary services such as schools, markets, public parks, and playing fields. It represented the largest housing initiative in the city.

Not long afterward, Romañach enters into a decade long partnership with his well-connected colleague Silverio Bosch. Four years later, in 1949, they received the National College of Architects' Gold Medal for the Jose Noval Cueto residence, considered by Richard Neutra as one of the best examples of rationalism in Cuba for its merging of characteristic elements such as ribbon windows, open plan, pilotis, and taut skin with tropical foils. The house is unique both for its architectural resolution as for its adaptation to Cuba's tropical climate.

Two extruded rectangular boxes, extensively sheathed in glass, sit on either side of a courtyard, all below a hovering concrete brim, which protects walls from the sun. The roof plane, punctured over the courtyard, frames views of the sky. Tenuous bridges connect the volumes perched on pilotis. As in colonial antecedents, main rooms face the courtyard and are located on the piano-nobile; services and the pool area are on the ground floor- shielded from sight by a perforated garden wall and cooled by the water's presence. Vegetation meanders into interior living spaces. High ceilings prevail and day lighting and cross ventilation easily attained given the judicious orientation of the building. Measured uses of local materials enrich spaces and save it from an otherwise unadorned interior canvas. Ornamentation is minimal, mainly via stone and metal details and the restrained and unexpected use of color. *House & Home* magazine published the house in August 1952. The article states, "Gropius was enthused by his recent visit to Havana, calling the house a fabulous built space, illustrating that beauty and functionalism derived from climate control are not mutually exclusive."[116] The Noval Cueto residence shares these common traits as well as its overall compositional resolution with Paul Rudolph's Leavengood Residence (1950-51).

Figure 100. Ana Carolina Font Residence, Havana, 1956, Mario Romañach

Figure 101. Ana Carolina Font Residence, Havana, 1956, Mario Romañach, interior view

Aside from his interest in developing a dialectical dialogue between modernity and Cuban traditions, Romañach developed a parallel interest in Japanese architecture, evidenced in some of his subsequent projects. The houses for Ana Carolina Font (1956) and for Rufino Alvarez (1957) serve as examples of how Asian influences are seamlessly stitched into designs, alongside colonial and rationalist threads.[117]

Upon arrival at the Font residence, offset stepped terraces greet the visitor, leading to the main entrance. The dumbbell shaped plan generates entry- and garden-facing courtyards. The entry hall and main staircase act as the hinge in between the adjoining rooms arranged at half levels. Asian inspired 'mamparas' separate the light filled entry hall from the main living areas. Their wood lattice

Figure 102. Jose Noval de Cueto Residence, Havana, 1949, Mario Romañach

Figure 103. Jose Noval de Cueto Residence, Havana, 1949, Mario Romañach, interior view

Figure 104. Jose Noval de Cueto Residence, Havana, 1949, Mario Romañach, plans

pattern permits a degree of privacy while facilitating cross ventilation and diffused day-lighting into the adjacent rooms. The delicate lattice pattern repeats on interior doors and outdoor screens, adding visual interest. Metal rods pierce floating wooden stair treads, one of many handsome modern details found throughout the residence. Unlike the Noval Cueto residence where sheets of glass predominate several facades, here openings are punched deep into the masonry walls; in other few instances, set in slightly recessed panels. Structural elements are expressed. Butterfly roofs float above the lateral arms of the composition, a reinterpretation of sculpted colonial enclosures. A continuous band of stained glass clearstory windows are sandwiched in between the roof and the walls, bathing spaces with polychromatic hues. Grouped across upper floors towards the garden are colonial inspired wooden persianas, creating a more permeable façade in contrast to the rather hermetic street elevation. Textural qualities of brick, stone, wood, ceramics, and stained glass are introduced and combined in new ways.[118]

In 1953, Romañach designed a residence for Ms. Evangelina Aristigueta de Vidaña. The design earned the *Gold Medal of Design* from the National College of Architects in 1955 as well as significant accolades from Richard Neutra. The L-shaped plan extends over a lush oversized lot in a posh outlying neighborhood of the capital. A porch is implied at the main entrance by a recessed plane, and a slot in the extended roofline allows sunshine to wash the wall and call attention to the adjacent entry stair. A columnar system and box trusses consent spaces, air and light to flow freely between graduating floor levels, which in turn simultaneously allow for both visual continuity and spatial definition of the more public spaces.

As in the Noval Cueto residence, the garden façades are more transparent than the street facing elevation. Structural bays are expressed throughout and a vertical reveal at the inlaid brick walls adds visual interest. A ribbon of clearstory windows stretches across the garden facades, protected by the projecting roofline. Wooden persiana doors allow cross ventilation, control day lighting, and provide access to the landscaped courtyard or to the many terraces, which

Figure 105. Evangelina Aristigueta de Vidaña Residence, Havana, 1953, Mario Romañach

Figure 106. Evangelina Aristigueta de Vidaña Residence, Havana, 1953, Mario Romañach, rear view

Figure 107. Evangelina Aristigueta de Vidaña Residence, Havana, 1953, Mario Romañach, rear view

Figure 108. Evangelina Aristigueta de Vidaña Residence, Havana, 1953, Mario Romañach, interior view

wrap around the house. The dominant roofline is an important actor in the design as it visually engages the landscape and suggests outdoor rooms. Its depth fluctuates, protecting walls and shading seating areas. Parallels can be drawn between this project and Neutra's early Case Study houses, his design for the "House with Five Courtyards," as well as design investigations by Alvar Aalto. Comparisons can also be made with Niemeyer's 1943 Kubitcheck house in Pampulha, Brazil, with its similar plan, section, incorporation of natural materials, and expressed angled roofline; where the Niemeyer and Romañach houses differ is in their respective relationships between indoor and outdoor spaces.

Figure 109. Oscar Kubitschek Residence, Pampulha, 1943, Oscar Neimayer

Working independently, in 1956, Romañach designed an apartment building for Ms. Aristigueta de Vidaña in the neighborhood of Miramar. The four-story reinforced concrete structure sets a new precedent in apartment building design in Cuba for its compositional characteristics and use of materials. A narrow sliver separates the two main rectangular masses with the principal stair, elegantly floating up within an intersecting, light-drenched, protected central patio. Half of the ground floor is semi-porous, its perimeter skin defined by inset clay-tile screens that camouflage a carport; they are a hybrid between traditional screens and a Corbusian brise-soleil. Each façade differs within the clearly expressed structural elements and brick infill walls, lending each elevation visual order on the one hand and plastic qualities on the other, thanks to the playful placement of persiana-clad bay windows and projecting screened terraces. Within the apartments, these jutting compartments, dressed in wood lattice or clay tile screens, control light and capture breezes, naturally cooling the unit while allowing for private outdoor living within a suburban setting, and conversely, providing greater connectivity with the outdoors from within the dwelling. Apartment interiors are simple, with few walls so natural ventilation is unimpeded. Narrow horizontal bands of clearstory windows are set back slightly to filter the blinding tropical light. This is the first instance in which Romañach utilized stained-glass windows. As with the previous buildings, Romañach's creative adaptation of colonial elements with Japanese influences and rationalist thinking parallel Neutra, and Le Corbusier, resulting in a unique synthesis - a truly modern vernacular proposition.

Figure 110. Apartment Building for Evangelina Aristigueta de Vidaña, Miramar, 1956, Mario Romañach

Romañach went on to design other apartment buildings including one for the Goods and Bonds Investment Co., completed in 1958. In addition to his private sector commissions, between 1955 and 1958, Romañach collaborated with Nicolas Arroyo Marquez, another very notable mid-century modern regionalist architect, on the development of a "Pilot Plan" for Havana in conjunction with Josep Lluis Sert's Town Planning Associates office for the National Planning Board. As a part of these efforts, they, along with architect Gabriela Menendez, designed a new Presidential Palace. The proposed siting was irresponsible but its handsome architectural proposition was informed by local precedents; buildings were placed around a courtyard, with a progression of terraces and outdoor rooms, all under a brutalist 'parasol', not unlike Sert's later US Embassy in Bagdad[119] or the concept developed by Rudolph at the Umbrella House in 1953.

Figure 111. Presidential Palace proposal, Havana

In 1959, Romañach immigrated to the United States. Primarily dedicated to academia, he taught at Harvard, Yale, Columbia, Cornell, and was program Chair at the University of Pennsylvania. In the 1970's, he collaborated on the 'curricular development plan' for the School of Architecture at Simon Bolivar University in Caracas Venezuela. Throughout this period, Romañach received several awards and recognition, including a *Certificate of Merit* by the AIA for the design of the Spanish Pavilion for the World's Fair held in New York in 1964. Later accolades included Citations for Design Excellence and the prestigious induction into the US National Academy of Design in 1979.

Figure 112. Medical and Surgical Center, El Vedado, 1948, Max Borges

Figure 113. Max Borges receiving the Gold Medal Prize, 1948

Max Borges

Born in Havana, Max Borges Recio graduated from Georgia Tech in 1939 and completed his graduate studies at Harvard the next year. By 1942, the precocious Borges, son of Max Borges del Junco, a reputable architect, was licensed in Havana, spending the first years of his career working in his father's office redirecting it toward rationalism. In 1948, at the age of 32, Borges Jr. received the Gold Medal Prize from the National College of Architects for the design of the Medical and Surgical Center situated in El Vedado. Articulated volumes result in a visual medley, woven together with strong horizontal lines created by thin projecting rooflines, accompanied by ribbon windows. The design announced Borges' yet inchoate sensibility toward the tropics, more clearly developed and voiced in forthcoming projects.

Between 1951 and 1954, Borges intervened on three occasions on an existing building site to expand the popular Tropicana Cabaret in Marianao. In the first project, he invited famed Spanish architect, Felix Candela, to collaborate.[120] A new dance hall was wedged between the existing building and the splayed property line, the resulting spatial geometry responding to these contrasting forces and making evident Borges and Candela's command of innovative structural systems. Five telescoping concrete shells vary between 12.7 and 28 meters and vault over cascading semi-circular terraces, which lead to the round dance floor and band shell that terminate the composition. At night, the dark painted shells, visually accented by rows of lights, blend into the night sky and the stars beyond. The shells slightly overlap and gaps between them frame views of the lush canopy of trees which tease the building.

Figure 114. Tropicana Cabaret, Havana, 1951, Max Borges

Figure 115. Tropicana Cabaret, Havana, 1951, Max Borges

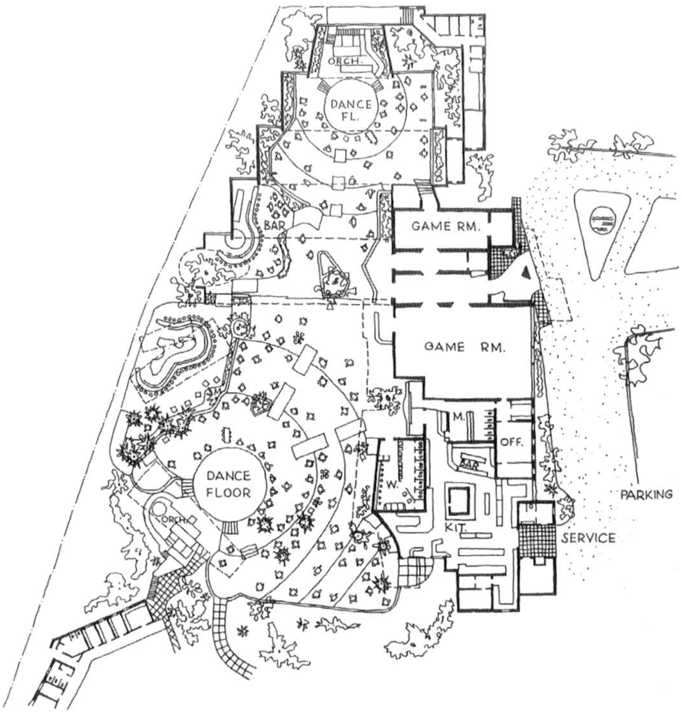

Figure 116. Tropicana Cabaret, Havana, 1951, Max Borges, plan

Furthermore, planters filled with existing and new tropical foliage, penetrate along the inner edges, adjacent to the stage, and by the main entrance, reinforcing the notion of an indoor-outdoor room. For its celebration of the tropical ambience and for its dynamic spatial qualities, the *Salon Arcos de Cristal* (Cristal Arches Hall - 1951) is a hallmark of innovative design in the tropics.

The next addition to the same site, the 'Under the Stars' Hall followed in 1952. It is an outdoor reflection of the earlier project, with a circular dance floor and radiating seating terraces. The open-air salon is anchored by the stage's sculptural backdrop, conceived as a representation of a mathematical formula.[121] The final addition to the site was the 1954 glass encased Casino, with a series of galleries covered by vaults and hyperbolic paraboloids connecting all of the buildings within the site. For its excellence in design, Borges was awarded another Gold Medal Prize by the National College of Architects in 1953. The completed complex is later included in Henry Russell Hitchcock's *Latin American Architecture Since 1945* exhibit (and catalog) at New York's Museum of Modern Art (MOMA) in 1955. The Tropicana Cabaret becomes one of the most recognized Cuban buildings of all time, indebted to Candela and Borges' innovative contributions and design excellence.

In 1953, Borges collaborated once again with Felix Candela, designing an addition to the existing Nautical Club in the Náutico neighborhood. Here again reinforced concrete vaults drape over the main hall, their undulating waves mimicking those of the sea beyond, a view of which they serve to frame. The open-air shells are suspended off parabolic arches, expressed on the outer roof with their legs piercing through, sidestepping across the hall, seemingly out onto the beach. Stouter proportions are ingratiated by a spatial luminosity, as in Tropicana, made possible by the slivers left between each vault, allowing natural light to bathe across each of the underlying spaces. The scale and rhythm of the vaults lends the project a civic presence, rivaling the adjacent historical structure.

Candela and Borges collaborated on a few other occasions, including the 1957 Nuñez Bank, and in that same year, with Candela as well as his brother Ernesto Borges, a tomb for the Nuñez Galvez family. The collection of projects designed by Candela and Borges inspired local architects to experiment with structural systems as a formal endeavor, including the Escuelas de Arte designers nearly a decade later. Prior to Borges' abrupt departure from Cuba in 1960, in conjunction with his brother, he added another half dozen buildings to Havana's skyline, including the nine-story Pártagas mixed-use residential building, but in none of these instances does he supersede the conceptual and constructive qualities achieved in his earlier projects.[122]

Figures 117 & 118. Indalecio Pertierra Building, Miramar, 1952, Frank Martinez, elevation and rear view

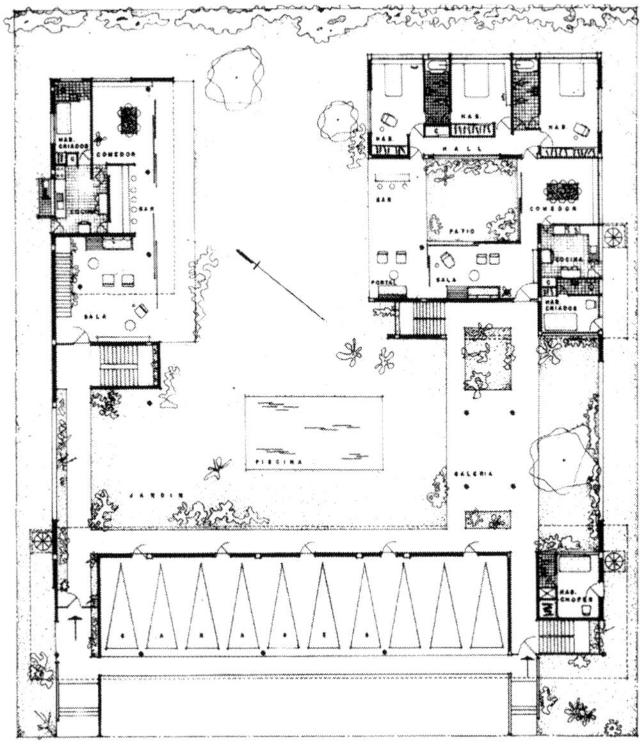

Figure 119. House for Eight Siblings, Miramar, , Frank Martinez, first floor plan

Frank Martinez

Slightly younger than the other leaders of this era, during his short-lived career on the island, Frank Martinez Justiz developed paradigmatic examples of Modern Regionalism in Cuba, often bridging between Corbusian strategies and a locally attuned pragmatism. After an initial membership in the ATEC group[123] and a brief period of collaboration with colleague Nicolas Quintana, Martinez strikes out on his own with the design of an apartment building in 1952.

The Indalecio Pertierra building, better known as the "*House for Eight Siblings*," is located on an interior lot, a half block from the sea, in the Miramar neighborhood. Martinez developed a U-shaped courtyard scheme with a four-story bar building parallel to the street, a three story courtyard building anchoring the NE corner, and a two-story duplex completing the northern boundary of the site. By breaking up the mass, dwellings are conceded greater privacy and in addition, natural ventilation is guaranteed. Loggias and terraces provide ample outdoor living spaces, accommodating a variety of social gatherings between the families. Permeable elevations fronting the main courtyard, developed with an abundance of sliding wooden persiana doors, further extend living spaces outdoors. The central courtyard is landscaped and focuses on a common pool area. Three external staircases provide access to the varying units. The front bar building contains three apartment, one per level, above a garage at grade that is screened from view by a garden wall. A limited flow of breezes permeates into the courtyard through systematic apertures located above louvered doors and two lateral 'zaguans.'[124] On the NE corner of the site three additional units, one per level, surround a smaller patio, warranting comfortable interior spaces. In this early project, Martinez experimented with colonial design features to temper inclement conditions and also with the courtyard type; tools which he further explores in forthcoming projects.

In 1954, Martinez designed a house for Ms. Emma Justiniani (pictured on next page) in the emerging neighborhood of Nuevo Vedado, bordering the Almendares River, and characterized at its outer reaches by steep slopes. The building sits perpendicular to a precipice and to the street. On the backside of the lot, a terrace slides out, hovering over the bluff. Ground floor pilotis accommodate a carport, service quarters, and lateral stairs leading to the main level. At the straight-run lightweight stairs, the volume is drawn back, suggesting a courtyard.[125] A deep overhang protects the glass sheathed recessed wall. The generously proportioned open plan living area faces the back terrace, and an ample bedroom looks onto the street. The location of persiana windows guarantee cross ventilation in all rooms. They are coupled with large expanses of glass throughout to increase daylighting. Locally harvested woods

Figure 120 & 121. Emma Justiniani Residence, Nuevo Vedado, 1954, Frank Martinez

and exposed stacked concrete blocks add a richness of textures. In this project, Martinez relies on a Corbusian prototype while alluding to colonial precedents with its implied lateral patio and the usage of persianas.

The next year, the design of a duplex for sisters Olga and Isabel Perez-Farfante in Nuevo Vedado, would become one of Martinez's most recognized and published buildings. Situated along the edge of a bluff, he re-adapted the courtyard type, transforming the typical 'patio' gallery into a bridge element, with the courtyard unusually placed, facing onto the street. The transparent Corbusian piloti system at grade affords commanding views across the site towards the river farther below. Following late-colonial precedents, the ground floor is assigned utilitarian functions. A pair of delicate staircases also inhabits this level, leading visitors from the "grand porch" to the dwellings.

The building is divided into three distinct volumes and is of particular interest due to the ambiguity of the stacked rooms sandwiched in between its bookends. When enclosed by the folding wooden persiana doors these spaces function as interior living rooms. When the doors are left ajar, the space serves as a gallery, affording unobstructed views of both the street and the Almendares River, and in either instance, allowing adjoining living spaces to capture the prevailing breezes, thusly for its flexible characteristics it is a truly 'tropical room.'

Each upper level houses an apartment, with living spaces to one side of the implied courtyard and sleeping quarters to the other. Given the thinness of the building, main rooms have windows on perpendicular walls, further cooling the spaces naturally. Floor to ceiling wooden persianas attenuate the harsh tropical light and the roofline projects far beyond

Figure 122. Apartment Building for Olga and Isabel Perez-Farfante, Nuevo Vedado, 1955, Frank Martinez

Figure 123. Apartment Building for Olga and Isabel Perez-Farfante, Nuevo Vedado, 1955, Frank Martinez, interior view

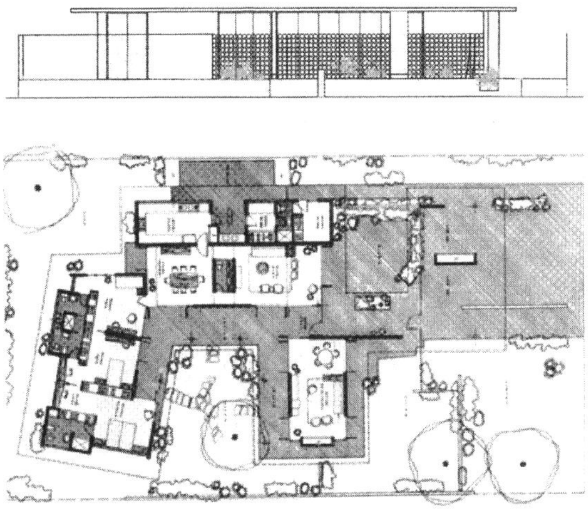

Figure 124. Manuela Ofelia Viamontes Residence, Havana, 1957, Frank Martinez, elevation and plan

the perimeter walls, casting welcomed shadows onto their surfaces. Set in a stacked pattern, exposed concrete blocks, accompanied by wooden persianas and fixed-plate glass, stretch between columns, and between floor and roof slabs, adding visual richness, and corroborating the structural order.

Although it can be argued that the breakdown of the building's mass attempts to play off the street's incremental reading, nevertheless this construction is less successful in its ability to integrate into the characteristic morphological syncopation of the neighborhood, whereby buildings typically present their narrowest frontage towards the street. Nonetheless, for its architectural successes, this project was deservingly awarded a *Diploma of Honor* by the College of Architects in 1955.

Over the coming years, Martinez developed a more acute interest in the relevance and reinterpretation of colonial precedents and in authenticating their resurgence. Consequently, his building designs aligned more closely with the spirit of those local traditions. Courtyards became the generator of form and most projects are developed on one level, likewise a byproduct of expansive flat lots. Pilotis disappeared. In their place, sliding planes along with porticoes dominated the compositions and mechanisms inherent to the tropical house play a more central role including: mamparas, ornate wooden lattices/screens, stained glass windows, clay tiles, exposed wood beams, stucco surfaces, brick walls, and persiana windows and doors. Interior and exterior spaces continued to flow into each other. Martinez designed two residences in 1957 that adhere to this synchronized methodology, the Efrain Torrente House and the Manuela Ofelia Viamontes House, both constructed in the Biltmore (Siboney) neighborhood.

The quintessential 'traditional' regionalist house is the Stanley Wax Residence (pictured on next page), completed in 1959. It is a direct descendant of Eugenio Batista's earlier initiatives and is clearly rooted to a national identity. At the porte-cochere entrance, the predominant themes are first disclosed, with the appearance of a garden wall that defines the sector. The wall slides below a soaring roof plane, intermingled with filigreed sliding wood panels and articulated brick walls. The pattern is repeated within the precinct and the interiors, with walls of varying heights, transparencies, and finishes, affecting the quality of light and the textural values in these spaces. In the bedrooms, large bay windows ensure plenty of daylighting and cross-ventilation. The central courtyard's colonnade serves as an extension of interior living spaces with paired persiana doors leading into them from various rooms. Added terraces, porticoes, and courtyards gyrate around the perimeter of the main building, each with a distinctive tropical character. Despite its clear '*Cubanidad*,' Neutra's influence is decipherable as are Japanese inspirations, all effortlessly woven into the design, from the macro to the micro scales.

Figure 125. Manuela Ofelia Viamontes Residence, Havana, 1957, Frank Martinez

Figure 126. Stanley Wax Residence, Havana, 1959, Frank Martinez

Figure 127 & 128. Stanley Wax Residence, Havana, 1959, Frank Martinez, view towards courtyard

The last four projects completed by Martinez prior to emigrating followed along the same lines, with a slightly more literal adoption of colonial precedents, as these houses also "land onto the ground"[126] plane and embrace the lateral courtyard as an organizing element. These projects include a house for Francisco Pacios in the Biltmore neighborhood (1957), a two-story residence for Eloisa Lezama Lima (1957), the Issac Rhimer house (1960), and a home for Carlos Taboada (1960).

In recognition of his accomplished trajectory and talents, satisfying the three elemental thresholds of Architecture - *beauty, integrity, and utility,*[127] Martinez was acknowledged with the *National Architecture Prize* in 1960.[128]

Manuel Gutiérrez

Born in the province of Pinar del Rio in 1925, Manuel Gutiérrez Balmaseda graduated from the University of Havana in 1948 and within three years, he became a faculty member of the same School of Architecture. He remained there through the coming year before moving onto another academic post at St. Thomas Villanueva Catholic University where he remained until 1959.

His first significant commission arrived in 1954, a residence in Nuevo Vedado. The house for Paulino Ingelmo reveals empirical and Miesian influences that Gutiérrez continues to explore over the coming five years. The three-story building straddles two terraces, resolving in section two contrasting goals. The back pool/garden level is elevated to accommodate at grade access from the main living rooms, while the lower front corner terrace allows for a carport and services to be slipped under the building. The entry court slopes to meet the street at grade and is defined by a low retaining wall, which intersects a rusticated stonewall that, in turn, marches along the sidewalk across the front

Figure 129. Paulino Ingelmo Residence, Nuevo Vedado, 1954, Manuel Gutiérrez

Figure 130. Paulino Ingelmo Residence, Nuevo Vedado, 1954, Manuel Gutiérrez

Figure 131. Paulino Ingelmo Residence, Nuevo Vedado, 1954, Manuel Gutiérrez, view of garden elevation

perimeter. From the entry court, a flight of stairs cantilevers out from the body of the main house, inviting visitors to the 'piano-nobile'.

The building is composed of three bays, with a slightly wider center; its modulation is suggestive of the classical 'a-b-a' proportioning systems. The elongated structural piers lend the building a monumental scale. Projecting roof and floor planes partner with the leggy piers to create wrap-around galleries, protecting the entire building from direct sunlight. Sandwiched between the jutting planes are combinations of wooden persiana doors and sections of stacked concrete block masonry walls. On both upper levels, a narrow transom runs along all the façades below which tall wooden persiana windows predominate. On the top floor, the wider transom houses 'persianas de Miami,' the industrially produced glass and aluminum awning windows that were initially produced and shipped from Miami during the post war era.

On the main floor, the living space is an open plan, and given the abundant use of persianas along its two longitudinal façades as well as on one of its short ends, the room is unified with the surrounding environment, both from a sensorial and a visual perspective. A deep, shady back porch extends the living spaces directly out to the garden. From an end bay, a perpendicular one-story wing, housing all needed services, slips out via a thin umbilical cord; it's brick construction contrasting the lightness provided by the main building's pre-stressed concrete columnar structure. Above the principal living spaces, each bay accommodates a bedroom, separated by custom-built closets that do not meet the building envelope, further facilitating cross-ventilation. To some extent, because these storage features read as furniture pieces, dividing a large space into compartments, they loosely recall the 'mamparas' of yesteryear. The project is a mature expression of the

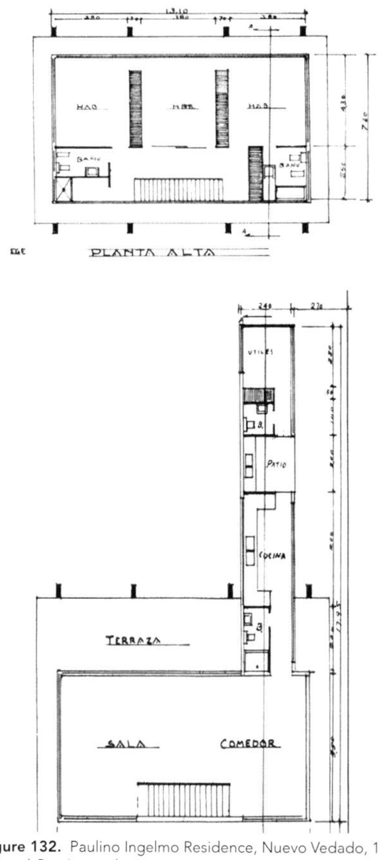

Figure 132. Paulino Ingelmo Residence, Nuevo Vedado, 1954, Manuel Gutiérrez, plan

Figure 133. Petra Verdera Residence, Alturas del Vedado, 1955, Manuel Gutiérrez

architectural acumen of the young designer - a rejection of puritanical rationalist dogma as much as of folkloristic colonial traditions. Instead, Gutierrez aspired to all the possible vicissitudes of crossbreeding cultural and structural explorations, which in the Casa Ingelmo result in an innovative, refined expression with international resonance.

In 1955, Gutiérrez designed a house for Petra Verdera in the Alturas del Vedado neighborhood, once again exploiting structural systems and their sculptural potential. The site is located at an intersection. Lengthwise, the building seemingly bridges across the site, intersected by a lower level parking garage court, revealed by a modest opening along the rusticated perimeter garden wall.[129] Two raised gardens flank the parking court, their retaining walls defining the lower space.

From the corner of the site, pedestrians access a deep porch, located under the first of five expressed structural vaults that skip across the entire building. The roof cantilevers beyond the envelope, protecting the large expanses of glass found between the vaults and the wood persiana windows that dominate the longitudinal street façade. The reinforced concrete vaults rest over metal piers braced by cables. Four of the five vaults are of equal dimensions but the nave dedicated to the living and dining spaces is twice the width. The plan is straightforward, conforming uses to the structural grid, with most spaces afforded windows on two sides to ensure cross ventilation and natural day lighting. Here again, custom built-in furniture divides interior spaces along column lines while not impeding cross-ventilation. Upon completion, the project was recognized as the *Best-Low Cost Residence* by the College of Architects, rewarding Gutiérrez for his design innovations.

Gutiérrez designed a residence for his family on a corner lot in the Jaimanitas neighborhood in 1956, following the trajectory of his previous projects by combining a rectilinear rational plan with an animated roofline. The parti is straightforward, with services banked towards the street and parallel living and dining areas facing the interior side yard. Less evident is pedestrian access to the residence, which is located to a side, within the deep corner porch that functions primarily as a carport. In this project, folded roof plates dialogue with a solid, over-scaled, diamond-shaped shield, introducing a grander scale to this otherwise modestly proportioned residence. Solid lateral walls extend out into the landscape, adding privacy and casting desired shadows. Upon them, rests the giant rhomboidal panel, which presses against the valleys of the overlapping roof plane. An interesting shifted volumetric reading results as the upper mass negotiates with the projecting panel, the void of the carport and the garden wall. Aligned with a small pool located in the garden porch, floating stairs drift up behind the glass curtain wall, meeting a catwalk,

Figure 134. Petra Verdera Residence, Alturas del Vedado, 1955, Manuel Gutiérrez, interior view

which traverses across the living room's double height space toward the bedrooms.

The coming year, Gutiérrez broke away from regulating concepts reliant on rectangular prisms and moves towards experimenting with other pure geometries, studying their additive potential as well as their deconstruction. Gutierrez further explored the relationship between form and function, employing combinations of differing square and circular elements; the latter forms, according to Cuban scholars, are attributable to FLW influences, but perhaps also, whether consciously or not, to pure indigenous geometries such as 'bohio' dwellings.

In his 1957 residential project for Mr. John Fernandez in the Biltmore (Siboney) neighborhood (pictured on next page), once again a modular system guided the design, but now with greater compositional complexity. A series of square volumes with intersecting corners house different functions- living, dormitories, and services. Floor plans correspond to the inherent logic of the modular structural system. Rooflines offer cues of the differing functions- flat over services and sculptural over the main volumes. Hyperbolic paraboloids gingerly kiss exposed brick piers centered on elevations; roof ends soar freely above the disintegrating corners composed of glass and wood persiana windows. Diagonal tethering of the pods does not impede fluidity or reading of rooflines. In the dormitory pod, projecting closets visually anchor the composition while creating deep shadows that protect the vertical persianas sitting in between. The combination of deep overhangs, recessed planes and the corner placement of fenestrations respond effectively to a variety of climatic nuisances. This project's village-like composition faintly recalls traditional indigenous villages of the island but also shares similarities with Alfred Browning Parker's Coconut Grove 'Jewel-in-the-Treetop' residence completed that same year, both architects referencing Frank Lloyd Wright.

In 1959, Gutiérrez designed a four story prefabricated structure to house the School of Electrical and Mechanical Engineering Workshops and Laboratories (pictured on pages 144 and 145) at St. Thomas Villanueva Catholic University. He deployed a similar system of rhomboidal forms to that employed in his Jaimanita home two years earlier. The prefabricated method of construction iterates his quest for both structural expression and an economy of means. The modular system comprises massive beams, which span the building's width between the diamond shaped end panels. These bookends rest on projecting beams and double as giant brise-soleil to protect the recessed glass skin. The plasticity of the composition is rendered by the repetition of its components, whose structural function is also plainly legible. At its entrance, in sync with the rhomboidal pattern, folded plates reach out to welcome visitors. This project was Gutiérrez's last on the island, a fitting summary of his innovative responses to structural, financial, and climatic considerations.

Figure 135. John Fernández Residence, Siboney, 1957, Manuel Gutiérrez

Figure 136. School of Electrical and Mechanical Engineering Workshops and Laboratories, 1959, Manuel Gutiérrez

Figure 137. School of Electrical and Mechanical Engineering Workshops and Laboratories, 1959, Manuel Gutiérrez, interior view

Shortly prior to his final departure, Gutiérrez was invited to lecture at the University. He did so expressing his further alignment with Wrightian thought, underlining that industrialization should be at the service of society and not vice versa, quoting FLW: "*Industry should go to the house, not the house towards industry.*"[130]

Two years later, in 1961 Gutiérrez immigrated to Puerto Rico, where he designed prefabricated housing, executing well over 1000 dwellings for seven development projects. Eventually, he relocated to Miami in 1977. In 2004, the Florida Chapter of the American Institute of Architects awarded Gutiérrez the "*Taste of Time*" award for the conceptual relevance and validity of his 1954 Paulino Ingelmo residence. At the award ceremony, he stated, "My principle has always been to resolve physical and spiritual needs by means of constructive truths." The next year, he received the same award for his design of the School of Electrical and Mechanical Engineering Workshops and Laboratories at St. Thomas Villanueva Catholic University. Upon his death a year later, his friend and colleague, Nicolas Quintana expressed a sense of loss, "*His works were truly a renewal, with high aesthetic quality and human dimension. We have lost one of the indispensable names of Cuban architecture.*"[131]

Figure 138. School of Electrical and Mechanical Engineering Workshops and Laboratories, 1959, Manuel Gutiérrez

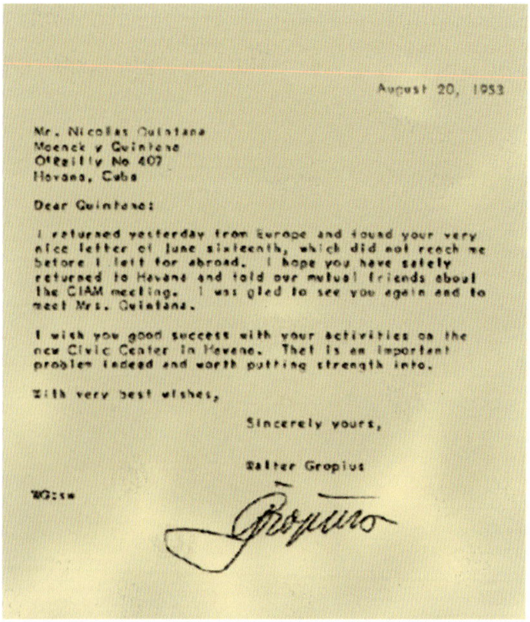

August 20, 1953

Mr. Nicolas Quintana
Moenck y Quintana
O'Reilly No 407
Havana, Cuba

Dear Quintana:

I returned yesterday from Europe and found your very nice letter of June sixteenth, which did not reach me before I left for abroad. I hope you have safely returned to Havana and told our mutual friends about the CIAM meeting. I was glad to see you again and to meet Mrs. Quintana.

I wish you good success with your activities on the new Civic Center in Havana. That is an important problem indeed and worth putting strength into.

With very best wishes,

Sincerely yours,

Walter Gropius

WG:sw

Figure 139. Letter to Nicolas Quintana, 1953, Walter Gropius

Figure 140. Rivero Residence, 1956, Nicolás Quintana

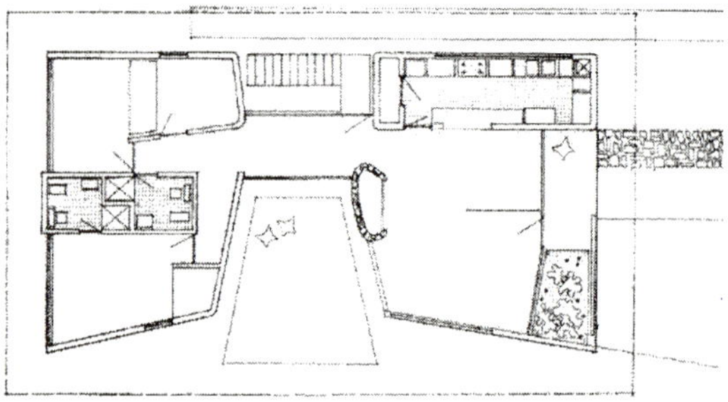

Figure 141. Rivero Residence, 1956, Nicolás Quintana, plan

Nicolás Quintana

Born in 1925, Nicolás Quintana y Gómez is the son of a prominent family living in Havana. His father, a reputable and established architect, led one of the city's largest practices, Moenck & Quintana. The young Quintana established a name for himself early on, when along with his peers Ricardo Porro and Frank Martinez, he burns Vignola tomes at the University of Havana in 1944. According to Quintana, "*the Vignola event was like a bolero that quickly turned into a conga, from something controlled to something wild...from three of us to a whole school*"...and ironically taking place in the courtyard of a building designed by his indignant father.[132] While in school, he was influenced directly by his professors Pedro Martinez Inclán and Eugenio Batista, forefathers to Cuba's modern regionalist movement, as well as by eminent visiting scholars, Richard Neutra and Walter Gropius, which he befriends later in life. According to classmate Ricardo Porro, Quintana and their friend Frank Martinez both received academic accolades from Walter Gropius for their rationalist approach to design in their studio projects, whereas Porro was castigated for his more 'individualistic' expressions.[133]

Quintana expanded his professional circles attending several CIAM conferences, the first while still a student, exposing him early on in his career to leading world designers driving the fields of architecture and planning. During a lecture several decades later, Quintana recalls, "*During the colonial era, architectural styles arrived with a delay of half a century in relation to Europe. But, just as was happening in the arts, with [Wilfredo] Lam and others, in the fifties we sat at the table with Neutra, Gropius, with Le Corbusier, with Sert... but, we were also dining with Cuban painters, writers and sculptors. We were traveling, experiencing great architecture with our own eyes and we were reading all the latest books and magazines. For all these reasons and more, it was a very exciting period... and our generation was completely up to date.*"[134] On another occasion, Quintana adds: "*it was an 'ajiaco social' (social melting pot), where we would meet and exchange ideas, resulting in an unusual capacity to draw from different sources*"[135] of inspiration, cultures, and knowledge.

Following their graduation, Martinez and Quintana collaborated briefly in 1950 on the design of Martinez's own house. However, upon the death of the elder Quintana, Nicolas joined Miguel Angel Moenck in the practice as co-director. Nonetheless, although working independently, during the few years in which both Quintana and Martinez practice in Cuba, several of their commissions shared common pursuits and characteristics albeit with varying results. For example, Quintana's Casa Rivero of 1956 was composed similarly to the Perez-Farfante duplex, with lateral wings, connected by a gallery, and centered on a redefined courtyard; although, the similarities end there. The Perez-Farfante project is more restrained than the Rivero residence in its use of materials, geometries and differs as well in its engagement of the terrain. The later Ramírez Corría residence by Quintana and Martinez's Stanley Wax house coincide in more aspects, including their

Figure 142. Ramirez Corría Residence, 1957, Nicolás Quintana

Figure 143. Ramirez Corría Residence, 1957, Nicolás Quintana

Figure 144. Ramirez Corría Residence, 1957, Nicolás Quintana

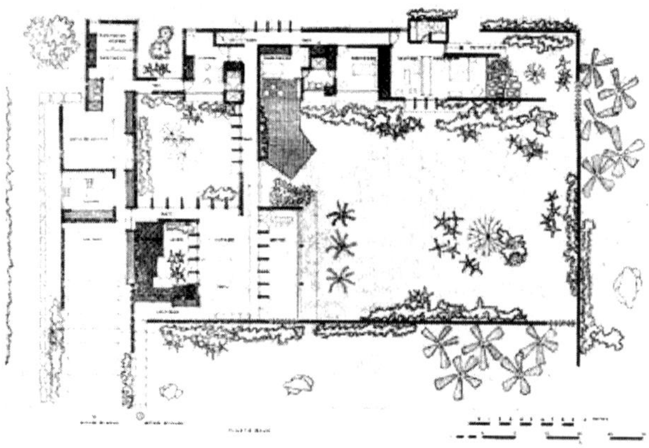

Figure 145. Ramirez Corría Residence, 1957, Nicolás Quintana, plan

Figure 146. Alicia Blanco Residence, Havana, 1954, Nicolás Quintana

multi-courtyard design, with perimeter ancillary spaces and extruded planes gliding below hovering rooflines, amidst tropical foils learned from Cuban traditions.

In 1954, Quintana designed one of his most noteworthy commissions, a residence for Alicia Blanco. The linear building sits along a sloping site, its mass nestling service areas underneath the far end, as well as an entry porch at midpoint. Tucked laterally, a sidewinding stair leads from the porch up to the piano nobile's gallery, which connects the shifted arms of the functionally segregated composition. An intersecting wing located above the porch, accommodates the main living space with a narrow screened porch at its end. The room captures 180-degree views and prevailing breezes thanks to the alternating floor-to-ceiling persiana fenestrations with fixed plate glass windows. In a bow toward Wrightian connectivity with the landscape, a low-lying roof establishes a strong horizontal reading, its extra depth protecting the ribbon of clearstory windows immediately below. Reinforcing the building's horizontality, a smooth stucco garden wall extends from the landscape across the entire elevation, reading as a plinth. Exposed stacks of concrete block fill the remaining wall surfaces, a common feature in both Quintana and Martinez's early career.

Minister of Public Works and his colleague, Nicolas Arroyo, appointed Quintana to the National Planning Board in 1955. Quintana directed planning objectives for the resort town of Varadero in collaboration with Josep Lluís Sert and for the historic colonial town of Trinidad, in collaboration with Lidia Cabrera. Whereas in the first, Sert's office took the lead, in the latter, Quintana and Cabrera worked closely to envision a "Venecia criolla," a project that peaks the interest of Cuban magnate Julio Lobo and the Rockefeller family.[136]

As a collateral benefit to his rising public stature, Quintana reaped several public sector commissions in Varadero Beach including: Hotel Kawama - Cabanas (1955), the Residencial Yacht Club - Cabanas, Main Entrance (1957), and contracts for several houses, including one for Gerardo Fundora (1956) and another for Eugene Curran (1957).

In the Hotel Kawama, Quintana designed several cottages, each fitted with two suites, one per level. The rectangular volumes have a shed roof with exposed wood beams across their entirety, extending out over a generous front porch to facilitate outdoor living. To safeguard privacy, cottages are strategically sited, with two elevations virtually solid, whereas the opposite faces are rather transparent, with interspersed panes of glass and wood persiana windows or doors. Quintana employed a local stone in the construction of the walls and wood and concrete were utilized in the construction of the

Figure 147. Hotel Kawana Cabanas, Varadero Beach, 1955, Nicolás Quintana

Figure 148. Residential Yacht Club, Varadero, 1957, Nicolás Quintana

Figure 149. Residential Yacht Club, Varadero, 1957, Nicolás Quintana, seaside cabanas

Figure 150. Residential Yacht Club, Varadero, 1957, Nicolás Quintana, entrance

detached lateral access stairs.[137] According to Quintana, his attention to wood details throughout paid homage to his renowned furniture and cabinetmaker grandfather.[138] The design's relationship to the region's traditional architecture is as easy to identify as is its connections to modernity. Investigations initiated in this project, linking tradition and modernity were furthered in his neighboring Residential Yacht Club in 1957.

In the Residencial Yacht Club Cabanas project, reinforced concrete vaults are expressed along a rectilinear beachfront building. Of the seven bays, four are dedicated to cabana spaces enclosed by sliding wood persiana doors and glass panels. Suggestive of colonial three bay precedents typically located on the piano-nobile, the second story also accommodates an arcade. The building's narrow terrace and garden wall define its precinct. The playful form and outward focus appropriately converses with the sea's waves. The expression of the structural vaulting, which results in a distinctive silhouette along with its similar beachside siting, makes this building a taller sibling of Paul Rudolph's Sanderling Beach Club in Siesta Key of 1952-53. A checkerboard of one and two story cabanas, bound by lateral rows of similar buildings, are bookended by the entry gate and the beach front building.

In step with his contemporaries, Quintana continued to search for the essence of Cuban architecture. This objective can be seen in two projects in 1957, the Mardonio Santiago residence in the Biltmore neighborhood and the villa for Carlos Ramírez Corría in the suburb of Marianao. Ramírez Corría coveted a contemporary Cuban villa, and Quintana delivered a successful example, demonstrating that the International Style can intersect local elements of identity, resulting in a sophisticated design. The traditional patio anchors the house around which, smaller courtyards transition between the building's wings and the perimeter white-washed brick garden walls, which complete the precinct. The relationship between the garden wall and the building proper fluctuates. Some volumes fuse into the garden walls, whereas others punch through forcefully. Rooflines also engage the garden wall in different ways, in one instance caressing its top and projecting far beyond the plane, lending a very sculptural quality to the overall project as it casts dramatic shadows, further enlivening the elevation and cooling the micro-climate.

When moving around in the house's open plan, five courtyards, terraces, porticos, and gardens are ever-present, imparting a sense of airiness and connection with the surroundings. The dining room is located in accordance with traditional colonial architecture in relation to the courtyard and is distinguished by its tall proportion. The room mediates between a wide porch and a small entry courtyard, which in turn is naturally cooled and visually anchored by a reflecting pool. At the intersection of two hallways, a linear stair leads up to the library and art gallery. The precious contents of these rooms are protected by the use of oversized vertical appendages on the building's skin, which model the harsh light.

Other traditional elements utilized include lattices, wood persianas, and stained glass panels that provide a handsome interplay of light and color. A staccato of vertical whitewashed brick fins protect elongated windows from the sun in the main volumes while adding a grander scale. A more intimate measure is assigned to the private wing of the residence, at times facing sheared off or rotated courtyards.[139] Volumetric articulations differentiate uses, underlined by the silhouette of the folded plate roofs, resulting in an interesting juxtaposition between Miesian planning strategies, Caribbean playfulness, and Corbusian plastic qualities.

The following three years were filled with important commissions for Quintana, including several residences: houses for Eugene Curran (1957), Carlos Quintana (1958), and Aida Fundora (1958). In these later projects, he further refined hierarchical legibility through volumetric expression of functions and again reinterpreted traditional elements to foil the tropical climate or add needed privacy. With the addition of natural materials such as wood and stone, he created comfortable and intimate environments.

Prior to departing Cuba in 1960, Quintana's final curtain call arrived at the request of the president of the National Bank. Moenck & Quintana took over a project for the National Bank Headquarters, commenced by another architect who had left the island shortly after the 1959 Revolution. The firm redesigned the building and tackled a plan for the adjoining plaza fronting the Malecon at the Caleta de San Lázaro. After several personal and professional disagreements with the next president of the bank, Che Guevara, Quintana "el gran burgues,"[140] immigrated to Venezuela prior to the project's completion. As a reflection of political and economic priorities, the bank building was later readapted into a hospital. When Quintana departed, he left 23 projects behind, completed in the span of less than a decade.

In Venezuela, Quintana worked on urban-scaled projects primarily, and he later settled in Puerto Rico collaborating on several civic projects. Upon arrival in Miami in 1986, he joined the faculty at the University of Miami and later moved on to Florida International University, where he was conferred the title of *Scholar in Architecture and Urbanism.*

During this twilight period, Quintana collaborated with UM Professor Felipe Préstamo, FIU Professor Juan Bueno, and other colleagues across the Straits on a study entitled, "*La Habana y sus Paisajes,*" which sought to identify the paradigmatic urban characteristics of the city that are worthy of preservation and emulation. A proposed project he did not see to fruition. His obituary read: "*Nicolas Quintana, one of the architects of the modern movement that flourished in pre-revolutionary Cuba, left his mark on the magnificent indigenous expression of modern architecture "with his ear to the ground.' Architect and intellectual, tireless lecturer, a disciple of José Lezama Lima, [... [he] received numerous awards for the work. Still, he lamented, "Amid the accomplishments and the general recognition, within me is a deep sadness. Continually I ask myself: Why not in Cuba, in my country?"*[141]

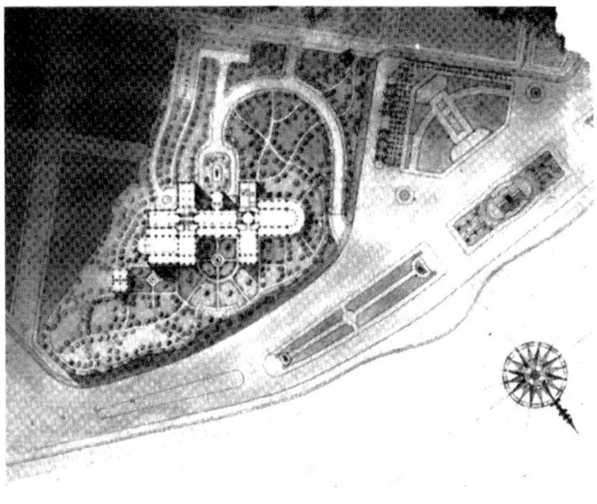

Figure 151. National Hotel of Cuba, Havana, 1930, McKim, Mead and White

Figure 152. Villa Paula, First Cuban Consulate, Miami, 1926, C. Freixa

Crisscrossing the '*charquito*'[142]

The waves of cultural influence between Florida and Cuba lapped back and forth between shores, at different intensities and not always symmetrically, but certainly for several centuries; each wave leaving behind traces of cultural and architectonic expressions. During a long period, the flow became a trickle only to intensify in the nineteenth century, with the introduction of the Monroe Doctrine in 1823,[143] causing US national interests to veer south officially. By the turn of the century, several American firms, such as Carrere & Hastings and Schultz & Weaver, secured important commissions in Havana, yet period records indicate that no architect working on Cuban design projects hailed from Florida. Similarly, there is evidence of only one Cuban architect practicing in Miami, Mr. Freixa, who designed a 'villa' for the Cuban Consul in the Lemon City neighborhood.[144] Given higher number of Cuban immigrants, the cities of Tampa and Key West proved to be the exception to this pattern. Long before the end of the Spanish-American War, each established a cultural and architectural dialogue with the island. Commercial and political interests amplified, soon followed by cultural and professional exchanges, increasing the interactions with Havana, and gradually migrating towards Miami as it began to emerge as a tourist destination and a growing economy.

Prior to WWII, regional architectural referencing between Havana and Miami were limited and commonly driven by promotional rather than conceptual pursuits, but the character of those conversations quickly evolved after the Art Deco era, a period that drastically alters the urban landscape of both locations and that shepherds a later epoch of exchange. During WWII, both cities prospered because of economic circumstances directly related to the conflicts. Escalating sugar prices catapulted Havana's economy and incentivized a building wave, whereas an inordinate amount of soldiers stationed in South Florida remain after the war, catalyzing the region's growth. These triggers ignited local economies and development, the groundswell logarithmically multiplying in the following decade and a half. At the end of the global conflicts, both cities were poised for dramatic social, economic, cultural, and especially physical change.

Dermal banter, driven by commercial and marketing interests of pre-war days, gave way to more significant and plainspoken dialogues. And whereas, for centuries Cuban architects maintained their primary focus on trans-Atlantic or in more recent decades on Northeastern U.S. and Latin American destinations for sources of avant-garde inspiration, after WW II their attention was distracted as Florida's bourgeoning towns prosper and so too grows its population of capable architects. Aside from gleaning lessons regarding hotel and retail design, Cuban architects became more aware of efforts by Florida architects to merge rationalism with their vernacular heritage. Conversely, South Florida architects continued to draw inspiration from Cuba's colonial architecture, yet they became more focused on the contemporary reinterpretations of those precedents and their elements. These regional interests arose as the International Style emerged in earnest during the postwar era, and architects in Cuba and Florida questioned the wisdom of its applications in the tropics. Architects on both sides of the Straits searched for an architecture that could contrast the universalizing tendencies of the style, searching for meaningful interpretations of places and traditions within the parameters of a contemporary vocabulary. A continued awareness of climatic considerations remained a driving force in architecture, unleashed by an increased sense of experimentation with post war technologies and new materials, reflecting a renewed local and global confidence in the future. External streams of thought amalgamated with internal priorities, laying the seeds for Regional Modern architecture in Cuba and Florida.

Greater interaction facilitated a more direct professional dynamic between architects in Florida and Cuba, coinciding with comparable pursuits to find a local modern identity and climatically attuned architectural character, although their cultural priorities were different. Wireless telegraph and the proliferation of telephones facilitated communication,

Figure 153. Advertisement

Figure 154. University of Miami student tours, 1938

Figure 155. Aeromarine Airways, 1922

added professional publications created greater awareness, international congresses fostered exchange, and new modes of affordable transportation enabled direct contact and site visits. Throughout the 1950's, the 'intersect' between Florida and Cuba, facilitated by such mobility and communication compressed distances and accelerated learning from each side, as well as incremented a sense of familiarity.

Professionals in the region paid closer attention to concepts, projects, and/or designers on the opposite shore of the Straits,' at times, pro-actively engaging peers, thusly expanding the definition of regional and referential boundaries. Questions related to Modern Architecture's adaptability to the tropics in fact led to analogous investigations of character and identity, drawing professional pursuits in closer alignment, with mounting professional appreciation for emergent, regionally derived principles, and design. A series of corresponding explorations occurred in the two locations, in a few instances with parallel outcomes. In addition to locally grown values, formal and informal dialogues further the development of a Modern Regionalism in the Caribbean.

Upon analysis of projects designed by Cuban and Florida architects and their corresponding timelines, it can be posited that in several instances, in addition to external forces, ideas crisscrossed the Florida Straits; the dialectic resulting in similar compositional solutions. Meant to foment sensitive and interactive relationships between buildings and the environment, design conceptions searched for open-ended regional design strategies, drawing from vernaculars near and far, historic and current. The cross-pollination flowed freely from one shore to the other, directly or indirectly, at times fertilizing designs with innovative multicultural solutions. There are a few instances in fact where projects in these two locations seemed 'informed' by 'neighboring' examples. Sources of inspiration mutate, are appropriated and/or their architectural characteristics become more comparable. Although few period records substantiate this claim, the parallels between the projects seem to speak for themselves and suggest at a minimum an awareness of objectives and proposals, with Rudolph serving as a frequent point of reference. For example, an early instance of mirrored efforts occurred between Paul Rudolph's 1947 Finney Guest House, 1950 Leavengood Residence, Mario Romañach's 1949 Jose Noval de Cueto residence, and Frank Martinez's 1955 duplex for Olga and Isabel Perez-Farfante. Interestingly, in all instances, the courtyard type is transformed, no longer insular, but rather engaging the surrounding environment, all paying homage to Corbu's Domino House, lifted off the ground. A more traditional interpretation of the courtyard house can be seen in Martinez's 1959 Stanley Wax Residence, Rufus Nim's 1949 Binder Residence, 1953 Stillman Residence, Romañach's 1953 Aristigueta Vidaña Residence, Quintana's 1957 Corría Ramirez Residence, and in innovative hybrid's by Rudolph in the 1953 Umbrella House and Marion Manley in the 1949 Bell Residence. Interestingly, houses by Martinez, Nims, Romañach, and Quintana were also tying Japanese influences into their designs, folding external design currents into their regionalist objectives.

These are not the only examples of possible cross-pollination within the region. Rudolph's 1950 Cocoon House began a volleying of ideas regarding the reinterpretation of a basic element of design: the louvered persiana window and door, typical of Southern and Caribbean colonial architecture. Alfred Browning Parker attested to his assimilation of the Cuban derivation. The banking of these windows by several of the architects including but not limited to Parker, Rudolph, Nims, Martinez, Polevitzky, Gutierrez, and Romañach resulted in novel 'breathable' walls as Parker himself defined them. Very tropical and very modern.

Parallel investigations into structural systems and their whimsical expression were grafted in particular from Brazilian contemporary architecture and in some instances directly from Felix Candela. However, projects were again nourished by regional readings. For example, similar forms and siting in Rudolph's and Quintana's designs, are more analogous to each other than to external sources of inspiration. This can be appreciated in Rudolph's Sanderling Beach house and Quintana's Residential Yacht Club beachfront cabana building, or less directly in Gutierrez's Petra Verdara Residence. In each instance, strong compositional and plastic qualities are distinguished and partnered with tropical foils. Similar structural expressionism is evident between Rudolph's Rubin Residence of 1951 and Gutierrez's 1957 house for John Fernandez. Common denominators between these two residences include, butterfly roofs, floating volumes, clearstory lighting, deconstructed corners, and extruded persiana windows.

Regional Dialogue

In 2004, as a part of related research, this author interviewed several Cuban born architects, including Manuel Gutiérrez and Nicolas Quintana. The Quintana conversation began with a description of his early career in Cuba, which as he described was enriched by his participation in CIAM sessions in 1947,[145] 1953, and 1956.[146] These congresses allowed Quintana to meet with the pioneers of Modern Architecture. Not to diminish the importance of those external influences on his career, Quintana also placed great emphasis on what he defined as the "*healthy conversations and intersecting ideas*" across the region during the postwar era, which in his estimation trickled into the first years of the 1960's.

As an example, Quintana narrated that, on the first leg of his honeymoon, and surely to his bride's utter delight, he detoured and met Paul Rudolph in Siesta Key, at the Cocoon House site. He was on an "architectural tour" along the eastern seaboard, eventually meeting with Gropius as well. According to Quintana, the meeting between him and Rudolph transpired at the commendation of Walter Gropius, their common mentor. The session allowed them to "become familiar with their current projects and to discuss projects by colleagues, to exchange ideas and discuss design philosophies." He narrated that they concurred on the necessity of moving away from the dictums of CIAM and searching for an architecture that was more directly rooted in local realities and attuned to the climate. According to Quintana, the two corresponded occasionally. He underlined the meeting's subsequent impact on his personal career and his admiration of Rudolph's oeuvre. A critical regionalism, by then characteristic of Rudolph's work, was certainly the conceptual backbone to the work for a growing number of lesser-known architects practicing in Florida and perhaps Cuba. In the case of Quintana and his compatriots, their pursuits were additionally nourished by what he termed "*the perennial essence*" of Cuba's architectural and cultural legacy.

Some period publications corroborate the premise of a lively regional dialogue. A feature article in a 1949 issue of Arquitectura magazine describes that the American Institute of Architects South Florida Chapter invited Dr. Cristobal Martinez Marquez, president of the Colegio de Arquitectos (College of Architects), as a guest of honor to their Annual Forum. That year the president of the AIA chapter, Alfred Browning Parker, who had already traveled and met colleagues in Cuba on two previous occasions, hosted the Cuban delegation and together they toured the city, including recently completed projects. During the Forum, Martinez Marquez lectured on the works of his contemporaries and according to the article, "*lead[s] in a discussion regarding common practices, innovative technologies and common building typologies that would be suitable for a "'tropical' building."* *In closing, the article states:"... it is undeniable that Havana and Miami have influenced each other respectively, given our proximity and the facilities we have today to communicate.*"[147]

Figure 156. Postcard from the VII Congress of Pan-American Architects, Havana, 1949

At the Seventh Pan-American Congress of Architects, held in Havana, the topic of locally receptive and accountable architecture was a prevailing theme. Architect Manuel de Tapia-Ruano pointed to the need for architects "*to develop sustainable architecture, characteristic of their respective country and context.*" Papers delivered by two Cubans, historian Joaquin Weiss and architect Victor Morales, called for "*schools of architecture to broaden the study of materials and methods of construction that would search for national and regional solutions.*" It is noteworthy, that at the same Congress, a University of Miami building by Robert Law Weed et al received a silver medal for its "*thoughtful tropical design.*"[148]

At the 40th Annual Convention of the Association of Florida Architects, held in West Palm Beach Florida in 1955, an exhibition featured current projects from across the state. The College of Architects of Havana was invited to show an exhibition on contemporary Cuban architecture, which had just recently been displayed at the Architectural League of New York City,

"LA ARQUITECTURA BAJO EL SOL"

FRENTE A POSIBILIDADES INFINITAS

Por el Arq. NICOLAS ARROYO

UN DISTINGUIDO ARQUITECTO DE LA HABANA, PROFESIONAL DE GRANDES EXITOS Y MIEMBRO DEL CONGRESO INTERNACIONAL DE ARQUITECTOS, HIZO USO DE LA PALABRA DURANTE EL ALMUERZO CELEBRADO EN LA 40a. CONVENCION ANUAL DE LA F.A.A. Y AQUI ESTA SU MENSAJE.

DISCURSO ORIGINAL EN INGLES PUBLICADO EN LA REVISTA "THE FLORIDA ARCHITECT", TRADUCCION DEL ARQ. EMILIO DE SOTO.

El Arquitecto Nicolás Arroyo en la Convención de Arquitectos de la Florida exponiendo su tema: "Arquitectura Bajo el Sol"

El Arquitecto se preocupa fundamentalmente de las necesidades de los pueblos. Para poder satisfacer estas necesidades, debe comprender el pasado y reconocer y evaluar las fuerzas sociales y económicas contemporáneas que dan forma a su propia sociedad. Debe tener perspicacia para captar los cambios que se efectúan en el mundo que le rodea. Y, al conocer las necesidades de sus semejantes debe aplicar sus observaciones a la organización del espacio que sirve esas necesidades.

La historia ha probado que la Arquitectura verdaderamente creadora siempre crece y se desarrolla naturalmente, consciente de las necesidades del hombre; debe reflejar el carácter de su vida, su trabajo, sus ratos de ocio, en una expresión verdadera de la sociedad en que convive.

Esta relación del Arquitecto con la sociedad en que vive no ha cambiado a través de los siglos. Ha sido, y seguirá siendo una medida básica de la comprensión que muestra el Arquitecto hacia los hombres y su habilidad para resolver sus problemas. Y si, al resolver estos problemas, se hace énfasis en proveer un ambiente mejor, en realidad es de mayor importancia el método utilizado para resolver dichos problemas y conseguir esos resultados.

Y esto es cierto por cuanto la forma utilizada para resolver el problema no ha cambiado a través de los años. En términos de aspectos visuales y usos diferentes del espacio y los materiales, pudiera parecer que el método ha cambiado. Pero no es así... ese método de que hablamos en que se remonta a la antigüedad no es basado en la improvisación, sino al contrario, en proceso organizado de investigación y análisis; en desarrollo orgánico creador, organización del espacio tridimensional, concebido simultáneamente en términos de economía, eficiencia estructural y apariencia armoniosa.

Exposición de Arquitectura en West Palm Beach, Florida. Planeada primeramente para ocupar una sala como la que reproducimos, la que se originó con motivo de la 40º Convention Show, llenó tres amplias galerías. Una mención especial fué ganada por la "Philip Julian's Educational", exponiendo una serie de dibujos a tintas para hoteles en Pittsburgh y Atlantic City, New Jersey.

EXPOSICION DE ARQUITECTURA EN LA FLORIDA

Por el Arq. EMILIO DE SOTO Y SAGARRA

A principios del mes de noviembre tuvo efecto en Palm Beach, Estados Unidos, la 40 Convención Anual de la Asociación de Arquitectos del Estado de la Florida. Era invitado especial un arquitecto cubano, Nicolás Arroyo, a quien se le había asignado el tema de "Arquitectura bajo el sol", que desarrolló con verdadero acierto y el mismo se reproduce en este número de ARQUITECTURA.

El Colegio Nacional de Arquitectos de Cuba fué invitado a enviar la Exposición de Arquitectura Cubana que tanto éxito alcanzó en la Architectural League of New York, en el mes de octubre pasado.

La Galería Norton (museo de arte y antigüedades) de West Palm Beach cedió dos de sus más amplios salones para celebrar esta Exposición de Arquitectura.

Desde los problemas de proyectos arquitectónicos de estudiantes de la Universidad de la Florida, hasta las más recientes obras de importancia en todo el Estado fueron presentadas en la referida Exposición.

La Exposición de Arquitectura, integrada por proyectos, fotografías y maquetas, fué cuidadosamente presentada.

Los premios adjudicados obedecían a un programa por categorías, correspondiente al carácter de la obra.

Figure 157. "Architecture Under the Sun" and "Architecture Exhibition in Florida" Articles, *Arquitectura* Magazine, 1955

where there was a growing appreciation of their work. A wing of Palm Beach's Norton Museum was set aside for their parallel exhibit. This invitation and homage illustrates the awareness, appreciation, and worth of the professional endeavors of Cuban designs.

Cuban architect Nicolas Arroyo was invited as keynote speaker to the convention. His intervention was entitled: "***Architecture Under the Sun***." In it, Arroyo stated, "*so as to satisfy the needs of a people, architects must recognize the social and economic forces at play and in turn reflect the character of a place, as an honest reflection of its people's values. To understand these needs he must understand the past, recognize and evaluate contemporary social and economic forces which model his own society. He must be attuned with the changes across the globe and in light of the needs of his countrymen apply those observations which may address their needs... History proves that truly creative architecture grows and develops naturally, conscience of the needs of man; reflecting the character of his life, work, moments of leisure and expressing the true character of the society within which he resides.*"[149]

These are but a few examples of the lobbing that occurred during this period. Toward the end of the era, finally one regional architect enjoyed a short window of opportunity to influence directly the built landscape of both Miami and Havana.[150] By 1957, accomplished architect Igor Polevitzky had designed several hotels in Miami Beach when he became active in the design of at least two projects in Cuba, one of which came to fruition. His Habana Riviera Hotel used the resort hotel culture of Miami Beach as a template. To this day, the Riviera rises stoically along the waterfront Malecón, as a prominent, commercially scaled example of Caribbean Modern Regionalism and sadly underlines the dialogue's abrupt disconnect and protracted hiatus.

'Disconnected'

Upon closer inspection, this experimental and exciting period reflects comparable architectural pursuits as well as divergent cultural agendas. The usage of similar architectural elements, typologies, and even language, underline their professional synergy and an analogous search for an authentic, tropically anchored architecture across Florida Straits. Often the islanders strove to reinterpret their colonial and cultural heritage in an unsentimental manner within the paradigms of a contemporary architecture. Notwithstanding some common bonds, the search for architecture's 'essence' was vastly different in Havana than across Florida - justly so, as one region was in its infancy, and the other was rediscovering its extensive urban and architectural history and re-inventing its national image.

Despite the merits of their creative pursuits, one common error must be underlined. In both locations, period buildings often did not engage the urban realm in a contributing manner, often standing unnecessarily apart from the fabric of the city, or ignoring its morphological characteristics and in the case of Havana, at times eroding the essence of its urban codes. This, coupled with the growing trend toward sprawling 'sub-urbanism,' contributed to the scarring of both urban landscapes to some degree. But that said, in Havana, there are many handsome examples of modern buildings respectfully inserting themselves into the fabric of the city, illustrating that the form based codes which guided her formation did not impede creative architectural expression.

By the early 1960's, a worldwide homogenizing of 'Modern' conventions spread on several fronts, suffocating regionalist priorities. Ironically, just as the automobile, before it had altered the design of cities and towns resulting in less sustainable communities as distances dilated and uses were segregated, so too another invention of the Industrial Revolution moved architects in this region farther away from locally attuned sustainable architecture: the air-conditioner. At a time when crude oil as an energy source seemed infinite and mechanical systems guaranteed comfort levels, passive systems were progressively abandoned altogether as air-conditioners became inexpensive. Additionally, social or economic agendas seeking to increase affordable housing stocks efficiently across the globe, came to rely on generic typologies and prefabricated panel systems. This resulted in unfortunate manifestations in South Florida and Cuba, replicating projects from Detroit, the Bronx, Czechoslovakia, or Moscow, yet alien to the tropical environment and furthermore, disconnected from cultural constructs.

The 'Regionalist' sensibilities of mid-century dwindled in both locations, giving way to economically driven solutions and even further mechanized and standardized building conventions. Localized circumstances diverted attention toward differing priorities. Then, channels of communication, the dialogue and the exchanges the regionalist professionals had previously benefitted from were effectively truncated; curiously enough, by another common denominator: the Cuban Missile Crisis and the multiple Cuban Exile waves of the 1960's.

Nonetheless, the preceding collegial exchange of ideas between Modern Regionalist practitioners in Florida and Cuba nourished pioneering and analogous investigations by discerning mid-century academics, students and practitioners that were respectfully searching for authenticity and pursuing a 'tropically' anchored architecture. Modern Regionalist structures remain in both locations, testaments to the ideals and accomplishments of their designers. Today they should be safeguarded. Their thoughtful designs provide valuable models and lessons of a modern, sustainable architecture. Respectful of local traditions and realities, prevalently informed by climate, distilled by humble pursuits for genuineness, and in some cases, enriched by healthy professional interactions amongst neighbors, their collective efforts were fed by a shared curiosity, which afforded all cultural richness. The body of work that surfaced was not only aware of international modern currents but was often informed by vernacular precedents, representing another link, in a long continuum of locally calibrated architecture; where designers responsibly tackled many of the same issues that are once again relevant today as society and professionals wake up to the limitations of natural resources and the adverse impact that buildings and sprawling cities have on our global climate. Those parallel efforts in Cuba and Florida, possessing common constructive traits, resulted in notable twentieth century contributions to the built heritage of both locations and evidence Mid-Century Modern Regionalism's engaging dialogue within the Caribbean Basin. From those not so distant 'eloquent' conversations, inspiration and hope are drawn.

Endnotes

[1] Miguel Bretos. "A Life-long Conversation between Florida and Cuba" Lecture, *Tracing Parallel Cultural Experiences between Cubans and Cuban-Americans*, Symposium, Lowe Art Museum, September, 2001.
[2] Allan Shulman, *The Making of Miami Beach* (Rizzoli International, 2000).
[3] US Census Bureau, Count: 528, 542, http://www.demographia.com/db-state1900.htm (October, 2010).
[4] Mid-century regionalist architects will abundantly reference wood frame vernacular in the coming decades.
[5] *Florida East Coast Railway*, http://en.wikipedia.org/wiki/Florida_East_Coast_Railway (October, 2010).
[6] *Modern Florida*, http://www.glencoe.com/sites/florida/student/socialstudies/fl_online/modern_florida.html#growthandchange (October, 2010).
[7] Beth Dunlop, *Miami Trends and Traditions* (The Monacelli Press, 1996), 15.
[8] Thanks in part to the San Diego World's Fair celebration of Mediterranean Revival Architecture. Beth Dunlop, "Inventing Antiquity: The Art and Craft of Mediterranean Revival Architecture," Florida Issue, *The Journal of Decorative & Propaganda Art*, Vol. 23, 2002, 190-207.
[9] Beth Dunlop, "Inventing Antiquity: The Art and Craft of Mediterranean Revival Architecture," Florida Theme Issue, *The Journal of Decorative & Propaganda Art*, Vol. 23, 2002, 190-207.
[10] Louis Perez, *Cuba and the United States: Ties of Singular Intimacy* (University of Georgia Press, Revised 2003), 32.
[11] Mario Coyula, Joseph Scarpacci, and Roberto Segre, *Havana: two faces of the Antillean Metropolis* (John Wiley & Sons, Ltd., Revised 2002), 3.
[12]Kenneth Treister, Felipe Prestamo and Raul B. Garcia, *Havana Forever - a pictorial and cultural history of an unforgettable city* (University Press of Florida, 2009), 89.
[13] The 1899 census reveals that Cuba's total population was 1,572,797. *Antecedentes, Evolución y Estructuras de Apoyo*, http://www.historyofcuba.com/history/time/timetbl2d.htm (October, 2010).
[14] Liliana Llanes, *1898-1921: La Transformación de La Habana a Través de la Arquitectura* (Giraldilla Editorial, Letras Cubanas).
[15] Roberto Segre, *El sistema monumental en la Ciudad de La Habana: 1900-1930*, http://www.habanaelegante.com/Fall2004/Ronda.html (November, 2011).
[16] Nicolás Quintana, "Arquitectura y Urbanismo en la República de Cuba, 1902-1958" http://lasa.international.pitt.edu/Lasa2001/QuintanaNicolas.pdf (November, 2011).
[17] Emilio Roig de Leuchsenring, *La Habana- Apuntes Históricos Tomo II*, Editoria del Consejo (Nacional de Cultura, 1963), 277.
[18] Jose Gelabert-Navia, "American Architects in Cuba: 1900-1930," *The Journal of Decorative and Propaganda Arts, Wolfson Foundation of Decorative and Propaganda Arts*, 1986, 133-149.
[19] Jose Gelabert-Navia, "American Architects in Cuba: 1900-1930," *The Journal of Decorative and Propaganda Arts, Wolfson Foundation of Decorative and Propaganda Arts*, 1986, 132-149.
[20] Eduardo Luis Rodriguez, and Maria Elena Martí Zequeira, *La Habana, Guía de Arquitectura, Agencia Espanola de Cooperacion Internacional*, 1998, 140-141.
[21] Forestier had been the head of urban planning in Paris before moving to Havana for a period of five years. He led a team of French and Cuban planners, architects and landscape designers. The objective of their *Plan de Embellecimiento y Ampliación de La Habana* (The Expansion and Beautification Plan for Havana) was to fuse the city's patchwork of neighborhoods by a formal network of roads, which anchored existing civic sites with proposed ones, all the while celebrating the lush landscape and waterfront edge.
[22] Narciso Menocal, "Lo Cubano in Cuban Architecture, 1924-1964," *Herencia Magazine*, Vol. 7, No. 1, Summer 2001, 39.
[23] Mario Coyula Crowley, "Razón y pasión, ¿La impronta del maestro? Racionalismo, regionalismo crítico y modernidad apropiada en la arquitectura cubana de la primera mitad del Siglo XX. Cuba: una identidad en movimiento," Archivo Cubano, http://www.archivocubano.org/corbu_01.html (November, 2011).
[24] A term coined by Martinez Inclán in the publication *La Habana Actual* and later appropriated by Carlos Miguel de Cespedes.
[25] In collaboration with Rafael Fernandez Ruenes and Jose Martinez, completed in 1930.
[26] Roberto Segre, *Arquitectura en la ciudad de La Habana: Primera Modernidad*, in collaboration with Carlos Sambricio, Madrid, 2000, 63-102.
[27] Primarily public buildings such as offices, ministries, hospitals, private sector office buildings, and residential condominiums.
[28] Juan de las Cuevas Toraya, *500 Años de Construcciónes en Cuba*, D.V. Chavín, Madrid, 2001.
[29] Cuban Scholar Mario Coyula considers Le Corbusier's influence on the island nation's architecture less pervasive, until the 1950's prevalent incorporation of '*brise-soleil*' elements.
[29] Bird Cage House, http://en.wikipedia.org/wiki/Birdcage_House (November, 2012).

[30] Roberto Segre, *Le Corbusier, Los viajes al Nuevo Mundo: cuerpo, naturaleza y abstracción. Cuba una identita en movimiento*, Archivo Cuba, http://www.archivocubano.org/corbu_02.html (September, 2010).
[31] The '*piloti*' and use of ribbon windows.
[32] Henry-Russell Hitchcock, *Latin American Architecture Since 1945*, New York Museum of Modern Art, 1955.
[33] Esther McCoy, *Case Study Houses: 1945-1962* (Hennessey & Ingalls, 1962).
[34] Mario Coyula Crowley, "Razón y pasión, ¿La impronta del maestro? Racionalismo, regionalismo crítico y modernidad apropiada en la arquitectura cubana de la primera mitad del Siglo XX. Cuba, Una identidad en movimiento," Archivo Cubano, http://www.archivocubano.org/corbu_01.html (November, 2010).
[35] Eduardo Luis Rodriguez, *La Habana: Arquitectura del Siglo XX*, Blume, 2001, 277.
[36] Rudolph C. Henning, *The Architecture of Alfred Browning Parker Miami's Maverick Modernist* (University Press of Florida, Gainesville, 2011).
[37] Ibid.
[38] Wayne Wood, *Jacksonville Historical Society*, Henry John Klutho, http://www.jaxhistory.com/klutho-book-1.html (October, 2010).
[39] Domin and King, *Paul Rudolph and the Florida Houses* (Princeton Architectural Press, 2002), 32.
[40] Domin and King, *Paul Rudolph and the Florida Houses* (Princeton Architectural Press, 2002), 33.
[41] Eric Nash and Randall Robinson, *MIMO: Miami Modern Revealed*, (Chronicle Books: 2004) 10, 37-40.
[42] Jan Hochstim, *Florida Modern: Residential Architecture 1945-1970* (New York: Rizzoli, 2004), 42.
[43] Associate architects: Paist and Steward.
[44] Jan Hochstim, *Florida Modern Residential Architecture 1945-1970* (New York: Rizzoli, 2004), 27.
[45] Primarily high humidity and mosquito infestations during half the year.
[46] In the end, Manley designs a total of 20 different buildings for the UM campus, on her own or in collaboration with others.
[47] The Servicemen's Readjustment Act of 1944 ("GI Bill").
[48] "La Gorce Building and Pentland Building Located on the University of Miami Main Campus Designation Report." City of Coral Gables, Historical Resources Division (November 18, 2010), 2-4.
[49] "University of Miami Moves Back to Boom-Bought Campus and into First Unit of All-Modern Educational Plant," *Architectural Forum 89*, no. 1, July, 1948, 76-82.
[50] Charles Leyden, "University of Miami Plans to Grow," *Miami Daily News*, February 17, 1946.
[51] Joyce M. Davis, *Lakeland's Unique Architectural Heritage*, Lakeland, Florida, Polk Museum of Art, 1987.
[52] Jan Hochstim, *Florida Modern Residential Architecture 1945-1970* (New York: Rizzoli, 2004).
[53] Casement, single, or double hung windows could not be left open in a downpour, making interiors hot and humid. The "Miami" awning window is hinged at the top of each panel and could thusly be left open during a rainstorm. Soon they are exported to Havana.
[54] More recently redefined as "Subtropical Modern" – a local interpretation of the International Style, specifically adapted to the local environment according to the afore sited Designation Report. "La Gorce and Pentland Buildings," *University of Miami Designation Report*, 2009.
[55] Robert Little will design the Ring Theater, Ashe Administrative Building, the Music School's Library, and Eaton Residential Hall.
[56] Snyder will design the University of Miami Neville McArthur School of Engineering building, wrapped in concrete and a gold-toned metal brise-soleil.
[57] Common name.
[58] *Alfred Browning Parker Architecture Archive Endowment*, http://www.uflib.ufl.edu/spec/architecture/abparker.htm (October, 2011).
[59] M. Ersoff, "An Architect Talks About His House," *Miami Herald*, May, 3, 1964.
[60] Damir Sinovcic, *Alfred Browning Parker, A Candid Conversation with a Celebrated Florida Architect*, http://www.designbook.us/magazine/issue/3/alfred_browning_parker (October, 2011).
[61] Examples include: wood frame construction, Florida Cracker houses, Chickee construction by Seminole/Miccosukee Indians.
[62] Parker is invited by this author to participate in the *Under the Sun* Symposium held at the University of Miami School of Architecture held in January, 2007. After the session, over dinner at the Woodsong Residence, this author interviews Parker.
[63] Parker did not clarify if this is the result of an economy of means or if it was due to the strained political relations that ensue years later.
[64] Frank Lloyd Wright, *House Beautiful*, November, 1953, 217.
[65] He writes to FLW: "Truly your life and work - your life-work - has been an inspiration in my thoughts these few weeks past. Not in sense of imitation have I enjoyed a few contacts with what you have done and are doing, but in thinking that I must do my utmost to live to the best that is within me." Rudolph C Henning, *The Architecture of*

Alfred Browning Parker Miami's Maverick Modernist (University Press of Florida, Gainesville, 2011), xvii.
[66] Elizabeth Gordon, "This is the House Beautiful," *House Beautiful*, November, 1953, 218.
[67] From then on, the house is referred to as the '1954 Pacesetter House.'
[68] Alfred Browning Parker, http://www.alfredbparker.com/bio%20page.html (October, 2011).
[69] Alfred Browning Parker, http://www.alfredbparker.com/ (October, 2011).
[70] Allan Shulman, "Igor Polevitzky's Architectural Vision for a Modern Miami," *The Journal of Decorative and Propaganda Arts 23*, 1998, 334-336.
[71] Allan Shulman, "Igor Polevitzky's Architectural Vision for a Modern Miami," *The Journal of Decorative and Propaganda Arts 23*, 1998, 336.
[72] Another group of mid-century modern regionalists had parallel pursuits. They included: George Reed, Peter Jefferson, and Dwight Holmes.
[73] Ibid.
[74] Allan Shulman, "Igor Polevitzky's Architectural Vision for a Modern Miami," *The Journal of Decorative and Propaganda Arts 23*, 1998, 334-359.
[75] Ibid.
[76] "Bird-Cage House," *Life Magazine*, June 5, 1950, 63-65.
[77] *82 Distinctive Houses from Architectural Record* (F.W. Dodge Corporation, Publishers, 1952), 62-63.
[78] The tile color has been referred to as 'Malecón-blue.' http://en.wikipedia.org/wiki/Hotel_Habana_Riviera (October, 2010).
[79] The Havana Hilton designed by Welton Beckett is completed a year later.
[80] Other pioneers of the Sarasota School included: Carl Abbott, Boyd Blackner, Bert Brosmith, Joseph Farrell, Frank Folsom Smith, Phil Hall, Mark Hampton, Philip Hiss, James Holiday, Gene Leedy, Victor Lundy, Bill Rupp, Louis Schneider, Tim Seibert, Roland Sellew, Ralph Twitchell, Tolyn Twitchell, Ken Warriner, Jack West, Ralph Zimmerman, and William Zimmerman.
[81] *Paul Rudolph*, http://www.trianglemodernisthouses.com/rudolph.htm (October, 2010).
[82] Christopher Domin and Joseph King, *Paul Rudolph: The Florida Houses* (Princeton Architectural Press, 2002), 30-44.
[83] *Paul Rudolph and his Architecture*, http://prudolph.lib.umassd.edu/introduction (October, 2010).
[84] Christopher Domin and Joseph King, *Paul Rudolph: The Florida Houses* (Princeton Architectural Press, 2002), 44.
[85] Ibid, 35.
[86] Ibid, 138.
[87] FLW is working on the FCU commission in Central Florida at the time.
[88] Christopher Domin and Joseph King, *Paul Rudolph: The Florida Houses* (Princeton Architectural Press, 2002), 126-130.
[89] Moholy-Nagy, Sibyl. *The Architecture of Paul Rudolph* (New York: Praeger Publishers, 1970), 42.
[90] Mark Lamster. "Paul Rudolph's Knock-Up Masterpiece," http://observersroom.designobserver.com/marklamster/post/paul-rudolphs-knock-up-masterpiece/25928/ (November, 2010).
[91] For more detailed information, refer to Narciso G. Menocal, "Lo Cubano in Cuban Architecture:1924-1964," *Herencia*, Vol. 7, No. 1, Summer, 2001.
[92] John A. Loomis, *Cuba's Forgotten Art Schools Revolution of Forms* (New York: Princeton Architectural Press, 1999), 1-3.
[93] Later appendix to the Second War of Independence is the Spanish-American War marked by a brief bellicose involvement by the US.
[94] Fernando Ortiz Fernández, http://en.wikipedia.org/wiki/Fernando_Ortiz (November, 2011).
[95] For additional information: *Cuban Fire: The Story of Salsa and Latin Jazz*, Isabelle Leymarie (London; New York: Continuum, 2002).
[96] For additional information: *Caribbean Dance from Abakuá to Zouk: How Movement Shapes Identity*, edited by Susanna Sloat (Gainesville, FL: University Press of Florida, 2002).
[97] For additional information: *Cuba Siglo XX: Modernidad y Sincretismo*. Las Palmas de Gran Canaria, Spain: Centro Atlántico de Arte Moderno; Palma, Spain: Fundació "La Caixa"; Barcelona: Centre d'Art Santa Mónica, 1996.
[98] Juan A. Martinez, *Cuban Art and National Identity: The Vanguardia Painters, 1927-1950,* (Gainesville: University Press of Florida, 1994).
[99] Mario Coyula Crowley, "Caminando por La Habana: una ciudad viva." *Archivos de Arquitectura Antillana*, Vol.5, No.10, June, 2000, 143-145.
[100] Joaquin Weiss y Sanchez, *Arquitectura Cubana Colonial: colección de fotografías de los principales y más característicos edificos erigidos en Cuba durante la dominación española, precedida de una reseña histórica-arquitectónica. La Habana, Cultural,* (1936). See also by Weiss: *Arquitectura Cubana Contemporánea* (1947), *Medio Siglo de Arquitectura Cubana* (1950).
[101] Ibid.
[102] Narciso G. Menocal, "Lo Cubano in Cuban Architecture, 1924-1964," *Herencia*, Vol. 7, No. 1, Summer, 2001,

38. (See for more detailed information regarding the traditionalist, functionalist and the expressionist camps.)
[103] Ibid.
[104] Ibid.
[105] Refer to: Leonardo Morales, "La casa cubana idea," Induction Speech, National Academy of Arts & Letters meeting held on November 25, 1934, (Havana: Molina y Cia. Printing, 1934). Also refer to: Eduardo Luis Rodríguez, "La renovación clasicista de Leonardo Morales," *La Habana. Arquitectura del Siglo XX.* Historian Narciso Menocal considers that this position became so widely accepted that in a brief period it became second nature.
[106] Leonardo Morales, "La casa cubana ideal," Speech delivered in November 1934 to the National Academy of Arts and Letters (Havana, Imprenta Molina y Cia, 1934) as referenced by Eduardo Luis Rodriguez in "Theory and Practice of Modern Regionalism in Cuba," *DOCOMOMO*, No. 33, September, 2005.
[107] For more detailed information regarding the National Schools of Art, reference: John Loomis, *Revolution of Forms. Cuba's forgotten Arts Schools* (Princeton Architectural Press, 1999).
[108] John Loomis, *Revolution of Forms. Cuba's Forgotten Arts Schools* (Princeton Architectural Press, 1999) 57-62.
[109] A documentary entitled *Unfinished Spaces* by Co-Directors Alysa Nahmias and Benjamin Murray provided footage of the state of neglect these masterpieces are currently found in, (2011).
[110] Reference: Eduardo Luis Rodriguez, "Theory and Practice of Modern Regionalism in Cuba," *DOCOMOMO*, No. 33, September, 2005 and Narciso G. Menocal, "Lo Cubano in Cuban Architecture, 1924-1964," *Herencia*, Vol. 7, No. 1, Summer, 2001.
[111] Eduardo Luis Rodriguez, *Modern Architecture 1925-1965, The Havana Guide*, Princeton Architectural Press, 2000. x, xii, xiv.
[112] For more detailed information, refer to Eduardo Luis Rodriguez, *Modern Architecture 1925-1965, The Havana Guide*, Princeton Architectural Press, 2000.
[113] Alejo Carpentier, Prologue to *Ecue Yamba O, La Habana: Ediciones Arte y Literatura*, 1977, pg. 11 as reference in Eduardo Luis Rodríguez, *Modern Architecture 1925-1965 The Havana Guide*, Princeton Architectural Press, 2000. pg. xi.
[114] Vernacular term: "to become like the natives; to assimilate."
[115] Nicolas Quintana, *Arquitectura y Urbanismo en la República de Cuba (1902-1958) Antecedentes, Evolución y Estructuras de Apoyo*, http://lasa.international.pitt.edu/Lasa2001/QuintanaNicolas.pdf, (June, 2012).
[116] "Caribbean Mansion," *House & Home Magazine* (August, 1952), 117-119. As referenced in: Francisco Gomez Diaz, *De Forestier a Sert, Territorio y Ciudad* (Madrid: Abada Editores, 2008), 515.
[117] Eduardo Luis Rodriguez, *La Habana Arquitectura del Siglo XX* (Barcelona: Blume, 1998), 285-87.
[118] For further information on Mario Romañach, refer to Eduardo Luis Rodriguez, *La Habana Arquitectura del Siglo XX* (Barcelona: Blume, 1998), Chapter 10, 268-291.
[119] Francisco Gómez Díaz, *De Forestier a Sert, Territorio y Ciudad* (Madrid: Abada Editores, 2008), 558.
[120] Francisco Gómez Díaz, *De Forestier a Sert, Territorio y Ciudad* (Madrid: Abada Editores, 2008), 439.
[121] Eduardo Luis Rodriguez, *Modern Architecture 1925-1965 The Havana Guide.* (Princeton Architectural Press, 2000) 152.
[122] Francisco Gómez Díaz, *De Forestier a Sert, Territorio y Ciudad* (Madrid: Abada Editores, 2008), 445.
[123] This group focuses on urban design issues and is led by Pedro Martinez Inclán.
[124] Entry breezeways.
[125] Eduardo Luis Rodriguez, *Modern Architecture 1925-1965 The Havana Guide*, (Princeton Architectural Press, 2000), 231.
[126] Francisco Gómez Díaz, *De Forestier a Sert, Territorio y Ciudad* (Madrid: Abada Editores, 2008), 451.
[127] Joaquin Weiss, "Medio Siglo de Arquitectura Cubana," La Habana, University of Havana, No. 24, November, 1950, 24.
[128] *Arquitectura Magazine*, Vol. 325-326, August-September, 1960.
[129] This bridging strategy is developed more eloquently in his 1959 house for Mr. Santiago Cintra.
[130] Francisco Gómez Díaz, *De Forestier a Sert, Territorio y Ciudad* (Madrid: Abada Editores, 2008), 467.
[131] Wilfredo Cancío Isla, "Arquitecto Cubano logra prestigioso premio," *El Nuevo Herald* (June 30, 2005), as referenced in Francisco Gómez Díaz, *De Forestier a Sert. Territorio y Ciudad* (Madrid: Abada Editores, 2008), 467.
[132] Julio Estorino, "Interview with Nicolás Quintana," University of Miami Libraries, Digital Collections, Cuban Heritage Collection Digital Collections, *The Luis J. Botifoll Oral History Project*, Tape 1, http://merrick.library.miami.edu/streaming/botifollvideo.php?interview=chc5212000024 (June, 2012).
[133] Gustavo L. More, "Ricardo Porro: Ciudadano del mundo," *Archivos de Arquitectura Antillana*, Vol. 20, January, 2005.
[134] Nicolas Quintana, "A History of Cuban Architecture," *Tracing Parallel Cultural Experiences between Cubans & Cuban-Americans* Symposium, Coral Gables, Florida, Lowe Art Museum, September, 2001.
[135] Julio Estorino, "Interview with Nicolás Quintana," University of Miami Libraries, Digital Collections, Cuban

Heritage Collection Digital Collections, *The Luis J. Botifoll Oral History Project*, Tape 2, http://merrick.library.miami.edu/streaming/botifollvideo.php?interview=chc5212000024 (June, 2012).
[136] Julio Estorino. "Interview with Nicolás Quintana," University of Miami Libraries, Digital Collections, Cuban Heritage Collection Digital Collections, *The Luis J. Botifoll Oral History Project*, Tape 2, http://merrick.library.miami.edu/streaming/botifollvideo.php?interview=chc5212000024 (June, 2012).
[137] Ramon Recondo, "La Arquitectura del Movimiento Moderno Selección de Obras Registro Nacional." DOCOMOMO Cuba, Ediciones Union," *Colección Arquitectura y Ciudad*, 2011, 190-91.
[138] Julio Estorino, "Interview with Nicolás Quintana," University of Miami Libraries, Digital Collections, Cuban Heritage Collection Digital Collections, *The Luis J. Botifoll Oral History Project*, Tape 2, http://merrick.library.miami.edu/streaming/botifollvideo.php?interview=chc5212000024 (June, 2012).
[139] Francisco Gómez Díaz, *De Forestier a Sert, Territorio y Ciudad* (Madrid: Abada Editores, 2008), 478.
[140] According to Quintana, in his last meeting with Che Guevarra, when accused of complotting against the government and of being a member of the bourgeoisie, he clarifies: "*...my corner shopkeeper is bourgeois, I am a 'grand bourgeois.'*" To which Guevara suggests his swift exile or a trip to the firing squad. Quintana and his family leave the island almost immediately in January of 1960. Julio Estorino, "Interview with Nicolás Quintana," University of Miami Libraries, Digital Collections, Cuban Heritage Collection Digital Collections, *The Luis J. Botifoll Oral History Project*, Tape 2, http://merrick.library.miami.edu/streaming/botifollvideo.php?interview=chc5212000024 (June, 2012).
[141] Elisabet Sabartés, "Nicolás Quintana Arquitecto La identidad de La Habana, La Vanguardia."- 06/06/2011, http://enmemoria.lavanguardia.com/obituarios/nicolas-quintana.html (January, 2012).
[142] 'Puddle'... term often used by locals to describe the small body of water between Florida and Cuba.
[143] Miguel Bretos. "A Life-long Conversation between Florida and Cuba" Lecture, *Tracing Parallel Cultural Experiences between Cubans and Cuban-Americans* Symposium, Lowe Art Museum, September, 2001.
[144] Paula Harper, "Cuba Connections: Key West-Tampa-Miami," *The Journal of Decorative and Propaganda Arts, Wolfson Foundation of Decorative and Propaganda Arts*, Vol. 22, 1996, 279-291.
[145] When he attended the Bridgewater Congress with Eugenio Batista, by his own account he is a "precocious student." From Interviews of Nicolas Quintana by Sonia Chao, 2001- 2004.
[146] From Interviews of Nicolas Quintana by Sonia Chao, 2001- 2004.
[147] Homenaje de los Arquitectos de Miami al Presidente del Colegio de Arquitectos de La Habana, C. Martinez Marquez "*Arquitectura Magazine*, Year XVII, No. 195, La Habana, October, 1949.
[148] Guillermo Zarraga, *El Desmembramiento de las Ciudades, VII Congreso Panamericano de Arquitectos,* December, 1950, 534-537.
[149] "Architecture Under the Sun," *The Florida Architect Magazine*, October-November, 1955.
[150] Schultz & Weaver, a New York based firm also contributes to both urban landscapes.

Image Sources

Figure 1. Image courtesy of Peter Augustus Jefferson
Figure 2. From: *Florida Architecture*, June 1949
Figure 3. Image courtesy of Jan Hochstim
Figure 4 - 6. Image courtesy of State Archives of Florida
Figure 7. Library of Congress Prints and Photographs Division Washington, D.C.
Figure 8. Sonia Chao Collection
Figure 9. Library of Congress Prints and Photographs Division Washington, D.C.
Figure 10 - 11. Image courtesy of University of Miami Otto G. Richter Library, Special Collections
Figure 12. From: Aristides J. Millas and Ellen J. Uguccioni, *Coral Gables: Miami Riviera, An Architectural Guide*, 2004
Figure 13 -15. Library of Congress Prints and Photographs Division Washington, D.C.
Figure 16. Photography by Peter Harholdt, 1999. Image courtesy of: Plymouth Hotel, Miami Beach
Figure 17. Sonia Chao Collection
Figure 18 -19. Image courtesy of University of Miami Otto G. Richter Library, Cuban Heritage Collection
Figure 20 - 21. From: Emilio Roig de Leuchsenring, *La Casa de Gobierno o Palacio Municipal de la Habana*, 1961
Figure 22. From: *A Book of Architectural Decorative Drawings* (New York: The Architectural Book Publishing Company, 1941
Figure 23. Image courtesy of Celia Garcia Collection
Figure 24. Sonia Chao Collection
Figure 25. Image courtesy of University of Miami Otto G. Richter Library, School of Architecture Collection
Figure 26 a-g. Photographs by Olivia Choy
Figure 27. Photograph by Eduardo Luis Rodriguez and courtesy of Eduardo Luis Rodriguez Collection

Figure 28. From: *Album de Cuba*, 1950
Figure 29. Image courtesy of Roberto Segre
Figure 30. Image courtesy of Juan de las Cuevas
Figure 31. Image courtesy of the Historical Museum of Southern Florida, Jay Spence Collection
Figure 32 - 33. Image courtesy of University of Miami School of Architecture Slide Collection
Figure 34. From: Stamo Papadaki. *The Works of Oscar Neimeyer*, 1950
Figure 35. Library of Congress Prints and Photographs Division Washington, D.C.
Figure 36. From: *Arquitectura* Magazine, 1954
Figure 37. From: *Arquitectura* Magazine, 1949
Figure 38. From: *Arquitectura* Magazine, 1952
Figure 39. Image courtesy of University of Miami Richter Library, Florida Collection
Figure 40. Image courtesy of John Howey. From: Joseph King and Christopher Domin, *Paul Rudolph: The Florida Houses*, 2005
Figure 41. From: *The Florida Tropical Home at A Century of Progress*, Catalog. 1933
Figure 42. Photograph by Steven Brooke and courtesy of Steven Brooke Collection
Figure 43. Image courtesy of the Historical Museum of Southern Florida, Marion Manley Collection
Figure 44. Image courtesy of University of Miami Otto G. Richter Library, Special Collections
Figure 45. Collaged images courtesy of Jan Hochstim
Figure 46-48. Images courtesy of University of Miami Otto G. Richter Library, Special Collections
Figure 49. Photograph by Ezra Stoller. Copyright, ESTO
Figure 50. From: William H. Nicolas, "Miami Expanding Horizons," *National Geographic* Magazine, November 1950
Figure 51. Image courtesy of University of Miami Otto G. Richter Library, Special Collections
Figures 52 - 55. Renderings courtesy of University of Miami School of Architecture student Troy Marrocco
Figure 56. From: "Two Residences in a Rock Pit," *Florida Architecture*, 1948
Figure 57. From: Joseph Barry, *The House Beautiful Treasury of Contemporary American Homes*, 1958. Photograph by Ezra Stoller
Figure 58. Photograph by Ezra Stoller. Copyright, ESTO
Figure 59. Photograph by Ezra Stoller. Copyright, ESTO
Figure 60-63. From: Joseph Barry, *The House Beautiful Treasury of Contemporary American Homes*, 1958
Figure 64. From: Joseph Barry, *The House Beautiful Treasury of Contemporary American Homes*, 1958
Figure 65. Photograph by Ezra Stoller. Copyright, ESTO
Figure 66. From: *Florida Architecture* Magazine, 1940
Figure 67. Library of Congress Prints and Photographs Division Washington, D.C.
Figure 68. Library of Congress Prints and Photographs Division Washington, D.C.
Figure 69- 71. From: *Florida Architecture* Magazine, 1957
Figure 72. http://en.wikipedia.org/wiki/File:Polevitzky_bird-cage_north_elev.jpg
Figure 73. From: *Life* Magazine, June, 1950
Figure 74. http://en.wikipedia.org/wiki/File:Polevitzky_bird-cage_interior.jpg
Figure 75 - 76. Image courtesy of Celia Garcia Collection
Figure 77a. Image courtesy of Roberto Segre
Figure 77b - 80. Photograph by Celia Garcia and courtesy of Celia Garcia Collection
Figure 81. From: Joseph King and Christopher Domin, *Paul Rudolph: The Florida Houses*, 2005. Image courtesy of James Deen
Figure 82. Library of Congress Prints and Photographs Division Washington, D.C.
Figure 83. Photograph by Ezra Stoller. Copyright, ESTO
Figure 84. Library of Congress Prints and Photographs Division Washington, D.C.
Figure 85. Photograph by Ezra Stoller. Copyright, ESTO
Figure 86. Library of Congress Prints and Photographs Division Washington, D.C.
Figure 87. Library of Congress Prints and Photographs Division Washington, D.C.
Figure 88. http://www.artfacts.net/index.php/pageType/artworkInfo/artworkID/18074
Figure 89 - 90. Images courtesy of Mario Coyula Crowley
Figure 91. From: *Album de Cuba*, 1950
Figure 92. Photograph by Eduardo Luis Rodriguez and courtesy of Eduardo Luis Rodriguez Collection
Figure 93. From: *Arquitectura* Magazine, 1940
Figure 94. Sonia Chao Collection
Figure 95. From: *Arquitectura* Magazine, 1956
Figure 96. From: *AAA Archivos de Arquitectura Antillana - Revista Internacional de Arquitectura y Cultura en el Gran Caribe*, Caribbean Architectural Records, June 2000

Figure 97. From: *Arquitectura* Magazine, 1955
Figure 98. Photograph by Eduardo Luis Rodriguez and courtesy of Eduardo Luis Rodriguez Collection
Figure 99. From: Government Plan for Public Works under Grau San Martin
Figure 100. From: *Arquitectura* Magazine, 1956
Figure 101. Photograph by Eduardo Luis Rodriguez and courtesy of Eduardo Luis Rodriguez Collection
Figure 102. From: *Arquitectura* Magazine, 1949
Figure 103. From: *Album de Cuba*, 1950
Figure 104. From: *Arquitectura* Magazine, 1949
Figure 105 - 108. Images courtesy of Roberto Segre. Photographs by Muniz
Figure 109. http://anavedobomgosto.blogspot.com/2010/02/kubitschek-house.html
Figure 110. Photograph by Celia Garcia and courtesy of Celia Garcia Collection
Figure 111. From: Emilio Roig de Leuchsenring. *La Habana Apuntes Historicos*, Vol. II
Figure 112. From: *Album de Cuba*, 1950
Figure 113. From: *Arquitectura* Magazine, 1954
Figure 114. From: *Arquitectura* Magazine, 1954
Figure 115. Image courtesy of Roberto Segre Collection
Figure 116. From: *Arquitectura* Magazine, 1954
Figure 117 - 119. From: *Espacio* Magazine, 1952
Figure 120 - 121. From: *Espacio* Magazine, 1954
Figure 122. From: *Arquitectura* Magazine, 1956
Figure 123 - 125. Images courtesy of Celia Garcia Collection
Figure 126. Photograph by Eduardo Luis Rodriguez and courtesy of Eduardo Luis Rodriguez Collection
Figure 127 - 128. From: *Arquitectura* Magazine, 1956
Figure 129. Photograph by Eduardo Luis Rodriguez and courtesy of Eduardo Luis Rodriguez Collection
Figure 130 - 132. From: *Arquitectura* Magazine, 1954
Figure 133 - 134. Sonia Chao Collection
Figure 134. Sonia Chao Collection
Figure 135. Image courtesy of Roberto Segre
Figure 136. Image courtesy of Juan de las Cuevas Archive
Figure 137 - 138. From: *Arquitectura* Magazine, 1956
Figure 139. Image courtesy of Nicolas Quintana
Figure 140. From: *Arquitectura* Magazine, 1956
Figure 141. From: *Arquitectura* Magazine, 1956
Figure 142. Image courtesy of Roberto Segre
Figure 143. From: *AAA Archivos de Arquitectura Antillana - Revista Internacional de Arquitectura y Cultura en el Gran Caribe*, Caribbean Architectural Records, June 2000
Figure 144. From: *AAA Archivos de Arquitectura Antillana - Revista Internacional de Arquitectura y Cultura en el Gran Caribe*, Caribbean Architectural Records, June 2000
Figure 145. From: *Arquitectura* Magazine, 1956
Figure 146. From: *Espacio* Magazine, 1955
Figure 147. From: Album de Cuba - Varadero, 1955
Figure 148 -150. Images courtesy of Nicolas Quintana
Figure 151. Image courtesy of Juan de las Cuevas Archive
Figure 152. Image courtesy of Historical Museum of Southern Florida, The Miami News Collection
Figure 153. Image courtesy of The Mitchell Wolfson Jr. Collection, The Wolfsonian Miami Beach
Figure 154. Image courtesy of University of Miami Otto G. Richter Library, Special Collections
Figure 155. Library of Congress Prints and Photographs Division Washington, D.C.
Figure 156. Sonia Chao Collection
Figure 157. From: *Arquitectura* Magazine, 1956

GREENER THAN GREEN:
mid-century Florida sensibility - a precursor to present day

Jan Hochstim

Figures 1. Parker Residence #3 "Pace Setter 1965," Gables Estates, Coral Gables, 1964, Alfred Browning Parker

The current fascination with energy conservation and sustainability may appear to populations born after the 1960s as a new direction our society is taking to save our planet from the ravages of a highly developed industrial age. While it is true that demise of the natural environment was not so much of a concern in the years immediately following World War II, the concerns for sustainability were driven then by forces based primarily on economics, logic and daring experimentation.

What we presently follow and demand by conscience and regulations, the so called "Green" architecture, was practiced in Florida in the postwar years by a small group of pioneering architects responding sensibly to conditions of building for a new generation of Americans coming back from the war looking for a new life in a subtropical environment and often doing it on a shoestring budget. It was also based on solutions to buildings that did not depend on traditional precedents, such as Colonial, Victorian or Spanish Mediterranean, that had little or nothing to do with Florida's subtropical climate. This was particularly true in single family residential designs that were built before the availability and affordability of air-conditioning. What these houses had in common was dedication to the principles of modern architecture espoused by such giants of the profession as Frank Lloyd Wright, Walter Gropius, Mies van der Rohe and Le Corbusier. Nowadays, such designs are referred to as *Modernism*, as if they belonged to an architectural style. But in reality there was no style. There were various approaches to design that differed dramatically from each other and responded to the well analyzed problems at hand, influenced at times by vernacular examples but not relying or copying previous styles. It must be stated however, that these designs were few and far between. The majority of residential projects, built by developers at that time, borrowed here and there such elements as open plans, glass jalousie windows, sliding glass doors and screened porches, originally created by the modern pioneers in response to the Florida climate and a new live style. However, even with the incorporation of logical elements, what the developers produced was endless suburbia filled with so called ranch style homes with unimpressive exteriors of 'choose your front' Colonial or Mediterranean masks to succumb to market demands. There were some exceptions in Miami, Sarasota, Winter Haven and Jacksonville where developers let a few talented modern architects produce enclaves of sensible examples of what Florida architecture should be.

Modern incursion in Florida has to be looked at in context of the prevailing residential designs of various regions of the state based on their climate and culture. While Florida's climate is generally considered hot and humid during summers and ideal in winters, there are slight variations from its southern tip in Key West to the northern border of Jacksonville as well as Pensacola in the western panhandle. These variations are reflected in the indigenous and vernacular architecture built from the time of the first settlements to the end of WW II. The northern and the northwestern parts of the state, with their cooler winters, display designs found in many southern states such as Georgia and Alabama. With the exception of Seminole and Miccosukee palm thatch huts known as Chickees, South Florida, which was settled much later than the rest of the state, produced architecture reflective of the Carribean models and borrowed from California Craftsman bungalows, and Mission and Spanish Mediterranean houses. Uniquely, Miami Beach in the late 20s and early 30s was exploring what was considered modern at that time, and now renown as Art Deco and Streamline Moderne.

Thus, with the exception of vernacular precedents reflecting strong Caribbean experience in the tropics, the designs of the young pioneers of the Modern Movement was in great contrast to Florida's architectural context. The residential Modern work that was produced varied from region to region. Based on these variations - really reflections of climatic, social and economical differences - Florida peninsula can be divided into South Atlantic Coast, South Gulf Coast, Mid Gulf Coast and Central and Northern regions. And yet, in order to produce the most sensible designs great variations of architectural expression emerged within each region.

In the South Atlantic region, which includes areas from Key West to Fort Pierce, and centers in the Miami-Dade and Broward counties, it is important to name just few of the numerous leading architects who propelled Modern designs in the post-war years to their national and international prominence: Robert Law Weed, Marion I. Manley, Igor B. Polevitzky, Alfred Browning Parker, Rufus Nims, Robert Bradford Browne, George F. Reed, Peter Augustus Jefferson, Robert E. Hansen and Donald Singer.

The South Gulf Region, with its hotbed in Sarasota, was unique due to the concentration of an artistic community that was quite receptive to experimentation in Modern architecture. Thus, unique and courageous developers such Philip Hanson Hiss dared to hire and encourage visionary architects, who are now known as the *Sarasota School*: Ralph Spencer Twitchell, Paul Marvin Rudolph, Jack West, Edward J. (Tim) Seibert, Ralph and William Zimmerman, Frank Folsom Smith, Victor A. Lundy and many young apprentices of Paul Rudolph, such as Mark

Hampton and Gene Leedy who opened up their architectural offices in other parts of Florida.

In the Mid Gulf Region, which stretches from Tampa Bay to Lake Wales, the architectural context was a mix of wood or brick houses with northern roots and variations of Spanish Mediterranean. However, the presence of Frank Lloyd Wright's Florida Southern campus in Lakeland provided incredible source of energy and inspiration to the young architects who got their training in Sarasota. Thus, Mark Hampton and Gene Leedy established themselves as the leaders of this region. Others contributing to the Modern sensibilities were William B. Harvard, John Howey, David Tudeen and Dwight E. Holmes.

In the Central and Northern region the leaders who produced remarkable examples of Modern residences were Alfred Browning Parker, Don P. Branch in Gainesville, and Robert C. Broward, Robert Griffith Ernest and William Morgan in Jacksonville.

In the hands of these modern pioneers across all regions of Florida there ran a common concern for blending of the inside with the outside, keeping the heat of the sun out, allowing maximum cross ventilation as well as utilization of local materials. While there were clear differences of individual expressions most of their designs can be placed in typological categories characterized as:

- Pitched Roof
- Screen Containers
- Solar Screens
- Floating Decks

Figure 2. Everglades Chickee

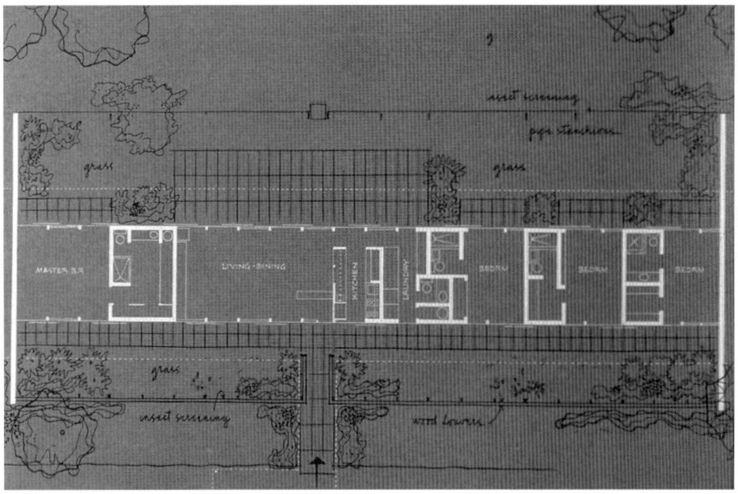

Figure 3. Messmore House, St, Petersburg, 1956, Rufus Nims

Pitched Roofs

The chickee huts, built by Florida's native population of Seminoles and Miccosukees are sensible responses to climatic and material concerns. These simple structures of cypress poles and roof framing clad with palm thatch offered the logical solution for shelter by providing raised floors to respond to flooding, open sides to maximize ventilation and large self-ventilating roofs for sun and rain protection. Many examples inspired by their logic and simplicity can be found throughout Florida with great concentration in the South Atlantic region. Of course the use of pitched roofs is not only influenced by Chickees. Many variations from simple hip roofs for a single structure or a grouping of pavilions with hipped roofs are found in the adaptation to the South Florida climate. So are simple gable roofs with open gables or modified hip roofs with vents in the Polynesian manner. It is important to mention that the modern pioneers in Florida did not specialize in one or the other roof type. They were utilizing the most appropriate form to solve conditions of the site and inhabitation.

It would be appropriate though to group the houses with similar roof forms for comparison and evolution of the types. One of the common characteristics that they all shared was maximization of cross ventilation. That was achieved by making the houses single room deep. There were no double loaded hallways or stacking of rooms. Circulation was provided on the exterior or on a parallel running walkway with walls opened by louvers to allow easy air flow. Bedrooms and open living room, dining, kitchen combinations were often arranged like links in a chain. Such arrangement made views and daylight available in every space from at least two sides (see Figure 3.)

Gable and Hip Roofs

Rufus Nims and his apprentices and later partners created some of the most straightforward houses that blended into the subtropical environment of South Florida. The Ratner Residence stands out as one of the earliest examples of modern gable roofed houses that derive their inspiration from the indigenous vernacular buildings.

Ratner house (Figures 4 & 5) follows the Chickee principle of a floor raised off the ground to avoid flooding and providing increased ventilation. However, rather than using a hip roof precedent this one utilizes a high pitched gable roof with open gables to allow for better cross ventilation. Exposed scissor trusses add to the drama of the raised interior space. Main rooms are strung along the waterside of the lot to allow for best views and ventilation. Only bathrooms and the kitchen face the landside but do not prevent cross ventilation to occur. Alternating full height glass panels and louvered French doors constitute the vertical enclosure making the interior unified with the natural context of the site.

Figures 4 & 5. Ratner Residence, Palm Island, Miami Beach, 1957, Rufus Nims and Robert Bradford Browne

Mc Clave Residence has great similarities to the Ratner Residence in that it is a long rectangle floating two feet above the ground with rooms stretched out along its long sides. But here there is a central Lanai area separating living-dining areas from the bedrooms side and the entire exterior is wrapped with a screened ship-like deck. The roof with its very large overhangs extending over the screened surround is a variation on a Polynesian roof, a modified hip with open gables. Exterior walls of glass and wood louvers have also glazed spaces between rafters and supporting beams making the roof appear to hover over the interiors. Like the Ratner Residence the response to the waterfront site and its nature is reflected in the building's form and the handling of environmental concerns.

Figures 6 & 7. McClave Residence, Key Biscayne, Miami, 1956, Robert Bradford Browne and George Reed

Alfred Browning Parker's approach to site and environmental factors produced spectacular houses that pushed the envelope of innovations and yet offered comfort and sense of belonging with the use of natural materials such as wood and local oolitic limestone. Mass Residence in Lake Worth is a daring utilization of a gable roof forming the entire cross section of house by the use of 30, 60 and 90 degree triangle. The length of the house wrapped by continuous balcony and shielded by generous cantilevered wooden canopy allows ample views and air movement. Additionally a narrow strip at the top of the gable serves as a skylight and exhaust, accentuating the dramatic lofty space. The interior spaces occupy three staggered levels providing for privacy, visual excitement, ease of air flow and magnificent views of the waterfront location.

Honored by *House and Garden Magazine* as "Pace Setter 1965", (Figure 9) was the residence designed and built by Parker for himself in the exclusive Gables Estates community, on a spectacular bay

Figure 8. Mass Residence, Lake Worth, 1956, Alfred Browning Parker

front site overlooking Matheson Hammock Beach. He raised the entire house a full story above the ground allowing for hurricane flooding to wash under the house without damaging any important livable spaces.

Figures 9. Parker Residence #3 "Pace Setter 1965," Gables Estates, Coral Gables, 1964, Alfred Browning Parker

The rest of the site at ground level contains work rooms, three car garage, equipment and storage, all arranged in a "C" formation creating an arrival court. The space between the garage and the house forms an esplanade with the swimming pool above reached from the second level deck. The decision to move the pool away from the waterfront was a deliberate gesture not to place an artificial water feature in front of the natural bay. The second level, the main level of the house, is reached by a coral rock stairway rising along the main fireplace chimney in a manner used by Frank Lloyd Wright, Parker's idol. Living, dining, kitchen and children's bedrooms form a string of single depth spaces surrounded on the outside by a spacious balcony deck. The third floor, occupying only the central part of the plan, contains the master bedroom suite. All this was executed using a full hip roof with the third level sheltered under a slightly raised gable floating above the hip of the second floor.

Cooling of the roof is achieved by an ingenious ventilation system whereby there is a space between the upper and lower surface of the roof thus creating air passage to eliminate heat.

The vertical surfaces of the house are a combination of adjustable wood louvers, insect screens and glass inserts for winter. But light is not compromised by the louvers because a horizontal glass soffit protected from salt spray and mounted in the large roof overhang allows light to enter the house above the header beams. Specially designed muted green ceramic tiles are used to clad a large part of the north elevation and the roof is covered with similar color concrete tiles. With no pun intended this house was really green.

Hipped Pavilions

Rather than stretching the house into a long rectangle, like the Ratner Residence, to allow single room depth for ease of cross ventilation, a square base plan, opening to all four sides and sheltered by a generous hip roof may appear to stay closer to the nature of the chickee. This type of space organization still demands placement of rooms with at least two or three exposures to the outside and letting the remainder of the plan to be an open porch. Another variation of this approach allowing even greater flexibility is to form series of pavilions containing different functions of the house, thus allowing each space the maximum exposure to the outside.

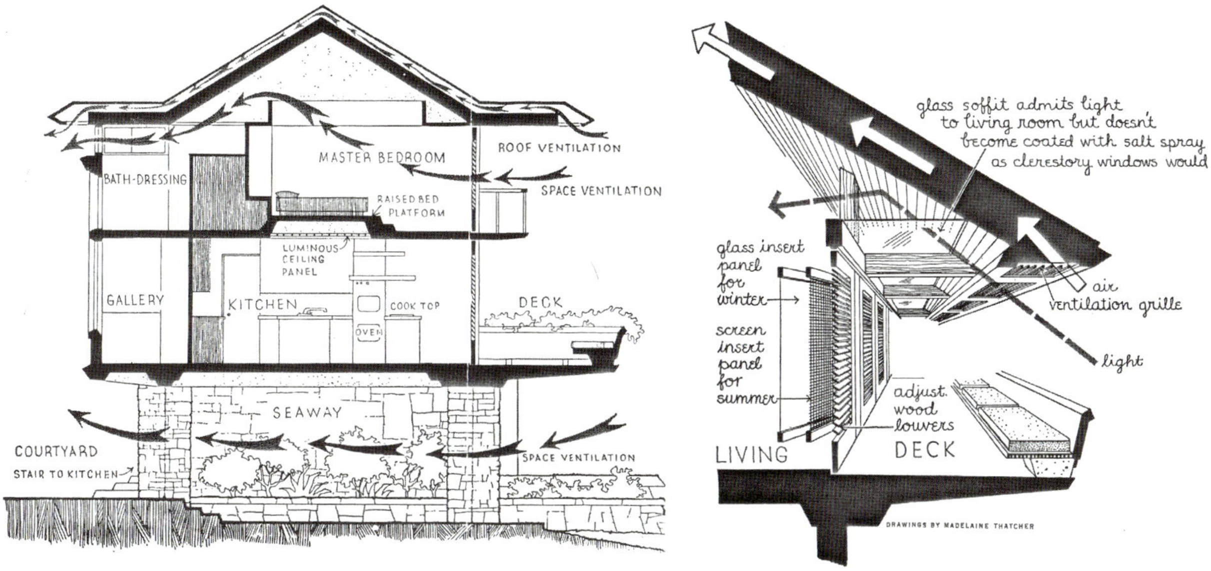

Figures 10 & 11. Sections

Figure 12. Borrows Residence, Key Vaca, Marathon Shores, 1957-60, Robert Bradford Browne and George F. Reed

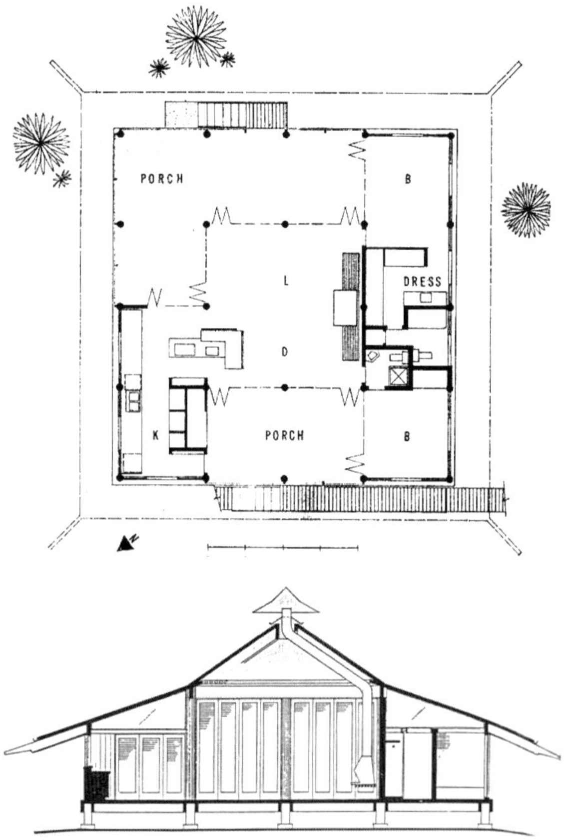

Figure 13 & 14. Borrows Residence, Key Vaca, Marathon Shores, 1957-60, Robert Bradford Browne and George F. Reed, Floor Plan and Section

Borrows House belongs to the first category, having almost all its spaces under a single square hip roof. Smaller similar roofed pavilions shelter the carport, boat dock and cabana. The main pavilion is raised slightly above the ground and its horizontal emphasis of the deck and roof's edge give it a sense of floating above the beach. The hip roof starts with a low pitch and then increases to a steeper angle, terminating with an exhaust lantern at the top. The roof is clad with standing seam metal, a sensible solution for longevity, reduction of weight and prevention of heat absorption so common with clay or concrete tiled roofs. The porch sides are screened and totally transparent providing excellent air and visual connection with its tropical surroundings.

For his mother's house Parker chose to utilize hipped roof pavilions not only to maximize exposure to the outside but to preserve precious trees on this densely landscaped Coconut Grove site. The house consists of two pavilions, one a double height main residence with living on the lower level and mezzanine sleeping loft above, and the other a single storey guest house. Both pavilions are raised off the ground and are connected to each other by a mosaic tiled terrace. Three sides of each pavilion are fitted with full height mahogany louvered Persiana doors that open completely unto cantilevered wood decks. What makes this design so successful is the preservation of privacy, maximization of ventilation – with three side of each pavilion open to breezes – and a sense of space and cooling that full height exposed hipped roof ceilings can offer.

Figure 15. Jewell Parker Residence, Coconut Grove, Miami, 1958, Alfred Browning Parker

Figure 18. Osman Residence, Key Biscayne, Miami, 1964-67 George F. Reed

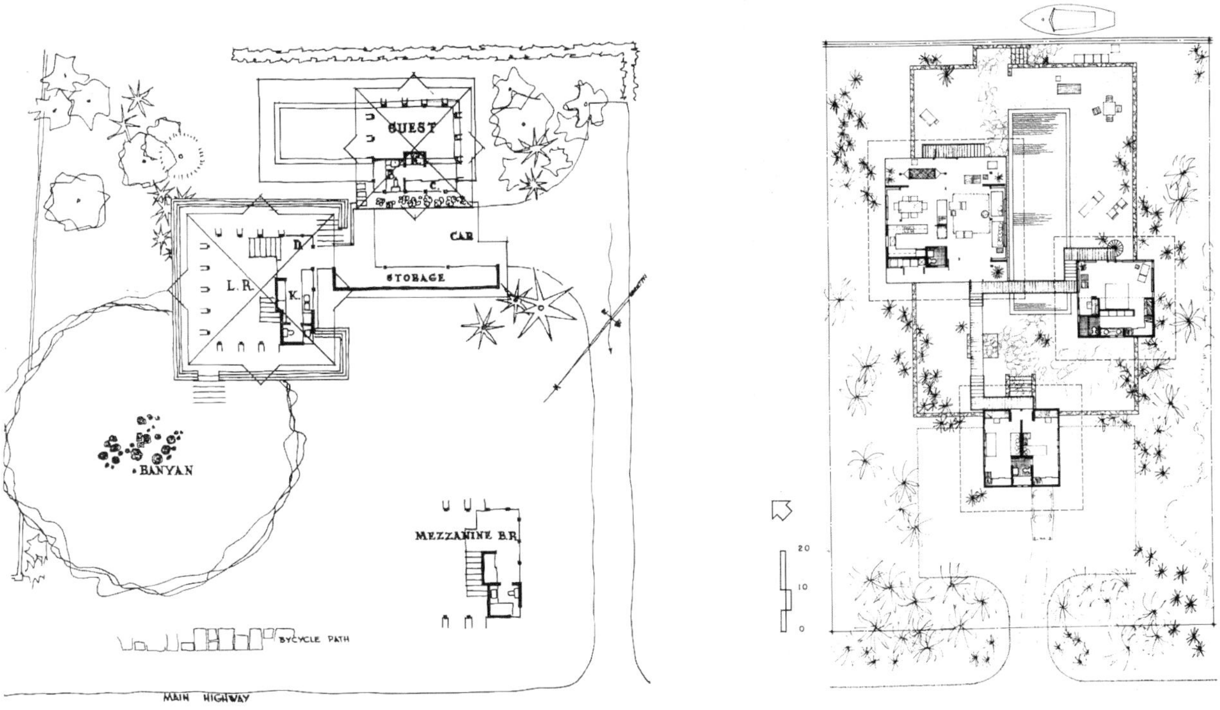

Figure 16 & 17. Jewell Parker Residence, Coconut Grove, Miami, 1958, Alfred Browning Parker, Site and Floor Plan

In a similar manner to Jewell Parker Residence, George Reed's Osman House takes advantage of splitting different functions of the residence into three perfectly square pavilions. Two small ones contain bedrooms for parents and children and the main large pavilion accommodates living, dining and kitchen. Floor to ceiling jalousie windows and French doors provide full ventilation and views. All pavilions are raised off the ground to prevent flooding, with the children's pavilion raised a full story to accommodate a carport. Connection between the pods is accomplished by raised wood decks and bridges. The clear advantage of the use of square hipped pavilions with their high ceilings and open sides makes this kind of design closer to the nature of the native chickees and their complete response to South Florida's landscape and climate.

A very dramatic raising of the house above ground is found in Peter Jefferson's Collins House. It is composed of two pavilions, in this case joined together at the ground level by an entry with stairway, gallery and a bedroom. The undersides of the raised pavilions contain an open loggia on one side and a two car carport on the other. The second floor above the loggia is one large open space for living, dining and cooking with both sides fitted with spacious decks. The upper part of the carport contains bedroom suites, which also have decks on all side to take advantage of the spectacular view of the site. Without compromising the need for cross ventilation, the privacy in this house is achieved by its elevated, above ground nature, and by the use of a ribbon of high placed windows in the bedroom services facing the street.

Figures 19. Collins Residence, Coconut Grove, Miami, 1961, Peter Augustus Jefferson

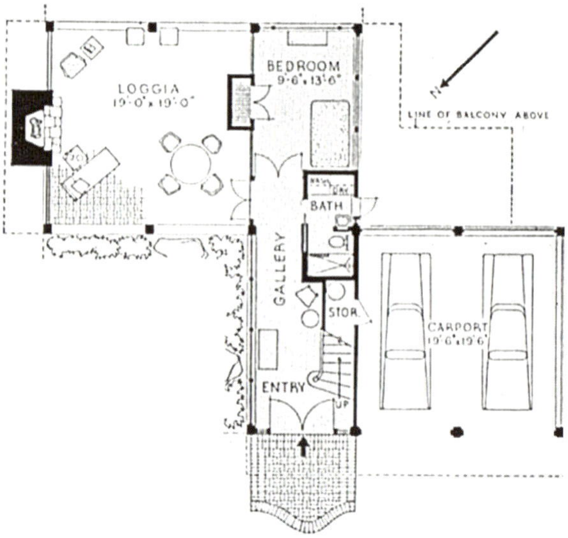

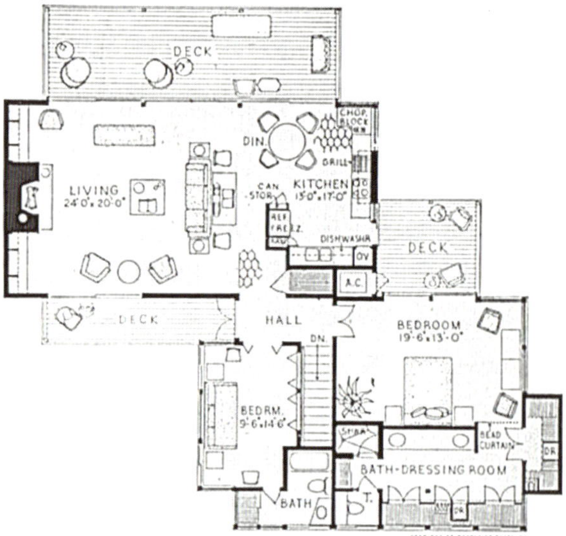

Figures 20 & 21. Collins Residence, Coconut Grove, Miami, 1961, Peter Augustus Jefferson, Floor Plans

Screened Containers

The fact of life in the subtropical climate is that man has to share the environment with a multitude of creatures, especially insects that make this coexistence less than desirable. But since living in such an environment before the advent of air conditioning required the use of window and door screens to keep the bugs out, this made the use of outdoors almost impossible during the hot summers when insects, especially mosquitoes were in charge of the outdoors. Traditional solutions called for screening of front porches, but this hardly allowed the desired freedom for the enjoyment of ones front or back yards.

Daring solutions to this problem in the post war years were provided in Miami by Igor Polevitzky. Why not place the house and its immediate outdoors areas within a huge screened container, thus freeing all the openings from the use of individual screens and making the outdoors use as easy as if the bugs were not there? Terraces for lounging, dining and swimming can now be a part of the home as they were meant to be.

In the Heller Residence, the first instance of wrapping almost an entire house with screening, Polevitzky located the main functions of the house such as living and sleeping on the first floor and placed an outdoor terrace over the living room and a cabana /guest room over the bedrooms creating a stepped-up space organization. At the opposite end of the house, an oval-shaped swimming pool is located half way between the first floor and the outdoor terrace and its cantilevered deck is reached by stairways from each level. The screened cage that envelopes the house is supported by closely spaced 2-by-8 pressure treated columns that carry steel open-web joists. The double height cage is intersected at two levels by the slabs of the pool deck and the second floor, thus contrasting the verticality of the screening with the horizontality of floors.

While such a dramatic use of screening was unique, what did become a standard of residences in South Florida was aluminum framed screened enclosure embracing the rear part of the house that contained the swimming pool and patio.

Solar Screens

In South Florida the conflict between allowing free flow of air through the house, maintaining precious views of nature and keeping out the heat of direct sunlight necessitated solutions involving ingenious handling of roof overhangs, adjustable window and door louvers and dramatic departure from even such devices. In Sarasota Paul Rudolph led the way with the most innovative and attractive means of controlling direct sunlight. Among his earliest examples is the Healy Guest House, know also as the "Cocoon" because of the ingenious use of new roof material.

Figures 22 & 23. Heller Residence ("Birdcage House"), Biscayne Island, Miami Beach, 1949, Igor B. Polevitzky

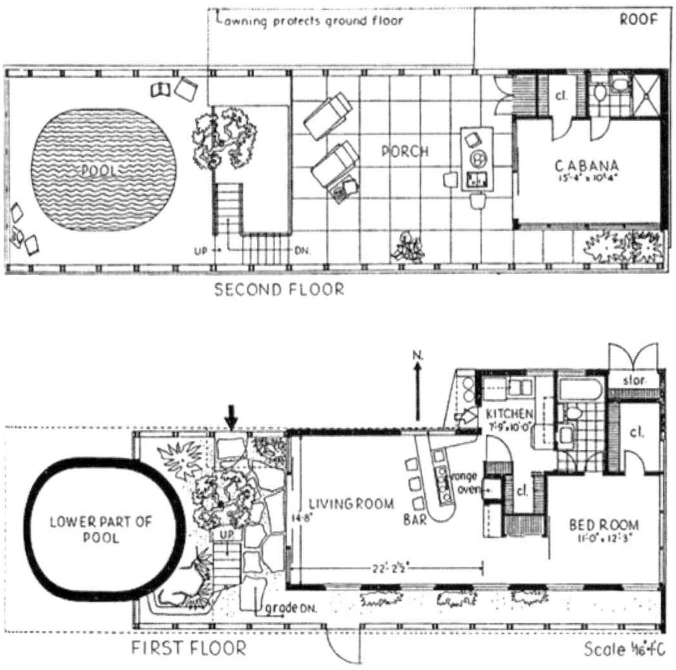

Figures 24. Heller Residence ("Birdcage House"), Biscayne Island, Miami Beach, 1949, Igor B. Polevitzky, Floor Plans

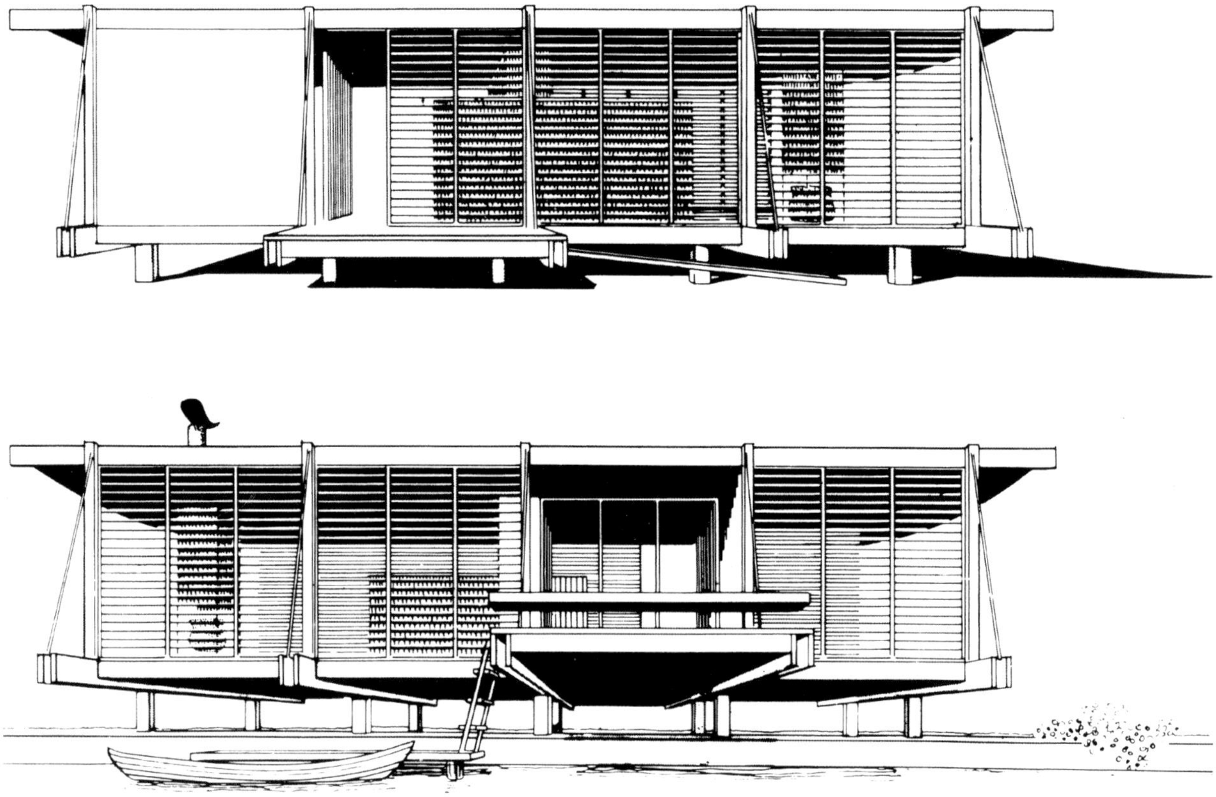

Figure 25. Healy Guest "Cocoon" House, Siesta Key, Sarasota, 1950, Ralph Spencer Twitchell and Paul Marvin Rudolph

The house situated on a narrow strip of land and backed on a bayou is a cottage made famous for its innovative roof. However, not having any roof overhangs along its long street side and waterside facades it is an excellent example of controlling sun rays from entering the house by the use of floor to ceiling adjustable wood louvered windows. This system also provides for privacy, which is in conflict with the need for cross ventilation. It is only logical that the house had to be raised off the ground for flooding protection, which also assists in the process of cross ventilation.

Like the "Cocoon" House, the Walker Guest House was meant for temporary stays in the area. Inspired by standard use of swinging shutters for sun protection and for securing the house while it is not being used, Rudolph created external wood trellises by extending roof beams on sides of this square house and setting them on wood columns. With three bays on each side of the house forming open porches, Rudolph placed swinging panels hinged to the edge of the roof. Each panel can be kept in either horizontal position or at any angle, including closing the sides of the house completely. The mechanism for lowering and raising the panels was achieved by ingenious counterweights suspended from the edge beams. The flexibility of this arrangement and the clarity of the geometry make this little house a foremost example of possibilities of mitigating the environmental factors in the subtropical climate.

The "Umbrella" house designed by Rudolph for Philip Hiss, a progressive developer responsible for much of Sarasota's residential modernism, presents the challenge of protecting the house from sun radiation by putting a box of the dwelling inside another box, a huge pergola. The house, a simple two storey rectangle sits inside a much larger rectangular enclosure that runs perpendicular to the house and contains the swimming pool and patio. The roof of the pergola is supported on thin columns forming the outside box. The top of the pergola is covered with closely spaced wood slats that cast an ever-changing shadow pattern on the house and patio. This unique solution to the sun problem is formally reminiscent of the screened box enveloping the "Birdcage" house in Miami Beach by Polevitzky.

The spatial organization of this house is dictated by its narrow lot and need for privacy. A daring carport and entry are tucked under the second floor bedrooms, with the rest of the house, a double height living, dining and kitchen and screened porch forming the rear. Protected from sunlight by very large roof overhangs with protruding joist

Figure 26. "Umbrella" House, Lido Shores, Sarasota, 1953-54, Ralph Spencer Twitchell and Paul Marvin Rudolph

ends the sides and rear are sheathed with full height sliding glass and screen panels. It is the front of the house that makes a unique statement about sun screening. A projecting vertical panel "floating" in front of the bedroom windows and running the full width of the house is made of a wood grille of thin vertical and horizontal strips dense enough to provide sun protection without acutely compromising views from inside. While the use of external sun protecting grills has its origin in India and North Africa it did not become a widely accepted method of protecting interiors from sun radiation in architecture of the West until just recently. Lately solar panels made with perforated metal grills used by leading world architects have become the latest trend in many building types throughout United States and Europe.

Figure 27. Walker Guest House, Sanibel Island, Fort Myers, 1952-53, Paul Marvin Rudolph

This three storey house takes the expression of sun protection to the most dramatic level by covering the entire glazed ends of the narrow sides of the house and central openings on its long sides with oversized wood louvered panels. The louvers are pitched to the outside for optimum sun angle protection. The resulting heavy horizontal striping that characterizes the exterior is just as pronounced from the inside. This striking and quite effective response to climatic conditions makes this house an excellent example of what it takes to design in Florida.

Figure 28. Harkavy Residence, Lido Shores, Sarasota, 1957-58, Paul Marvin Rudolph

Floating Decks

Ever since 1914 when Le Corbusier demonstrated with his Maison Domino what design freedoms are offered by the use of concrete many architects adopted the principle of horizontal slabs raised above

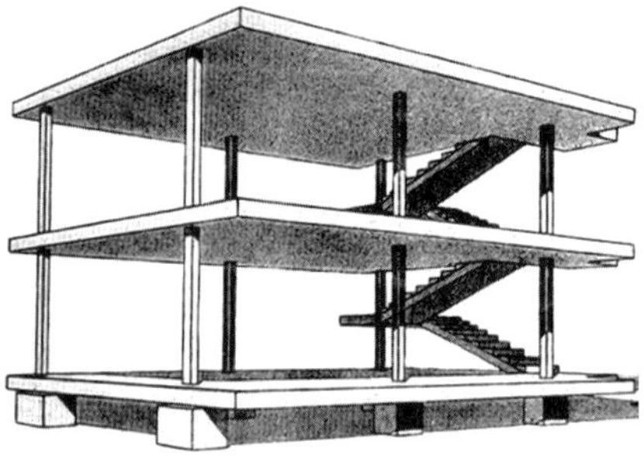

Figures 29. Maison Dom-ino

ground and supported by slim columns. Such construction method provided complete freedom of arrangement of interior partitions, exterior walls and windows, no longer bound by traditional masonry bearing wall restrictions. During the post war years in Florida, young pioneering architects picked up on Le Corbusier and utilized his ideas for adaptation to the local climate. The possibility of floating floor slabs above ground for flood protection and increased air exposure, in combination with the freedom of opening completely all sides of the house to the breezes and views, made all the sense in the world and beats the traditional system of walls sitting heavily on the ground with small holes punched in walls serving as windows.

Rufus Nims was one of the most innovative architects in whose office he trained future leaders of Miami's modernism. He experimented with various construction systems to make the contemporary house harmonious with South Florida climate, utilizing the latest technological advancements. Adler Residence is a foremost example of applying Le Corbusier's principles of freedom of design using concrete slabs in planning for the sub tropics. It consists of a rectangular concrete slab raised off the ground supported on eight thin freestanding concrete columns with edges of the slab cantilevered to create interior and exterior circulation. The roof slab echoes the floor, forming a protective canopy. The ground level is reserved for carport, cabana and utilities while the second floor is a single depth bedroom suite and a combination of kitchen, dining and living. An exterior concrete staircase, reached by walking under the house, connects to the upstairs and becomes a sculptural feature of the generous sized patio with a circular swimming pool. The side of the house facing the bay and parts of the front consist of alternating full height glass or adjustable wood louvered panels. For practical reason the remainder of the exterior walls consist of solid wood panels suspended between floor and ceiling strips of horizontal glass windows.

Figure 30. Adler Residence, Hibiscus Island, Miami Beach, 1952, Rufus Nims

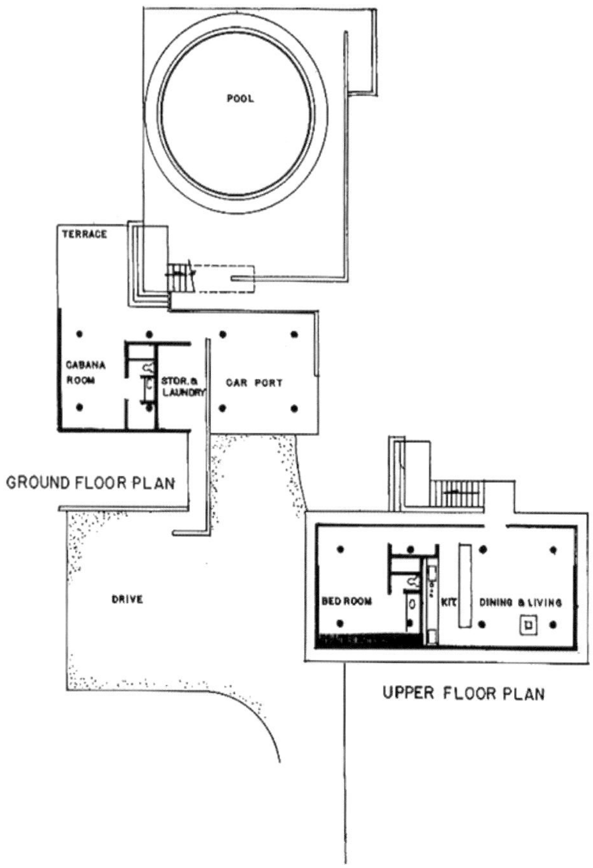

Figure 31. Adler Residence, Hibiscus Island, Miami Beach, 1952, Rufus Nims, Floor Plan

Responding to the nature of the site, climate and need for privacy this utilization of the concrete slab technology solves many of the problems attempted with greater difficulty using more conventional residential forms. The novel architectural form resulting from applying this technology is an important addition to the development of residential design.

As was his habit, Parker not only designed but also built this house with his own hands. Located on a (rare for Miami) sloping site terminating on Biscayne Bay, he took a total advantage of the topography by creating a split level arrangement of spaces distributed on four planes. This was a move intended not only to follow his idol Frank Lloyd Wright's organic principle of site adaptation but to take advantage of views, cross ventilation and privacy. One enters the house via a couple of steps above the carport and arrival court. Dining room and kitchen are located at this level. Seven steps above it is the main living room and master bedroom level with a balcony forming the waterfront edge. Directly below this level are children bedrooms. On a flat roof deck above the master bedroom, and reached by climbing an exterior staircase to a slightly sloping roof of the dining room and few more steps to the deck, is a study/guest room poised like a little glass pavilion. The roof deck serves as a dance floor and roof garden. While this spatial arrangement is unique for Miami it is the handling of vertical enclosure that is of special interest. To capture views and breezes Parker lined the entire length of the two main levels of the house with floor to ceiling mahogany Persiana doors with adjustable wood louvers. The house is clad with, very carefully selected by Parker, oolitic limestone laid in rich ashlar patterns to make it an integral part of the site. Viewed from the low part of the site the house expresses the strong horizontality of its construction method: flat concrete slabs floated on thin columns.

This is a direct utilization of Le Corbusier's principles, even to the use of the roof as a garden. This house received a double honor for being selected by *House Beautiful Magazine* as the "Pace Setter of 1954" and Frank Lloyd Wright, in a rare praise of another architect had glowing comments about this house's organic nature.

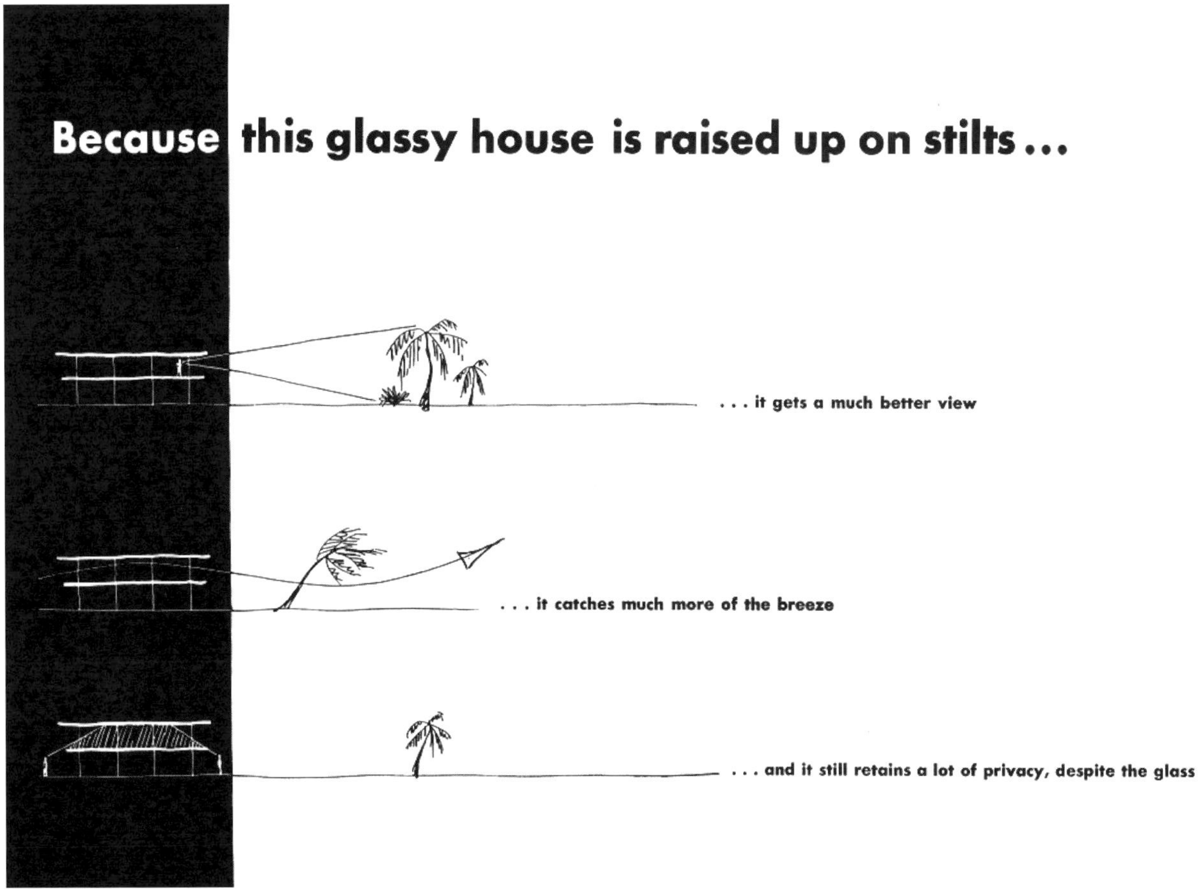

Figure 32. Diagram

Figure 33 & 34. Parker Residence #2 ("Pace Setter 1954"), Coconut Grove, Miami, 1953, Alfred Browning Parker

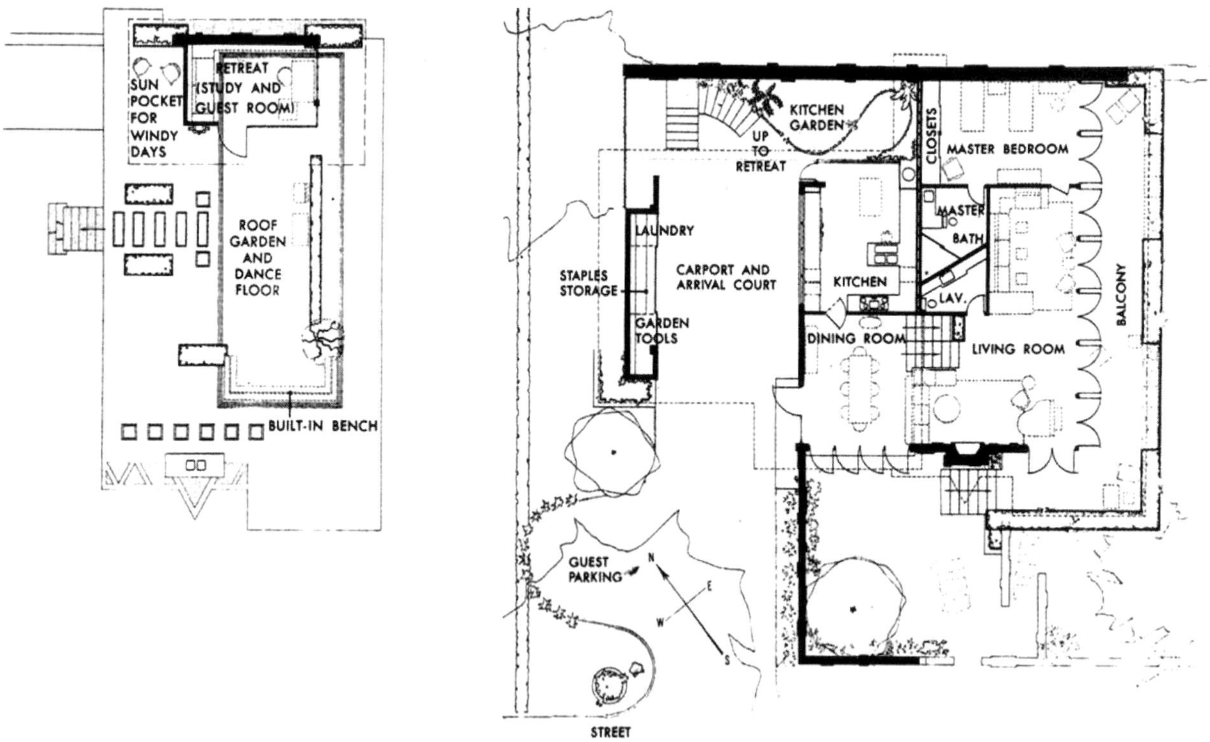

Figure 35. Parker Residence #2 ("Pace Setter 1954"), Coconut Grove, Miami, 1953, Alfred Browning Parker, Floor Plans

Figure 36. Parker Residence #2 ("Pace Setter 1954"), Coconut Grove, Miami, 1953, Alfred Browning Parker

Conclusion

In the 1960s whatever progress was made by these pioneering architects in the area of sustainability was virtually destroyed by the affordability of air conditioning. This new technological advancement made concerns for natural heat reduction and cross ventilation no longer an absolute necessity. Thus, consumers' lack of understanding of virtues of sensible design permitted developers to market sentimentality of traditional styles that proliferated in the ever expanding suburbia.

But it should be an important lesson that in response to social, economic, climatic and technological forces following World War II, the rich variety of solutions by architects throughout Florida showed that even when given problems with great challenges, there is nothing impossible. And it is a trend driven by necessity, intelligence, logic and talent rather than fashions. It is imperative that as a society we do not fall into the pit of replicating solutions that have little if anything to do with the problems at hand. One can invoke the famous statement by Louis H. Sullivan that "every problem carries and suggests its own solution."

THE TROPICAL HOME IN FLORIDA: minimalism, modernity and sustainability

Allan T. Shulman FAIA, LEED AP

Figure 1. The Barnacle (Ralph Munroe Residence), Coconut Grove, 1891-95

In the years following World War II, residential design in South Florida was immersed in regionalism, and a new type known as the Florida Tropical Home emerged. Tropical homes were products of the modern movement, but their design was strongly leveraged on Florida's subtropical climate, distinctive landscapes, and even its established residential vernaculars. These experimental hybrids were raised off the ground to protect from floods, shaded from the sun with adequate roofs, and designed to withstand hurricanes without becoming bunker-like. Building materials such as concrete, stone and wood were exploited in new applications and blended with innovative technologies like glass jalousie windows and plastic mosquito screening. This new and unique modern regional architecture eventually produced its own language as well as its own technology. Landscaped inside and out with native vegetation and well-ventilated to the point of being atmospherically transparent, the tropical home defined a way of living comfortably in the tropics in the years before central air conditioning became prevalent. Moreover, it tapped into the romantic ideal of Florida living, suggesting an open-air lifestyle in concert with the state's natural wonders. As a model of regional architecture, this serial experiment in sustainability was, in its directness and simplicity, far more radical than the current parameters of green design.

Fundamental to the development of the tropical home was the ideal, common in Miami, of constructing an authentic, organic, regional architecture. The roots of this ideal are as diverse as nineteenth-century American Transcendentalism and the turn-of-the-century Arts and Crafts movement in England and the U.S.[1] The organic ideal inspired architects to naturalize broader architectural vocabularies to meet local conditions. Lessons were drawn from early Miami homes, like that for Coconut Grove pioneer Ralph Middleton Munroe, now known as the Barnacle (1891). The Barnacle's lightweight wood construction, raised siting, wrap-around porch and pyramidal roof were models of environmental fitness. Even in the Mediterranean Revival style of the 1920s, whose heavy masonry architecture was poorly adapted to Miami's heat and humidity, sustainable approaches were suggested through the use of narrow building volumes, and by providing a ready vocabulary of indoor-outdoor spaces like patios, loggias, exterior stairways, and pergolas. The organic approach gained prominence in mid-century America through the writings and designs of Frank Lloyd Wright, especially his Usonian houses of the 1930s; however, the task of articulating an authentic architecture for Miami was complicated by the city's newness.

The problem and the opportunity of the tropical home fascinated a generation of postwar architects, who built hundreds of them between 1945 and 1965. Many were prototypes for a type of generalized mass production that eventually eluded the tropical home. A broad group of Miami's most talented architects were involved, the leaders of which were Alfred Browning Parker, Igor Polevitzky, George Reed, Rufus Nims, Russell Pancoast, and Wahl Snyder. Their distinct individual approaches defined Miami's emergent new typology of tropical residential architecture. In the process they also laid out an appropriate architectural identity for their subtropical city--one that was inherently sustainable.

Igor Polevitzky

Igor Polevitzky (1912-1978) was the first of Miami's modern architects to fashion an architecture based thematically on tropical prototypes. Working both before and after World War II, he emphasized the fluidity and ambiguity between indoors and out in improbably light structures. In a series of typological and tectonic experiments that began in the 1930's, Polevitzky amplified the region's characteristic patio and porch until these elements constituted the function, form and image of the home. He further experimented with the home's skin, progressively distorting and reducing the structural envelope from the white planar masses of the Bauhaus into pure volume, or little more than a frame. Polevitzky's transparent indoor-outdoor boxes, dubbed "birdcage houses" by *Architectural Forum*,[2] were recognized nationwide as one of the boldest innovations in tropical domestic architecture.

Figure 2. Sailing Baruch Residence, the "Tropotype" house, 1939, Igor Polevitzky and Thomas Triplett Russell

Polevitzky inaugurated his experiments in 1935 with the concrete "tropotype," a house model designed for the tropics and Miami in particular. The tropotype reinterpreted Florida's vernacular raised cottage type in the architectural syntax of the International Style using cantilevered concrete slabs to provide wrapping outdoor galleries and sunshades.[3] In the late 1930's, with partner T. Trip Russell, he initiated a new line of investigation.

Figure 3. Second Heller House (Birdcage House), Biscayne Island, 1949, Igor Polevitzky

Figure 4. Phillips Residence, Davis Harbor, Miami, 1952, Igor Polevitzky

Figure 5. G.I. House Group, Miami, 1946, Igor Polevitzky, rendering prepared for the South Florida Chapter of the American Institute of Architects' "$5,000 G.I. House" competition

The Greenwald Residence (1936), a.k.a. the "four-stage" house, comprised architectural spaces that thematically progressed from indoors to outdoors through nuanced degrees of enclosure.[4]

Polevitzky's prewar investigations of regional design prototypes expanded into postwar experiments with a low-cost house type designed especially for veterans. At Golden Shores in Sunny Isles, Polevitzky developed a minimalist house type whose basic rectangular module was narrow and one room deep, emphasizing economy, ventilation and connection with the outdoors. Building on ideas first proposed in a 1946 G.I. House design competition, he pioneered a regional approach to prefabrication in which the building's skin, including masonry wall panels and combined window/louver units, were fabricated in the shop and assembled in the field. Screening ran from the overhanging eaves of the wood roof to the slab, providing an inexpensive porch.

In both his prewar experiments and early postwar veterans' housing, Polevitzky tried to break open the masonry boxes that defined ordinary house construction in Miami. By the 1940's, eschewing the expense of a more plastic concrete architecture, Polevitzky turned increasingly to the elemental technology of the screened porch. This ubiquitous feature of the Florida home, typically constructed of wood framing and metal screening, became the typological generator of a new trend in residential architecture. Utilizing improved aluminum or wood framing systems, in combination with newly developed plastic screening systems, Polevitzky progressively innovated the basic rectangular house-box, first by appending a large outdoor living porch, then by transforming the box itself into an outdoor living porch, and later by sculpting the box-porch in relation to enclosed living areas. The plain use of screened walls on these light and airy structures gave the "birdcage" houses their name.

Polevitzky designed the first birdcage, a modest one-story rectangular house with a shed roof, in 1947. Based loosely on the architect's earlier G.I. house model, the first Heller House introduced a covered but open central space that bisected the narrow body of the house, drawing from the strategy of the vernacular Florida Cracker dogtrot. In the open-air center, Polevitzky assembled the essential features of year-round living; the kitchen, dining and living room were contained in a virtual breezeway that could be opened or closed, depending on the weather. The house was equally remarkable, however, for its large, screened patio, which functioned as a seamless extension of the convertible indoor living space. Constructed of aluminum framing and screened in stainless steel mesh, the patio also featured an adjustable roof made of a sliding aluminum awning that could be retracted under the eaves. As *Architectural Forum* remarked, the idea of a screened porch was here "extended to its logical conclusion."[5] Measuring thirty feet by nineteen feet, the patio was almost as large as the house and comprised two separate levels, a small pool and landscaping. The plans designated the patio – a recreational open space that was contiguous with the environment, yet sheltered from mosquitoes – an "outdoor living room."[6]

In the second Heller home for the same client, Polevitzky turned the relationship between house and porch upside down. Here, masonry walls were almost completely discarded, in favor of a taut, diaphanous box-like tent of Lumite plastic mosquito screening. Constructed on concrete platforms, its simple wooden frame and steel trusses supported a partly opaque and partly translucent flat roof. The screened box enclosed a tremendous outdoor area, including a garden shaded by an olive tree and a raised swimming pool. Whereas the aluminum frame of the first Heller house was expressive and even technologically progressive, the later Heller birdcage was neutral and vernacular, shrouding the enclosed spaces while conveying a subtle sense of texture. There may have been no more direct expression of the first underlying principle of the International Style: architecture as volume rather than mass. Only the raised form of a lozenge-shaped swimming pool seemed solid.

The elements of the house hovered on floating concrete decks that were, in effect, platforms for outdoor living. In this way, the second Heller birdcage elaborated on the notion of rooftop living that was popular in Miami before World War II. *House and Garden* emphasized the home's flexibility, noting that "each room within the screened enclosure takes a different approach to the Florida climate: the pool and its terrace are for sun, the deck for breeze, living room for shelter."[7]

The platforms thus offered stages for a variety of experiences, an extension of the nuanced system of enclosure Polevitzky had already introduced in his four-stage indoor-outdoor Greenwald Residence. A small "indoor" bedroom enclosed by exposed and waterproofed concrete blocks was located under the highest living deck, inverting the vertical hierarchy of the traditional American house and offering a refuge in inclement weather. For Polevitzky, the house implied the creation of a tempered outdoor environment for living, rendering most of the protective features of the traditional house mass nearly obsolete.

Polevitzky exploited the tectonic possibilities of the birdcage in a group of houses that tested the range of the birdcage as a building type, and of his own ingenuity in using long-span wood frames and metal trusses. The boldly constructed birdcage frame of the Phillips Residence (1952), the sibylesque strategy of the London Residence (1955) and the fully raised living area of the Gibbs Residence (1955) are standouts of this line of exploration. Each subsequent birdcage intensified the paradox between shelter and garden, solid and void, enclosure and openness. The intersection of more solid masonry construction with the screened frame of a birdcage formed a point of departure for these ambiguities. By emphasizing the interweaving, mirroring, interpenetration and vertical stacking of house elements, Polevitzky amplified the blurring of indoors and outdoors.

Wrapped in the sheerest of skins and unfolding in space, Polevitzky's birdcages reconceived of the Florida home as an atmospheric envelope. The central feature of this fundamentally humanistic ideal was reduction of the polarity between inside and outside. As a house type, the birdcages embodied the intertwining of the modern and primitive, the progressive and traditional: a leitmotif not only of a new regional architecture, but of postwar Miami's culture in general.

Figure 6. Alfred Browning Parker Residence (Pacesetter), Coconut Grove, Florida, 1953, Alfred Browning Parker

Alfred Browning Parker

Among Miami's modernists, Alfred Browning Parker (1916-2011) has been notable for his identification with the American tradition of organic architecture, in the manner of H. H. Richardson, Louis Sullivan, and Frank Lloyd Wright in particular. Like Wright, Parker creates buildings in the belief that architecture can be a harbinger of an authentic regional culture and civilization in Miami. Throughout his career, Parker has forged a dual identity as both a modernist architect and a student of the tropics. His postwar house projects, innovated to fit the characteristically lush landscapes of Miami's Coconut Grove, evidence a great sensitivity to materials and landscape. Parker used native oolitic limestone, wood, and concrete on structures that nestled among that area's wooded hammocks, stone ridges and coastal fringes.

Parker's homes of this era were not simply nativist in their use of materials; they harkened back to a model of self-sufficiency and austere frugality, and to a minimalist ethos. In 1944, Parker used his own labor to build his first Miami home, a rustic cottage that exploited Army surplus components and other materials not controlled by wartime authorities, like oolitic rock for walls and local pine, hand-framed for roofs.[8] A similar austerity can be found in Parker's Trop-Expansible House, designed in 1948 as a model starter home for returning G.I.s. It was unpolitic in the postwar to build more than one actually needed, and considered particularly clever to restrain the house to only its essential components and amenities. The compact Trop-Expansible home could be grown in two ways: its limited interior area could be quickly doubled by opening into an attached screened patio; only as needed, the owners could add on bedrooms and increase living space. In this way resource consumption was minimized, and scalable to real needs.

Figure 7. The Tropex-pansible Home project, 1948, Alfred Browning Parker

Parker's early work reveals a deep appreciation for the specifics of landscape and terrain, and even for the recuperation of difficult or tainted sites. The Chandler (1950) and Hopwood (1951) residences, for instance, were carefully integrated around the perimeter of a former rock pit. Parker transformed the pit floor into a sunken garden, with stairs and ramps connecting to the houses, which were cantilevered from the plinth of rock to enjoy the trade winds and views. The homes' varied, wood-constructed components, clad in the style of Wright's earlier Usonian houses with vertical board and battens, illustrate the architectural vernacular vocabulary of extensive wood decks, overhanging mono-pitch roofs, and projecting wood awning windows.

Parker explored varied typological approaches in the making of a well-ventilated tropical home. One strategy - having overlaps with the work of Marcel Breuer and other modernists - included programmatic dispersion. The Rockson Residence (1951) in Miami was functionally organized in three zones (bedrooms, service areas and living area), each constituting a separate clerestoried pavilion. These were linked with screened breezeways under connecting roofs.[9] Parker used an even more dispersed layout in the Coconut Grove house he designed and built for his mother, Jewell Parker, in 1958. This small compound had living and sleeping spaces assembled under one great pyramidal roof, and a guest house under another smaller one. The house's broad sheltering roofs provided a breezy retreat from Miami's heat; fully wrapping terraces and verandas extended the indoor living space into the yard.

Parker's speculative investigation of the tropical home found an apotheosis in 1954 in the residence he designed and built for himself in Coconut Grove. This terraced home broke with the vocabulary of wood construction Parker established in his early houses. In its place, he developed a language based on bold contrapositions of cantilevered concrete slabs, vertical oolitic limestone walls, and wood persiana (louvered) doors. The stone walls were notably fashioned of the same oolitic material as the bluff on which the house stood. Battered for effect, they anchored the structure and channeled views and airflow through its living spaces. Similar stone walls defined the property edges, and separated the different levels of the terraced site. The tray-like concrete floors were staggered to produce a split-level design that took advantage of the sloping site. Parker devised an unconventional internal organization, using half-level stairs to draw visitors from the dining room up to the main living level, where the terraces commanded views of Biscayne Bay. Here, all was warmth and natural materials: terrazzo floors, cork ceilings, mahogany doors, ashlar stone and wood paneled walls, as well as built-in wood furniture laced with open webbing, caning, or leather. Below the living area, literally carved into the rock of the coastal ridge, were the children's bedrooms. While most postwar architects abandoned the roof deck, preferring outdoor spaces closer to the ground and in screened enclosures, Parker furnished his roof with a 2,500 square-foot white tiled dance floor and what he called a sky garden, with built-in seating and a hibachi grill. The roof deck created an airy entertainment space where, as *House Beautiful* suggested, "You hose away the crumbs."[10]

Parker's house was a powerful synthesis of his own ideals, and virtually a manifesto of organic principles, tropical design and self-sufficiency. The comprehensive treatment of the structure, filling the entire November, 1953 issue of *House Beautiful* as its 1954 "Pacesetter," transformed this new synthesis into a closely-watched case study of authentic and modern Florida living. Parker's organic houses were calculated to spring from the earth; through rigorous experimentation with materials and form, Parker has been able to redefine the boundary between building and landscape.

Figure 8. Coslow Residence, Palm Island, Miami Beach. Rufus Nims, 1968.

Rufus Nims

In contrast to Polevitzky and Parker, Rufus Nims (1913-2005) took primary inspiration from exploring the structural systems appropriate to tropical architecture. Although he worked in a variety of materials, his explorations of concrete were especially provocative. Beginning in 1949, Nims designed a series of concrete houses that sandwiched a raised floor of open-plan living space between flat concrete plates. Later, he built homes that employed the structural properties of ferro-cement to create free-form concrete shells. Nims utilized simple, inexpensive and modern structural frameworks to produce technically innovative housing prototypes that synthesized the most functional and expressive possibilities of concrete.

Modern concrete homes departed from Miami's established homebuilding technologies, which by the 1940s entailed masonry construction in combination with wood framing. Nims eschewed these; exploiting the material for its economic, typological and atmospheric qualities, he pioneered its use in home construction, where the material served as a badge of both modernity and tropicality. His use of concrete further implied connections with the substance and spirit of tropicalist architecture in Latin America, where postwar architects were already using a concrete-based architectural syntax inspired by the work of Le Corbusier in the development of a new formal expression.

Nims developed his first concrete home prototype – a "concrete plate home" – in the residence for Charles Roman in the Morningside neighborhood of Miami (1949). Concrete plate structures comprised a system of smooth concrete slabs (with no visible beams) held aloft on columnar supports. Le Corbusier had theorized this construction type in his 1914 concrete house prototype, the Maison Domino. The sandwich logic of plate houses was indeed a modernist device; Nims' experiments with the type paralleled the contemporary work of architects like Mies van der Rohe (the iconic glass Farnsworth House in Plano, Illinois [1950]), Paul Rudolph (the Lamolithic and Revere prototype houses [1948] and the Leavengood Residence [1950-51]), and Oscar Niemeyer's Santa Barbara beach house (1948) and Canoas House (1953-54).

The raised wood houses of the vernacular Florida Cracker homestead were an even more direct inspiration for Nims. Feather-light in their repose on the wet Florida soil, their open walls and broad sheltering roofs resonated with modern architects involved in defining a regional architecture. Nims' conspicuously light and transparent plate houses can be understood as a modernist restructuring of the vernacular logic of raised living areas, sheltering roofs and breathable walls. Beyond the advantages of hurricane and termite resistance, the raised concrete house offered superior views and enjoyed better breezes and fewer bugs; it was also more private, notwithstanding the nearly total atmospheric transparency of its walls. The raised house also created shaded outdoor space in equal measure to enclosed building volume, and provided a natural space for the car. He conceived of the plate house as a "maison-type" for Miami, a transformation of its vernacular Cracker antecedents for modern times. It rationalized the relationship of the modern tropical home to Miami's waterfront landscape, where flood-prone neighborhoods promised potentially exotic, aquatic recreation. The type was so new to Miami that Nims fabricated

Figure 9. Hibiscus (Adler) Guest Cottage, Hibiscus Island, Miami Beach. Rufus Nims, 1952.

all the necessary formwork and built the house himself, a pattern of professional involvement and constructive autonomy he would repeat many times in order to realize his architectural vision.

When completed, the Roman House effectively floated over its suburban context, as well as its own lot. A ground-floor cabana and parking were tucked beneath the house and surrounded by landscaped patios. The discreet seclusion of house from the yard was enhanced by the single winding concrete stair that connected them. Its elevated living areas were circumscribed into the rectangular floor plate of a single concrete slab. Liberated from structural concerns by the twelve concrete piers that carried the roof and floor directly into the pilings, the house had an open plan that allowed rooms to flow freely into each other and out to the landscape. Surrounding the living area, panelized walls were recessed from the slab edge for protection from the rain. As a skin, these panels conveyed an array of tectonic impressions. Balancing privacy and transparency to the breezes, solid wood exterior panels floated between ribbon-like glass vent panels at the floor and ceiling levels. Full height walls of jalousie glass on the east side further ventilated the house, and transformed the view toward nearby Biscayne Bay into what Nims called "visual wallpaper." Green plastic screening, green glass and green curtains were employed to soften the light.

The increasing cost of formed concrete during the 1950s limited the application of raised concrete houses, although Nims continued to explore the constructive logic in more efficient applications. He experimented with sprayed lightweight concrete aggregate, often called ferro-cement or "shotcrete" construction. After World War II, the technique was commonly applied to the development of thin shell structures. The contemporary work of Pier Luigi Nervi in Italy, Felix Candela in Mexico and Milo Ketchum and Anton Tedesko in the U.S. had illustrated a radical new anatomy of structural forms. Nims was similarly interested in the intersection between efficient engineering and artistic form. His genius lay in exploiting, systematizing and devolving the technique to the scale of a home, where it responded to domestic economies and everyday living needs. At the Coslow Residence on Palm Island in Miami Beach (1968), Nims sheltered the house with an interconnected series of hyperbolic parabaloids, or "hypars," that formed a vaulted canopy of peaks and valleys. Under this canopy, the house was laid out organically into ameoba-like spaces free of the geometry of the vaulted roof. The organic spaces of the house merged into the landscape continuum of the site, abundant foliage, channeling breezes and the movements of body and spirit.

It is an irony of concrete construction that a material so heavy could be construed into a light and airy architecture so appropriate to the tropics. Nims decisively employed concrete's inherent potential to create a durable yet economical and livable shell, creating a variety of singular works that responded to the particular needs of individual clients. Idiosyncratic as they may be, these homes relayed broad ideals about domesticity in a hot and humid climate: Each can be viewed as a prototype, the seed of an idea for mass production. They defined, in their collective logic, an extraordinary synthesis of structure, space and lifestyle calibrated to create a new regional architecture.

The Shape of Things to Come

Polevitzky, Parker, and Nims a range of novel solutions that echoed back and forth among them and their peers, constituted a distinct new architectural culture in Miami. Reflected in newspaper and magazine feature articles, this culture was the basis for a real regional discourse on architecture and the environment. This discourse paralleled the discourses of modern architecture in other regions (the work of the Sarasota School and Brazilian modernists come to mind), but had a distinct Miami flavor; it contributed to the construction of an authentic identity that was at the heart of Miami's postwar quest for rootedness. The Florida tropical home ideal reached its apex in the 1960's, then quickly faded to obscurity as central air conditioning, security consciousness and a cultural drift toward material profligacy eroded its popularity and vitality. Today, very few of these tropical homes survive; of those that remain, fewer retain their original design objectives of atmospheric transparency. Beyond the physical remnants, the ideals themselves are little understood. The nature of the tropical home as a theoretical construct, as a lifestyle generator, and an aesthetic, has been overshadowed by today's discourse about sustainability, with its focus on metrics, technology, and generalized standards of comfort. In contrast, the tropical home was a visible badge of rootedness. It expressed, in its details and form, a lifestyle in tune with the climate. Most importantly, it explored what it means to live sustainably, not just technically, but spiritually.

Endnotes

[1] Both Transcendentalism and the Arts and Crafts movements were a response to perceived negative social consequences of the Industrial Revolution- particularly human alienation from nature and individual creative instincts. Transcendentalists like Ralph Waldo Emerson and Walt Whitman reacted to the mechanization of society by espousing principles of individual self-reliance in solitude with nature. Arts and Crafts design processes centralized natural imagery and championed a rustic authenticity that eluded assembly line mass production. As early as 1908 Frank Lloyd Wright described an "organic architecture" that sought to transfer nature's principles to the built environment. See Kimberly Elman, "Frank Lloyd Wright and the Principles of Organic Architecture," www.pbs.org/flw/legacy/essay1.htm
[2] "Bird-Cage House," *Architectural Forum* (May 1950): 92, 138-141.
[3] The "tropotype" model – so named because it was devised specifically to suit the Florida sub-tropics – was first designed as a house prototype for the Seaway Corporation and built in 1935 in Surfside. The idea was borrowed from the raised cottages common in the American Southeast. Polevitzky gave the scheme a modern face, constructing it largely of concrete and articulating it in cubic and planar terms. The living room and bedrooms were located upstairs, having access through wide French doors to a wrapping gallery; the kitchen, dining room and parking are on the ground floor. "A Tropotype Scheme for Florida," *Architectural Record* 87 (March 1940): 74.
[4] The Hartman Residence on Allison Island in Miami Beach (1939) was described as expressing four stages of indoor-outdoor living. Between the living room and backyard terrace, a sequence of spaces progressively unfolded toward the environment. "Four Stages of Indoor-Outdoor Living," *Architectural Record* 96 (November 1944): 68.
[5] "Tropical House with Aluminum Screened Porch for Outdoor Living," *Architectural Forum* (April 1948): 119.
[6] Ibid.
[7] "Wrapped in a plastic screen," *House and Garden* (July 1950): 54.
[8] "They built this house for $1,200…" *House Beautiful* 88 (March 1946): 106-107
[9] "A new architecture for tropical Florida: how to be comfortable (summer and winter) despite heat, glare, rain, rots, hurricanes and bugs," *Architectural Forum* 94 (February 1951): 131-139
[10] "The Starlight Roof," *House Beautiful* 95 (November 1953): 259.

Image Sources

Figure 1. *The Barnacle (Ralph Munroe Residence)*, Courtesy of History Miami, Ralph Munroe Collection.
Figure 2. *Sailing Baruch Residence*, Courtesy of History Miami, Igor Polevitzky Collection.
Figure 3. *Second Heller House (Birdcage House)*, Photograph by Ezra Stoller, Courtesy of History Miami, Igor Polevitzky Collection.
Figure 4. *Phillips Residence*, Photograph by Rada Photography, Courtesy of History Miami, Rada Collection.
Figure 5. *G.I. House Group*, Rendering prepared for the South Florida Chapter of the American Institute of Architects' "$5,000 G.I. House" competition, Courtesy of History Miami, Igor Polevitzky Collection.
Figure 6. *Alfred Browning Parker Residence (1954 Pacesetter)*, Courtesy of the Bass Museum of Art.
Figure 7. *The Tropex-pansible Home project*, Courtesy of the University of Florida, Smathers Libraries, Alfred Browning Parker Collection.
Figure 8. *Coslow Residence*, Courtesy of the University of Florida, Smathers Libraries, Rufus Nims Collection.
Figure 9. *Hibiscus (Adler) Guest Cottage*, Photograph by Jan Hankowski. From cover of *Florida Architecture* (1954-55).

TRADITIONS OF SUSTAINABLE GREEN ARCHITECTURE IN SOUTH FLORIDA

Thorn Grafton, AIA, LEED AP BD+C

A high point in the long evolution toward a sustainable architecture for South Florida was documented in a panel discussion about the work of three South Florida mid-20th Century Modernist Architects. Alfred Browning Parker, Peter Jefferson, and George Reed are architects renowned for their houses that become, along with their fortunate residents, part of the site and environment. This discussion, which I had the privilege to introduce and moderate, was revealing not only of their works but also of the philosophies behind the work. As an introduction to presentations by these distinguished architects, I was asked to provide my own perspective on the question of sustainability in our South Florida built environment.

The recent Green Movement in Architecture has spread across the landscape of design professionals like a forester's "controlled burn," eradicating harmful invasive species and reintroducing depleted nutrients into the soil. Clearly this initiative is necessary in South Florida in the first decade of the 21st Century - as we are catching our breath after unprecedented growth. Other than bringing some new residents and businesses downtown, we generally missed the chance to increase our long term sustainability, as only a few of the new projects were designed and constructed to green standards. Yet even if most of these projects had achieved high levels of LEED™ certification, that in itself will not allow us to achieve a truly sustainable architecture. For that, every designer needs broad perspective on the evolution of design over time in our unique place.

In a relationship with abundant nature, indigenous peoples of centuries past certainly built sustainable buildings. Relatively small populations and the use of simple technologies and available materials made this possible. As green architect and educator William McDonough taught us, the simple mathematics of ecological balance is expressed as Waste = Food. Seminole chickee huts - palm thatch over durable cypress logs notched and strapped together - were totally organic. They could be quickly deconstructed and reconstructed as needed to allow tribes to follow food or increase distance from threats. Indigenous peoples adopted lessons from nature to improve their survival, a practice known today as biomimicry. The structural design of chickees was informed by the way palms withstand hurricanes, by shedding their fronds, leaving the cylindrical trunks unaffected. Similar building techniques had been used by the indigenous Tequesta culture that disappeared shortly after Spanish explorers arrived. We have one structural record of their footprint of years of settlement here 2,000 years ago - post holes and basins cut into the limerock at the 38' diameter "Miami Circle." This site, whatever its purpose, was located at the confluence of river and bay, a location once abounding with life. Even today, my own estimation is that a 20 mile diameter circle drawn from this point at the mouth of the Miami River will encompass more living species than a similar 20 mile circle surrounding any other major North American urban area. An awareness of this historic biodiversity, now in recession, must bring additional responsibility to the environmental impacts of unchecked prosperity.

Figure 1. Chickee

Figure 2. Smiths Casino

Wood frame vernacular buildings started the architecture of early Miami. Of the many houses and commercial structures built before 1926, stellar examples include South Dade's William T. Anderson's General Store (Anderson's Corners) in 1912, and Smith's Casino, the first building on Miami Beach, other than squatter's cabins. This lovely delicate pavilion certainly

Figure 3. *Holmes Residence*, Courtesy of Peter Jefferson.

Figure 4. Vizcaya Museum & Garden, Coral Gables, Miami

looked like a LEED Platinum building – it sported a full windmill, cisterns and an elevated open deck under a steep pitched wood shingle roof. These simple buildings were built with our very few locally-available building materials (beyond the aforementioned Cypress), such as Dade County Pine and oolitic limerock. The pine, *Pinus Elliotti, var. Densa*, is the basic Southern Yellow Pine, growing slowly in the limerock under a thin layer of organic material. The growth rings are much closer together than the standard SYP, and the resultant density of the wood makes it resistant to termite infestation, if not in contact with the ground or leaky plumbing. Driving nails into this vintage lumber today requires drilling starter holes. The oolitic limerock, soft and white when extracted, hardens as it dries but remains porous so it is suitable only as a facing or for site walls. "Keystone" or coral stone is similar, yet because it is formed from the fossilized remains of living corals, the pattern of coral polyps appear when slabs are sawn. The slabs served as exterior pavers and wall facing in our Mediterranean Revival buildings and were sometimes filled with tinted stucco and honed to a smooth finish for use in Art Deco building walls in the 1930's. Sustainable these materials are not. Keystone was strip mined from Key Largo to Windley Key, and despite waning supplies, keystone is still sold today. Slow growing Dade County Pine ceased commercial production after WWII, as cheap concrete block was in full production. The few protected stands of local pine were devastated by Hurricane Andrew, though many young trees are visible again. Cypress in Florida is harvested and replanted on managed tree farms, yet the growth rate is slow enough and the commercial value high enough for us to keep an eye on protected natural Cypress stands.

The utilitarian wood frame vernacular buildings did not require architects or often rise to the level of architecture. A true architecture would first blossom here with Mediterranean-Revival design. On a slightly domed grotto ceiling in a garden pavilion at Vizcaya, hundreds of identically sized orange mollusk shells and bleached rose corals are concentrically arranged. At Vizcaya Museum & Garden, the 1916 architectural icon of our region defined by high style and gilded artifice imported from other times and places, there is this documentation of the natural history of Biscayne Bay integrated with architecture. That these animals were collected live and cemented in place to inspire us with the beauty and abundance of our resources, recalls John James Audubon shooting birds in the Keys and Everglades so that he could draw them with supreme accuracy. These examples reveal that our reverence for nature included an element of entitlement, which today we must reconsider.

The Mediterranean-Revival style is somewhat of an invasive species brought back from our travels and used without understanding. Early occupants of Mediterranean-Revival buildings could not always live comfortably in these

Figure 5. Pancoast Residence, Miami

stuccoed masonry buildings. My grandfather, architect Russell T. Pancoast, FAIA, began his career by designing over 50 such structures in the 1920's and early 1930's in response to the clamour inspired by the glamorous Vizcaya. He lived in a Med-Rev home of his own design, and his experience led him to abandon the style by the mid-1930's, and begin to advocate in the profession for architecture more responsive to our hot-humid climate. The Mediterranean seacoasts which provided inspiration for the style are considerably further north in latitude, drier, and with a larger daily temperature swing than South Florida. Buildings with thick walls transfer unwanted heat inward at night. Small windows don't promote cross ventilation, and a lack of overhangs requires them to be closed during frequent rainfall.

International influences in architecture helped produce our take on Art Deco of the 1930's. This evolution allowed some progress toward a more regional architecture, with breezy expanses of operable windows, protected from sun and rain by eyebrow overhangs. The new glass blocks translated bright daylight into visual poetry inside. Figurative representations of our abundant nature seemed appropriate to cast into facades or etch into fenestration, as this subtropical land increasingly catered to budget-conscious factory workers and other vacationing snowbirds. To paraphrase Leicester Hemingway, Ernest's brother, it was as if this new architecture that was replacing the stodgy Spanish style was helping to bring the Great Depression to an end. With their rounded corners, fluid lines and sense of whimsy, South Florida's Art Deco or Tropical Modern buildings made people feel optimistic again. This ability for the built environment to so positively affect the human spirit is an often overlooked aspect of sustainable design, suggesting the even more aspirational name of 'regenerative' design. South Miami Beach is a phenomenal fabric woven by multiple architects who were not collaborating as much as they were spontaneously improvising on a common theme. This was also the decade when the turkey vultures migrating from the cliffs of Hinckley, Ohio, adopted the ziggurat top of the Dade County Courthouse (1933) as their roost, with the stepped pyramid providing uplift at take-off. The macabre, but graceful visitors faithfully return from October to March each year. Our tallest tower became a symbol of symbiosis, though one the Chamber of Commerce never touted. Some of the black buzzards now alight on upper balconies of the new white condo towers… an image one might expect in a Carl Hiaasen novel.

Our timeline brings us to the three South Florida Architects who launched their careers in Miami after WWII. The conference had the added benefit of Architect Jan Hochstim's participation. He is Professor of Architecture at the University of Miami and the author of *Florida Modern*, a valuable book which traces the work of many Florida Architects, including these three. Hochstim followed presentations by Peter Jefferson, George Reed and Alfred

Figure 6. Mass Residence, Palm Beach, 1954, Alfred Browning Parker

Figure 7. Osman Residence, Key Biscayne, Miami, 1964-67, George F. Reed

Browning Parker with a deeper drilling into the techniques and environmental benefits of their work. *Florida Modern* documents the many examples of houses that would certainly earn high levels of green certification today, yet at the time were the product of creative intuition in an age before the widespread use of air conditioning. These three architects were part of a group that created locally-appropriate architecture through the design of naturally ventilated space, the use of regionally produced materials, and crafting harmony with site and landscape.

Alfred Browning Parker was a disciple of Frank Lloyd Wright. Parker's body of work translates Wright's principles of organic architecture to this climate perfectly, and he is perhaps the only South Florida architect whose work earned the written praised of the master himself (as quoted in *Florida Modern*). Often lifted into the breeze above open ground level rooms, Parker's houses were nonetheless solidly rooted to the ground with rustic keystone masonry for shear walls, columns and tiered garden patios. The interiors were also dramatically composed, with open mezzanines overlooking public spaces. Natural woods were used throughout the interior; heavy timber framing, tidewater red cypress paneling, cedar shingles, and tropical mahogany doors and furniture. As a young architect interviewing in his Coconut Grove office, he noticed my wide eyes admiring his large conference table, a giant piece of dark red wood about 5" thick with no straight edges. "We brought several of these slabs of Mahogany up from Honduras," Parker informed me. Then he went on to tell me how he had personally worked as a mason and carpenter on the building surrounding us, originally built as his first house in 1945 (he often performed physical work on houses he designed). Truly a master builder, those at the University of Miami conference were also treated to his skill as a storyteller (ask us about "The Turtle"). Parker in 1949 was my father's professor of architecture at the University of Florida. Amazingly, in 2009 at the age of 93, he was teaching architecture again in Gainesville, where he had recently completed a new house for himself.

A native Miamian, soft-spoken George Reed was an architect's architect. Although Reed passed away recently, his body of work remains a high water mark of skillful design, earning him over 20 design awards from his profession. Starting out apprenticed to the venerable Miami architect Rufus Nims, Reed's understanding of local climate and environment led him to invent an iconic typology for our area, which some have called the Pod House. The Osman House is a perfect example – three perfectly square pods covered with pyramidal roofs having substantial overhangs all around, yet each a different size and set at different heights above grade, connected with footbridges and arranged around a lap pool and interspersed with tropical landscape. The flexibility of the concept easily allows the incorporation of existing trees. He was able to maximize perimeter and porosity in a way that seemed beneficial to life. Reed's audacity was breaking the functions of a house apart and not covering the connections between them. "But what about the rain?" critics would ask. "Delightful, isn't it," he would respond.

Peter Augustus Jefferson's design education had enamored him of Wright's work, so it was not long after he moved to Miami in 1954 that he was working in Al Parker's office. Jefferson shared with Parker the expertise of having worked as a mason and carpenter. After a few years with Parker, Jefferson opened his practice in 1959. He began to produce well-crafted houses noted for the way outdoor living spaces extended the rooms within. His balconies, verandas, and loggias were integrally designed. Examples of Jefferson's work included in *Florida Modern* employ varying design responses to both jungle hammock and waterfront conditions. He and his wife Joan moved to Stuart in 1968 and opened a bed-and-breakfast with a captivating waterfront view. They were soon leaders in an initiative that created a walkable and commercially successful downtown that retained its small town character. Born in West Virginia and educated in Michigan, Jefferson nonetheless excelled in subtropical architecture.

Figure 8. Collins Residence, Coconut Grove, Miami, 1961, Peter Augustus Jefferson

Figure 11. Pancoast Residence, Snapper Creek Estates, 1960, Lester C. Pancoast

The work of these 3 architects became very influential to those who shared their belief that architecture could communicate a sense of what is locally appropriate and in balance with the natural world. One of those was Lester C. Pancoast, son of Russell and Kay Pancoast. The primary designer of a modern lakefront house for his architect / artist parents in Snapper Creek Estates (also shown in *Florida Modern*), Lester Pancoast's definitive influence was the fusion of building and landscape he found on travels to Japan. This house completed in 1960 was a long rectangle on a north-south axis, typically the incorrect orientation for a passive energy efficient house. However, the frequently open sliding glass doors allowed this house to become a wide air scoop for the prevailing breeze across the lake. A tall hardwood hammock shaded the house from the west. Wide covered areas (*Engawas*, in Japanese) protected the house, at waters edge on the east, and on the west partially covering a zen garden. Lester Pancoast left his father's firm to found his own in the late 1960's, and passion gravitated toward landscape architecture later in his career. In the years before his passing in 2003, he was also a prolific watercolor artist acclaimed for his images of tropical flora captured in radiant translucence.

Other sustainable design initiatives paralleled and followed the wisdom of these Mid-Century architects, although the overall trend in the region for decades to come would be conspicuously consumptive. The Miami Modern or MiMo movement, while not as cohesive as the Art Deco fabric, continued the idea of architecture as personification of community. Emerging post-war technology and materials advances were incorporated in architecture with a liberated sense of style and playfulness (occasionally venturing into Kitsch), as TV and the lure of the Tropics brought waves of tourists. Unfortunately, this was also the time we turned our backs on the previously pervasive solar hot water collectors of the 1930's, and cooking with natural gas, because, as the TV cartoon character Ready Kilowatt told us, "There's no match for flameless electric living!" Coal-fired power and gasoline were dirt cheap. Servicemen and women, thousands of whom had come to Miami for R & R during the war, came back to settle and raise families, and now there was a baby boom going on. I-95 cut through Overtown, and new connecting ribbons sent us toward the Everglades. The sprawl consumed farmland, shops mutated to wondrous malls, downtown was ignored – you get the drift.

The introduction of affordable building air conditioning technology during the late 1950's and early 1960's was motivated primarily by the laudable goals of convenience and comfort. However, as air conditioning became a de facto requirement for virtually all non-residential buildings, our architecture lost much of its regional character. An example of this design expediency was the mid-1960's addition of air conditioning to Miami Senior High School, designed for flow-through ventilation in 1927. The work included removing most of the large expanses of original steel projecting windows, leaving in their place masonry infill with a narrow aluminum window at each end of the opening. Also the decorative cast stone vents located high on hallway walls broken to install the ducts, and ceilings throughout were lowered. At the time this approach was easy to rationalize - the corroding window hardware made operation difficult, and air conditioning systems were not efficient, so less heat gain in a building with no overhangs was part of the design objective. Still, the sacrifice of daylighting in classrooms, and the loss of historic character in what would become a National Historic Landmark were challenges we inherited as architects for the historic rehabilitation and expansion of the school in 2006. To discover that it was my forbearer's firm that carried out the orders of the School District has provided a little extra personal motivation. Somewhat ironically, just before the Miami High air conditioning, the Pancoast firm completed the non-air conditioned Robert King High Towers, an award winning multi-story public housing development for the elderly. The building faces southeast and is only one apartment deep to maximize ventilation. The covered exterior walkways are subject to rain, and this design feature

Figure 9. Mailman Center, Miami, Russell Pancoast Architects

Figure 10. Miami-Dade Community College, Kendall Campus, Russell Pancoast Architects.

is now seldom repeated due to "inconvenience."

Later in the 1960's, as the scale of our civic and commercial buildings increased, an expressively bold and "brutal" architecture emerged. The unfinished concrete, with added textures or formwork revealed, took some getting use to for a culture accustomed to painted stucco. Some of the best examples are the early campuses of Miami-Dade Community College, the Mailman Center for Child Development and the iconic Miami Marine Stadium, all by Russell Pancoast's firm which by then was growing large. These met a key goal for green buildings – durability. Exposed concrete needs only an infrequent pressure cleaning. In the case of the Marine Stadium, the unprecedented clamshell cantilever is showing some signs of spall, to be expected with its feet planted in the saltwater of Biscayne Bay. Hilario Candela's heroic design has rallied not only local preservation heroes, but national and international ones as well to its defense. The question has arisen here before – will what the rest of the world considers an incomparable treasure rise up high enough on our own local list of concerns to save it?

An appealing idea - that the appropriateness and strength of design can inoculate buildings or even neighborhoods with the power to heal not only themselves, but in the process, the larger community. We saw this happen on south Miami Beach in the late 1970's and 1980's, with the creation of historic architectural districts and the institutionalization of a preservation ethic. A movement that was at first controversial and derided as anti-progressive, became over time an engine of sustainable development, yielding a triple bottom line of environmental, economic and social equity. This learning process has helped Miami become a crucible for architectural ideologies, both contrasting and complimentary. Among the many missteps is Miami's post-modern downtown Cultural Center, which was a revival of Mediterranean-Revival. Unfortunately the double revivals canceled each other out, and left us a hilltop fortification of culture centered on a vast and empty sun-drenched plaza. Furthermore, our biggest potential misstep would be to expand the Urban Development Boundary, and continue to rely on greenfield development.

From the early 1990's onward South Florida academic and design leaders have been defining the "isms" or doctrines on how to achieve sustainable urban environments. In the important goal of pedestrian friendly, diverse communities, the focus should be on synergistic locations and coherent scale of infill development. We need a more committed search for a viable relationship between original ecosystems and continued development. Both of these conditions should be actively mapped into the planning process to get at the essence of place. Green-washing and formulaic design can be thereby avoided.

Designers should also look to other hot and humid zones globally for inspiration. The work of Geoffrey Bawa of Sri Lanka is one such example. Bawa's buildings adapt comfortably to a hot-humid climate, without air-conditioning. Some of his walled houses in urban areas became sort of the inverse of Reed's pod houses – they covered larger portions of the lot but were perforated by a series of inner courtyards. Another typology Bawa used was the wide open but roofed second floor serving as living space, as the upper roof keeps the sun off the actual roof deck of the enclosed space below.

Protecting and restoring our planet's biodiversity is the core of a sustainable design challenge which is Here and Now. Buildings, city streets, parking lots, transportation corridors, storm drainage, and water treatment facilities will all be required to become living, regenerative systems. Our rooftops and buildings will need to provide most of the same ecosystem services as the natural ground – the production of food and energy, water filtration, and the stabilization of temperature and air quality. We will have to create massive systems to mitigate and hopefully heal the worst symptoms of climate change - the impending scarcity of food and water, and sea level rise. The many actions required to regain our global ecological balance always begin locally, and local sustainable traditions require daily redefinition.

Figure 11. South Florida Residence, XX Century, Alfred Browning Parker

Image courtesy of Thomas A. Spain

HISTORIC PRESERVATION
a 'green' alternative: case studies

HISTORIC PRESERVATION:
a green alternative[1]

Sonia R. Cháo

Although the Earth's surface temperatures have always fluctuated, their logarithmic climb, over the past century, are directly attributable to human and industrial activities that have altered the chemical composition of the atmosphere, influencing global climate patterns, the quantity, and quality of natural resources and human settlements. As buildings and cities are amongst the largest contributors towards global warming,[2] it stand to reason that sustainable architecture and urbanism, which address interconnected environmental, social and economic concerns, partnered with the preservation of historic, natural and cultural resources, are at the heart of the solution.

The Problem:
The 'anthropogenic degradation' of the environment

Climate change is a fact, and attempts to reduce U.S. energy consumption on a national scale are fundamental. Leading culprits associated with the anthropogenic degradation of the environment include: development patterns, infrastructure deficits, automobile-dependency, building designs, farming practices, and the production of goods. According to the U.S. Energy Information Administration, buildings are the largest consumers of energy in the nation. The energy needed for the construction and operation of North America's building stock represents over 70% of the utilization of energy derived from coal-fired power plants. The nation's appetite for energy consumption has not decreased in any significant manner, thus hundreds of additional coal-fired power plants are under construction, even though they are the most polluting source of fossil fuel derived energy. "Slowing the growth rate of GHG emissions and then reversing it over the next ten years is the key to keeping global warming under one degree centigrade (°C) above today's level. It will require immediate action and a concerted global effort."[3]

The Challenges:
Social Equity, Economic Development, and Environmental Conservation

Climate change affects a broad range of realities, including ecological systems, water supply, food production, coastal infrastructure, and human health, resulting in extreme weather conditions, rising sea levels, the scarcity of basic needs such as water and food, the scaring of the land and seas, and, the eradication of plant and animal species. Add to this mix the stifling reality of economic stagnation with widening gaps between the rich and the poor, social segregation, unsustainable human settlements patterns, energy-guzzling buildings and over-consumption of resources--with no end in sight for most of these practices - and, the future seems ominous indeed.

The Responses:
The Silent Partner - Historic Preservation

Researchers project that as global population rises so too will the rate of renovation and construction of buildings. Currently the U.S. building stock is approximately 300 billion square feet. Between 2005 and 2035, investigators foresee that 52 billion square feet will be demolished and 150 billion will be remodeled. If that sum is coupled with their projections that another 150 billion square feet will be new construction, then by 2035, three-quarters of the building stock will be new or renovated.[4] It thus makes sense that changes made now in the building sector will have a dramatic effect on the environment.

Therefore, the appropriate rehabilitation of buildings, including historic structures, can not only protect cultural and built resources, but can also contribute towards a healthier planet.

According to the National Park Service, historic preservation is inherently a sustainable practice. The rehabilitation of historic buildings viably connects built and cultural heritage to the preservation of natural resources. "A commonly quoted phrase, 'the greenest building is the one that's already built,' succinctly expresses the relationship between preservation and sustainability. The repair and retrofitting of existing and historic buildings is considered by many to be the ultimate recycling project, and focusing on historic buildings has added benefits for the larger community. Traditional materials are generally durable, the continued maintenance of historic buildings and features relies on local craftsmen rather than replacement parts, and these structures generally make up the heart of our towns and cities. For decades, preservation programs, like Historic Preservation Tax Incentives, have demonstrated that whole communities can be revitalized by rehabilitating individual buildings... In recognition of the role the built environment plays in energy use, [the National Park Service's] Technical Preservation Services [Division] develops guidance and technical information about how historic properties can incorporate sustainable practices to reduce energy consumption, while maintaining those characteristics that make historic properties significant."[5] Additionally, many historic buildings possess passive design elements in response to local climates, and as such, already benefit from a good dose of sustainable design features. Therefore, preserving older buildings recognizes their physical contributions to place-making as well as their embodied energy. According to Richard Moe, Executive Director at the National Trust for Historic Preservation, "it takes energy to construct a new home... it saves energy to preserve an old one."[6]

Just a few years ago, preservationists mainly pursued the recuperation and maintenance of cultural and built heritages, while emerging 'green' architects and builders strove to lessen mankind's adverse impact on the environment, reducing dependence on fossil fuels, primarily by technological innovation, recycling, and the creation of alternative energy sources. For a while, preservationists and green designers and builders were at odds, perceiving opposing goals. Yet, historic preservation is a green alternative.

Valuing, Preserving and Creating Sustainable Architecture & Urbanism

History is packed with significant examples of sustainable architecture and urbanism, which on the one hand deserve to be preserved, and on the other, can serve as valuable lessons for current architects and builders.

The exportation, adaptation, and mutation of those precedents have informed our evolving built heritage for centuries. Yet, for nearly sixty years, lessons from those paradigms of sustainability where shelved - thought irrelevant in a modern society - and as a result, urban revitalization strategists banked on the assumed devaluation of historic buildings to justify their demolition and architects altered their building designs, making them increasingly dependent on artificial and mechanical systems to control their environment, with little or no regard for their cultural inheritance, urban morphology, or a region's climate. Historic structures were razed as new building designs became increasingly divorced from these topics, culminating in exchangeable, vacuum-sealed, generic boxes that often seemed to arbitrarily land on the landscape. Historic neighborhoods scared by insensitively scaled and climate-illiterate buildings have resulted in some of the most blighted neighborhoods in our communities. And, the replacement parts - those 'containers' - are amongst today's greatest energy guzzlers.

During the latter half of the 20th century, professionals less readily assimilated the built inheritance nor its teachings of sustainable vernacular precedents than did the layperson. More recently though, a greater appreciation has been evidenced by a new generation of designers. Just as important teachings can be garnered from the design of traditional, mixed-use, pedestrian friendly, self-sustaining towns of previous centuries, so too can they be drawn from the acclimated building designs, spanning between our vernacular roots to more recent Mid-Century Modern Regionalist architecture.

Bridging between tradition and innovation, and looking at 'green', not as a trend, but rather as a part of a longer, historical continuum, allows for the preservation of and/or retrieval of design values that have naturally and traditionally accompanied building design - thus expanding current mainstream thinking.

Lessons from our past and more recent history are relevant to present and future generations of designers and offer alternative or complimentary concepts, to current technologically oriented methods, proposing that 'sustainable design' embrace urban and building traditions that conserve energy and materials, which incidentally often also represent more practical, affordable alternatives.

The Sustainable Traditions & Innovations of South Florida: worthy of preservation and of emulation

In the sub-tropics, Native Americans built light structures, which responded to the natural context in a practical manner. Constructions were elevated off the ground to keep them cool, dry, and insect-free. Local materials were used; walls were made of breathable reeds, topped by thatched roofs. The dwellings were often placed in clusters or concentric configurations, such as to reinforce a sense of community. The next generation of permanent immigrants that followed imported their building traditions to Florida, but wisely and quickly adapted them to respond to the hot and humid climate. In St. Augustine this entailed the adaptation of the Spanish courtyard house, to allow for protection from the sun, cross-ventilation and out-door living spaces. Later waves of immigrants from the Northeast often learned from their Caribbean neighbors. They accommodated their building traditions as well, resulting in elevated wood frame structures, outfitted with high ceilings, plenty of tall windows for cross-ventilation and screened porches, which also allowed for outdoor living; essentially acclimatizing their imported customs and influences from other places, to establish a new civilization and a sense of place. In like manner, in the early twentieth century, the catalog inspired 'California bungalows' that followed were adapted to the region, incorporating local materials and responding to the extreme climate, providing an expediency of experience rather than innovation, which by accommodation contributed handsomely to the incremental growth of the era. Even large-scaled office buildings of the period, provided their users with covered arcades, operable windows in tall rooms, with transoms above doors and roof top gardens, allowing for increased comfort. Mediterranean and Art Deco Moderne styles that ensued to a greater or lesser degree all made adjustments in response to the extreme climate of the region and often celebrated their connection to the tropical exterior in playful ways.

Many of the nationally acclaimed architects of the Modern Regionalist movement that followed were based out of Central and South Florida, including Marion Manley, Alfred Browning Parker, Igor Polevitzky, Robert Law Weed, Rufus Nims, Paul Rudolph, and a chorus of others. This generation of practitioners unsentimentally looked to the history of South Florida architecture in an attempt to develop a contemporary method and style of building that was responsive to geography and the climate of place, distinguishing them from most of their earlier and later peers of the Modern era. These Modern Regionalists were informed by the traditions of the past and experimented with the new materials of a post-war era, resulting in a sustainable architecture, which associated the past with the present.

With the advent of both the car, at the scale of cities, and the wide-spread commercialization of air-conditioning at the scale of buildings, new developments and buildings ignored useful preceding design strategies. As a result, to this day building and town designs greatly serve to further isolate our society and increase our dependence on fossil fuels. More often than not, those late XXth and early XXI century additions to our cities lead to 'non-contributing' buildings and places that do not add towards the formation of sustainable towns and buildings, rather they subtract from their essence. In the meantime, historic resources, which could be re-used, rehabilitated or restored, are bulldozed in the name of energy efficiency and/or economic revitalization.

Green Is More Than Skin Deep

Being 'green' is not an issue of 'style', nor should it be relegated to a mere discussion of technological inventions, reliant on performance based energy efficiency benchmarks alone. Rather it should be a more holistic pursuit, in which designs 'integrate' natural systems, urban systems, site and climatic realities, building design typologies, energy use, economic considerations, technology, as well as the human condition, while recuperating our built and cultural inheritance. As in past generations, today's designers can expeditiously learn and interpret the past, so they may be more consonant with, rather than destructive of the natural and built world, resulting in sustainable designs with measurable ecological impacts that consider both built inheritance and future legacies. An architecture and urban design that in short, is rooted to place, and increases the quality of life of present and future generations by embracing all scales and 'green' spectrums. Preserving historic buildings recognizes their physical contributions to place-making as well as their embodied energy and in addition, the passive methods they often employ respond to local climates and as such are models of sustainable principles.

A greater appreciation of historical assets and their intrinsic characteristics, as well as a re-examination of sustainable precedents, across our shared histories, in an integrated manner, from the macro to the micro scales, can expedite the incorporation of useful tools, while evidencing the splendid heritage from which we can continue to draw. In summary, 'sustainable design' bridges between tradition and innovation - it has for centuries. Therefore, 'Green' is not an isolated contemporary trend, but rather it is a part of a longer, historical continuum, thus allowing for the retrieval of design values that have habitually and naturally accompanied sustainable design - when in fact, it was not considered an 'innovation' but rather a logical response to place - thus expanding current thinking, which focuses 'sustainable' design primarily on 'novelty'.

These notions can be shared with professional and academic peers as well as with students of all ages, "to promote creative problem-solving, relevant to climate change - one which incorporates a deep understanding of the relationship between nature and design...".[7]

GREENWASHING

Greenwash is disinformation disseminated by an organization so as to present an environmentally responsible public image. Derivatives: greenwashing (n). Origin from green on the pattern of whitewash.
- Tenth Edition of the Concise Oxford English Dictionary

What are some of the problems related to the 'Green' labeling?

There are clear examples of companies where their core business is based primarily on an activity, which has been identified as significantly contributing to environmental pollution or destruction, and yet through clever marketing, present themselves as environmentally responsible. For example, oil and coal companies, whose products have been determined by UN scientists to be the largest source of man-made greenhouse gases, are by definition engaged in an environmentally unsustainable business, and thus to minimize the general public's perception of this fact, they are actively greenwashing when they claim to be good stewards of the planet. Scientists tell us that each ton of coal or barrel of oil burned adds to the risk of dangerous climate change, which over 160 countries have pledged to prevent in an international treaty. In short, there is a fundamental contradiction between the environmental (and legal) requirement to reduce carbon dioxide (CO2), and the production and sale of increasing quantities of coal and oil, the main sources of CO2. Similarly, forestry companies, which log in ancient forests, the richest terrestrial reservoirs of biodiversity on the planet, make it almost impossible to implement the commitments made by 165 countries to protect species in the 1992 International Convention on Biological Diversity. Currently, it is estimated that 50-100 species become extinct each day, and forest clearing is a major contributor. This is another example of how a core business can be in fundamental contradiction with a sustainable environment.[8] Oil, coal, and wood are all materials that are greatly consumed in either the manufacturing or maintenance of buildings. In a similar manner, within the design and building industries themselves, there are those that attempt to 'greenwash', be it in the design, manufacturing or building sides of the process, either by exaggerating the properties or potentialities of a given design, construction method or material. And, consumers of buildings are equally culpable of soothing their environmental conscious and image. For example, it is difficult to make the case that a residence for a single family, which consumes a large tract of land, and possess outrageous amounts of square footage, is in any way environmentally responsible solely because they have included some energy efficient systems or met minimum benchmarking standards. They are simply less bad. A much more realistic alternative exists, and is employed increasingly by environmental campaigners and heritage organizations in promoting alternatives to new development- the embodied energy of a historic property.

EMBODIED ENERGY

The energy required to extract, process, manufacture, transport and install building materials.
- Tenth Edition of the Concise Oxford English Dictionary

Studies show quite remarkably that despite very different approaches taken to producing new homes, in general, the total CO2 emissions have been very similar to their historic predecessors. Previous studies and much of the accepted thinking on domestic CO2 emissions had suggested that demolishing existing homes and building new homes to replace them contributed to an overall reduction in CO2 emissions. However, more recent studies instead suggest that this is not so, and that refurbishing existing homes and converting unused properties into new homes can yield CO2 reductions by preventing emissions from *embodied energy* that would arise from new building. Although embodied CO2 emissions related to building and developing and refurbishing homes are a relatively small proportion of the total CO2 emissions from housing, omitting them from future projections of domestic CO2 emissions is highly disingenuous; it leads to overestimating the CO2 savings new homes can make, and to underestimating the potential of refurbishing existing homes and returning empty homes to use to help cut emissions.

CONFLICTING CLAIMS

"New properties are "greener" than older ones"
- Sunday Times, October, 2006
"New homes are more environmentally friendly and sustainable than at any time in recent history"
- Home Builders' Federation, 2007
"New homes are over four times more energy-efficient than older homes and therefore 'greener'"
- Smart New Homes, 2007
"New homes can be up to eight times more efficient than a typical Victorian property"
- Peveril Homes, 2007

It is increasingly common for developers to make environmental claims for the buildings they produce. A significant body of opinion sustains that demolition of historic buildings and its replacement with new energy efficient structures is largely preferable in many cases to refurbishment. The grounds of this argument are that the operational (in-use) carbon emissions of highly efficient newly built structures, including the housing sector, can be far lower than those of existing buildings. These claims were not off the mark by much if one compared a home that pre-dated the use of high R-value insulation, energy efficient windows, and weather-stripping to those that currently include them. It is undoubtedly true for example, that new homes in general, are better insulated than homes built in the past; because at the time of their construction there were no mandatory standards governing energy efficiency or thermal comfort nor the same availability of construction materials. Nevertheless, many of those energy saving features, are retrofitted easily enough into a historic building. But, by the same token, generically designed buildings, which are devoid of the passive designs features of older homes, are by comparison arguably more expensive to upgrade to current 'green' standards than the historic ones that already incorporate those features. Other claims however are harder still to quantify. For instance, to justify supplanting historic homes with newly built 'green' homes, developers and regeneration planners sometimes use assertions of the superior environmental performance of new housing. This argument is frequently debatable, if not out-right untrue, given that a historic structure can integrate new 'green' features or technologies.

On other occasions, confabulations are employed to validate razing a neighborhood, and replacing it with new developments, when instead there are existing supplies of unused buildings that could be readily updated, rehabilitated, or used for a new function. The rehabilitation of neighborhoods and their increments can effectively heal the wounds of a historic neighborhood, which on the one hand is rich in built and cultural heritage, but on the other, might be suffering from 'missing teeth' in its urban fabric, that in turn have led to higher crime rates and economic destabilization. Equally questionable are the claims that new developments are essential to economic revitalization, when in fact the rehabilitation of existing housing stocks, in particular those that are tied to a community's history or identity are ripe for rehabilitation and could equally contribute to economic growth. At the other end of the spectrum, in the process of rehabbing historic buildings, the introduction of better insulation, water, and energy efficient features, and the removal of any toxic materials, such as lead or asbestos should be addressed.

Given that as global population rises, so too will the rate of renovation and construction of buildings, it thus stands to reason that changes made now in the preservation and green building sectors and a balanced partnering between them will have a dramatic consequence on the environment, thereby providing the tools for holistic and integrated sustainable design thinking that, through reshaping present approaches to design, would strengthen our community and nation.[9]

An Integrated Approach

According to Native American wisdom, we have not inherited this earth, but rather are here as mere guardians, sent to protect it, for the benefit of its rightful heirs, our children, and their children.

In light of the realities associated with global warming, current generations are going to leave future ones with a world vastly different from the world lived in today, if assertive action in the present is not taken to address the impact of the built realm on the environment. Present 'curators' of the planet, can address sustainable design needs more effectively by better 'integrating' noble yet 'parallel' endeavors and modifying development at all levels - regions, communities, neighborhoods, campuses, projects, and even single buildings - past, present and future.

Undoubtedly, to evade dangerous climate change, the design and construction of buildings and cities must be re-considered and consequently, architects, urban designers, and preservationists play a central role in limiting climate change. As in past generations, today's practitioners can effectively integrate past lessons into their projects, better connecting them to a place while reducing their ecological footprint, and embracing innovation. This requires an awareness of past successes, which can expeditiously inform design and building processes - looking both into the future and the past for inspiration as well as the rethinking of historic preservation, architecture and urban design values so they may be more consonant with, rather than destructive of the natural world.[10] This implies a methodology that in short, increases the quality of life of present and future generations by embracing lessons from past and current generations. This bridging between innovation and tradition, at all 'green' levels of the design spectrum, includes the preservation of historic buildings, which incidentally, right off the bat, often accomplished many parallel 'green' goals sensibly and cost-effectively, through passive design methods. If for no other reason, their presence in our communities is a reminder that sustainable goals are achievable.

BUILDING DESIGN AND CONSTRUCTION FACTS[11]

Sonia R. Cháo

- With so much attention given to transportation emissions, many people are surprised to learn that buildings are the single largest contributor to global warming.
- Data from the US Energy Information Administration illustrates that buildings are responsible for almost half (48%) of all energy consumption and GHG emissions annually; globally the percentage is even greater.
- Seventy-six percent (76%) of all power plant-generated electricity is used just to operate buildings. Clearly, immediate action in the Building Sector is essential if we are to avoid hazardous climate change.

Buildings constructed annually: 1,770,000

Buildings demolished annually: 290,000

Waste generated annually from construction and demolition: 136 million tons

Portion of construction waste that is recycled or re-used: 20 to 30%

Amount of waste generated during construction of average 2,000 sq. ft. house:
3000 pounds of wood; 2000 pounds of drywall; 600 pounds of cardboard

Amount of waste generated during construction of new single-family home: 4 pounds per sq. ft.

Portion of total energy consumption associated with buildings: 40%

Portion of electricity consumption associated with buildings: 72%

Portion of carbon dioxide emissions associated with buildings: 39%

Portion of Greenhouse Gas Emissions associated with buildings: 30%

Average reduction in energy use after retrofitting a historic building: 25%

Increase in average new house size from 1950 to 1999: 105%

Average embodied energy in existing buildings: 5 to 15 gallons of gasoline per sq. ft.

Average embodied energy in a 250,000 sq. ft. office building: 3.75 million gallons of gasoline

Average operating energy expended by a commercial building built in 1920: 80,127 BTU's per sq. ft.

Average operating energy expended by a commercial building built in 2000: 79,703 BTU's per sq. ft.

Endnotes

[1] This article was originally presented in 2007 and updated in 2011.
[2] www.architecture2030.org
[3] www.architecture2030.org
[4] www.architecture2030.org, March 3, 2007
[5] http://www.nps.gov/tps/sustainability.htm, October 6, 2011
[6] www.nationaltrustforhistoricpreservation.gov, August 1, 2008
[7] 2030 Challenge website: www.2030challenge.com
[8] http://www.stopgreenwash.org/, Greenpeace, October 4, 2010
[9] National Endowment for the Arts Grant Guidelines - *DESIGN: Access to Artistic Excellence*, www.NEA/Submission/NEA Grants for Arts Projects Access to Artistic Excellence Design.htm
[10] Ibid
[11] www.energy.gov, U.S. Department of Energy, November 21, 2011

THE CORAL GABLES MUSEUM:
a lesson in sustainable stewardship

Jorge L. Hernandez

In his acceptance speech for The Vincent Scully Prize of 2007, Richard Moe, the past President of the National Trust for Historic Preservation, proposed the concept of sustainable stewardship. Arguing that Americans comprise 5% of the world's population yet are responsible for nearly one quarter of global green house gas emissions, he called us to re-examine our actions and our relationship to nature and her bounty: our natural and cultural heritage. Because nearly half of the greenhouse gas emissions produced by Americans can be attributed to the construction and operation of our buildings, it is incumbent on all of us, but particularly architects and building professionals to reassess the relationship of architecture to nature. The most significant work on the subject is Vincent Scully's tome *Architecture: the Natural and the Manmade*. For this paper, I would like to present the views of two recent authors who have considered the subject.

W.G. Clark, the architect from Charleston who for many years was Chair of Architecture of the University of Virginia, proposed the concept of "replacement." He states that "architecture whether as a town or a building is the reconciliation of ourselves with the natural land at the necessary juncture of culture and place." For Clark, "architecture seeks not only the minimal ruin of landscape but something more difficult; a replacement of what was lost with something that atones for the loss." In the best architecture, this replacement occurs through an "intensification of place where it emerges no worse for human intervention, where cultures' shaping of the land to specific use results in a heightening of beauty and presence. These places would seem worthy of our existence." Every act of building represents a taking of both the fruits of nature, the raw materials of which buildings are made, and the surface of the earth, where buildings are sited. This act of taking must be tempered by its purpose.

Clark's concept is akin to the ancient concept of propriety in architecture: where we must not only build well but with prudence, a place of cultural heritage with permanence in mind. Clark never reaches the position where architecture can surpass if not at least equal the beauty of a natural setting. For Clark the act of replacement, high minded as it may be, is architecture's responsibility to atone for its taking - a necessary evil.

Alan De Botton, author of *The Architecture of Happiness* goes one step further. In his chapter, "The Promise of the Fields," De Botton completes Clark's concept of replacement by arguing that architectural beauty can at least parallel if not surpass the beauty of natural settings. He asks "would the world not be less beautiful without a Venice…or a Royal Crescent at Bath?" Of course, we can interject our own favorites. And, we can also turn the focus of the question towards the opposite pole. Would the world not be less beautiful or sublime without a Grand Canyon, Mount Everest, or The Great Barrier Reef? By setting his sights on the highest artistic expression which architecture can achieve, De Botton renews the classical concept of *bella natura* making it comprehensible to a modern ear. That concept is that human industry, intellect and action; armed with principles extracted from nature can craft of nature's bounty an intensely natural thing. A thing that is both natural and designed. A thing such as gold, frankincense or myrrh to which I would gladly add wine, perfume and architecture. For both De Botton and Clark, architecture must be tempered by purpose and consequence to be concerned with the common good. Yet it is De Botton's understanding of architecture as a work of our making based on nature that places architecture squarely within nature's folds.

This understanding leads us to appreciate the importance of the symbiotic relationship of our cultural and natural heritage. We realize that the term *green preservation* becomes a non-qualifier because in the end all preservation has been to some significant extent and will increasingly *be green*; and all acts of sustainability are aimed at the preservation of some thing. This reciprocal understanding of the natural content in works of architecture (buildings, landscapes, towns and cities) challenges us to recast an idea for the built environment which can once again be in harmony with the natural order of things, an order where preservation is paramount, where our historic buildings and landscapes are, as our elders, prized for their lessons and valued for their wisdom.

The Coral Gables Museum is a case study answering Richard Moe's call to sustainable stewardship. This 1939 Works Progress Administration Building by architect Phineas Paiste is on the National Register of Historic Places. Originally designed as the Coral Gables police and fire station, jail and courthouse, this structure named The Municipal Building was slotted for demolition but saved in the 1970's. After a long period where it served as city offices the building, now restored, will open as The Coral Gables Museum. The project is a LEED certified (silver) restoration and addition including the replacing of a parking lot with an urban piazza, the addition of a loggia open to citizens for daily use, a community room and a range of gallery spaces in both the historic building and the new addition.

To advance the legacy of George Merrick, the founder of Coral Gables, the mission of the museum is to celebrate the civic arts: art, architecture, landscape, history, preservation and the environment. The conservation and restoration of walls built solidly of load bearing coral stone (oolitic limestone) slabs was a unique challenge. The historic structure, the new addition and loggia, sculpture garden and piazza will contribute to the civic landscape of downtown Coral Gables.

ENDANGERED 1920'S BUNGALOW: saved from demolition and restored by Dade Heritage Trust

Becky Matkov

A house in Little Havana, considered the finest example of a Belvedere Bungalow in the City of Miami, was saved from the bulldozer in 2003 when the nonprofit organization Dade Heritage Trust (Dade Heritage Trust) used its Preservation Revolving Fund to purchase the structure.

The J. Jacob Hubbard House, located at 138 NW 16th Avenue, a block from the site of the Orange Bowl, had been built circa 1921 in the Lawrence Estate Land Company Subdivision. It was home to the last owners, Rolando and Mercedes Alvarez, for 40 years. They had raised their family there, enjoying the breezy front porch and sun-filled rooms. Health problems and a desire to live near their daughter in Orlando, however, made a developer's offer to buy the property, demolish the house and construct an apartment building sound tempting. They were delighted when Dade Heritage Trust offered them a solution that was equally attractive financially and would preserve their memory-filled house.

Bungalows, a common architectural style from 1914 through 1920, are now fast vanishing in South Florida, with Dade Heritage Trust listing them on its "Most Endangered Historic Sites List."

The Hubbard/Alvarez Bungalow was extraordinary in that it had been changed so little. It was a classic "Belvedere" or "Airplane" Bungalow, with its use of wood shingles, Prairie style casement windows, intersecting gabled roof planes, decorative timbers and a second-story belvedere.

When Dade Heritage Trust Chief Executive Officer Becky Roper Matkov learned that the Hubbard-Alvarez Bungalow was imperiled at a City of Miami Historic and Environmental Preservation Board meeting, Dade Heritage Trust's Board decided to act. Empowered with a Preservation Revolving Fund, established with support from Miami-Dade County, Dade Heritage Trust offered to purchase the house and save it from destruction.

Dade Heritage Trust envisioned preserving the property as a model of "green restoration," using energy efficient and water-conserving building and landscaping practices.

The bungalow's original design was inherently "green." It was well sited on an elevated limestone ridge. Native materials were used, including Dade County pine and oolitic limestone, or "coral rock." Overhanging eaves and abundant windows and doors provided excellent cross ventilation. The high ceiling and extended rafters of the L-shaped front porch created an updraft that made sitting on the porch on even a hot July day cool and comfortable. The house even had an original cistern used to save water from the roof runoff.

By conserving the embodied energy and materials of the bungalow, and by preserving the bungalow's original architectural design, Dade Heritage Trust hoped to turn the bungalow into a demonstration project of how conservation and preservation can work together. Bill Murphy, then Dade Heritage Trust Board President, emphasized that the goal was not to just save one particular historic house, but to inspire others to sustainably preserve their historic buildings as well.

At an official closing on August 18, 2003 at the Dunwody White & Landon office of Dade Heritage Trust's pro bono attorney Tom Matkov, the Hubbard/Alvarez Bungalow became the property of Dade Heritage Trust.

After purchasing the house, Dade Heritage Trust held a "before" open house on September 20, 2003 to acquaint the community with the bungalow and with Dade Heritage Trust's plan to restore it.

Dade Heritage Trust then immediately nominated the Hubbard/Alvarez bungalow for historic designation by the City of Miami. On October 29, 2003 historic designation was approved by the City's Historic and Environmental Protection Board, thus ensuring the bungalow's protection from demolition for the future.

Under the leadership of then Dade Heritage Trust Board President Richard Heisenbottle a plan was developed by Architect William B. Medellin for restoring the house as a residence. LEED-certified Architect Sebastian Eilert donated his ideas for incorporating green building practices into the process.

Miami Dade College students, under the direction of Professor of Architecture Jose Vazquez, visited and studied the Hubbard/Alvarez Bungalow for its design. Drawings, photographs and models were made, and the house was featured prominently in an exhibit on Miami Bungalows held at the Historical Museum of Southern Florida from May 18 -September 9, 2007.

Demolition of the nearby Orange Bowl by the City of Miami in 2008 and plans for construction of a new stadium for the Marlins Baseball team made it less feasible to restore the bungalow as a single family residence. The Miami-Dade County GOB Preservation funding that Dade Heritage Trust was slated to receive for the restoration proved problematic, delaying Dade Heritage Trust's restoration progress.

In 2009, the environmental nonprofit organization Citizens for a Better South Florida, which had been looking for new headquarters, made an offer to purchase the bungalow. The contract was contingent on Dade Heritage Trust securing a zoning variance and performing specified construction work.

Dade Heritage Trust applied for a City of Miami historic preservation overlay for the bungalow, notifying neighbors

Dade Heritage Trust Treasurer Walter Alvarez, Dade Heritage Trust President Bill Murphy, Attorney Thomas J. Matkov, Dade Heritage Trust CEO Becky Roper Matkov, and Sellers Mercedes and Rolando Alvarez at the signing of the bungalow sale.

Contractor Hugh Ryan onsite.

Walking through the newly restored Hubbard/Alvarez Bungalow is Miami-Dade Commissioner Bruno Barreiro, Miami Commissioner Frank Carollo and DHT CEO Becky Roper Matkov.

Cutting the ribbon to dedicate the restoration of the Hubbard/Alvarez Bungalow are Arsenio Milian, Chairman of Citizens for a Better South Florida, Miami-Dade County Commissioner Bruno Barreiro, Dade Heritage Trust CEO Becky Roper Matkov, Miami Commissioner Frank Carollo, Miami-Dade Commissioner Katy Sorenson, Contractor Hugh Ryan, Miami Commissioner Francis Suarez and Dade Heritage Trust Chairman Walter Alvarez.

and property owners and appearing before City boards to secure approval for the variance, which enabled the single family home to be used as an office.

Architect William Medellin revised the original residential restoration plans to make the structure ADA compliant for office use. This involved building a handicap ramp, widening some doorways and redesigning and appropriately equipping the downstairs bathroom.

Hugh A. Ryan Construction Company was the contractor for the renovation. The goal was to retain as much as possible of the original structure and fixtures.

The wooden floors throughout the house were too badly damaged by termites to salvage, so new red oak floors were installed. The deteriorated second floor jalousie windows, which were not original, were replaced with metal impact resistant casement windows. These were custom designed to match the original wooden casement windows downstairs. The downstairs windows were repaired and made operable once again.

A central air conditioning system was planned by an engineer to be as unobtrusive as possible. Equipment was housed in closets on the first and second floors, and an L-shaped soffit was run in the first floor bedroom with ductwork opening into the walls of the dining room and living room, thus leaving intact their beamed ceilings. A cage was placed over the outside compressor to prevent theft. An attractive steel fence, the design of which was approved by the City's Historic and Environmental Preservation Board, was installed around the yard for further security.

Green practices included using Benjamin Moore's "Aura", a low VOC paint, throughout the house on both the interior and the exterior.

A tankless hot water heater replaced the old hot water tank, freeing up extra space. A large, original laundry sink in the laundry room was repaired and retained for multiple uses. New energy efficient kitchen appliances were installed. Light fixtures in an Arts and Crafts era design were installed throughout the house, using energy-efficient compact fluorescent bulbs.

Dade Heritage Trust's original plans had included adding extensive native landscaping and restoring the cistern for irrigation use. Citizens for a Better South Florida, which has a mission of providing environmental education to underserved communities and encouraging environmentally green practices, plans to carry out these goals.

A dedication for the restored Hubbard/Alvarez Bungalow was held by Dade Heritage Trust on February 19, 2010. Dade Heritage Trust Board Chairman Walter Alvarez and Dade Heritage Trust CEO Becky Roper Matkov were joined by Miami-Dade Commissioners Katy Sorenson and Bruno Barreiro and City Commissioners Frank Carollo and Francis Suarez in the ribbon cutting ceremony, along with Arsenio Milian, Board Chairman of Citizens for a Better South Florida, the new owner.

Adaptive re-use of the Hubbard/Alvarez demonstrates the value of conserving, rather than demolishing. Its restoration saves an important part of Miami's architectural heritage, and its new use will be a resource and inspiration for the entire community.

complimenting passive design strategies

WHAT IS LEED?

Carolyn Mitchell, Founding President,
USGBC South Florida Chapter

Introduction

The way we build has a variety of detrimental side-effects on the environment and on human well being. Is there a moral obligation on the part of the design community to pay attention to these effects? How can an industry with such an assortment of participants, interests, specialized technical disciplines, and economic forces come to terms with the effect of its activities and its highly atomized responsibility for those effects? In the years since the 1992 Rio Summit on the Environment, the industry has become more aware of the environmental and health impacts attributable to building. Reassessment of wasteful energy and water use practices, depletion of raw materials, toxic pollution associated with the manufacture of building materials, and the approximately 135 billion tons of waste generated per year from construction activity alone have provoked the building industry's movement toward greater responsibility and a precautionary approach that amounts to a fundamental change in the way the building industry operates. But because the building industry is composed of such a diverse range of participants, making changes is necessarily a complex and challenging undertaking. The U.S. Green Building Council's *Leadership in Energy and Environmental Design* (LEED) rating system has emerged as a provocative and useful tool for changing the building practices that cause the most damage.

South Florida has long been focused on the impact of its rapid development on the Everglades, where loss of habitat was the impetus for the founding of Florida's environmental movement. Marjory Stoneham Douglas's 1947 book *The Everglades: River of Grass* drew attention to the deleterious effects of building in South Florida. Damage to this fragile ecosystem - the source of South Florida's water supply - was a costly mistake that government is now attempting to repair. Sprawling development of suburban neighborhoods destroys habitat and creates a lifestyle that has serious environmental implications on a more global scale. To live in the typical sprawl-burban development requires a car and this increased dependence on automobiles is a major cause of the CO2 emissions that are causing climate change. The intensity of energy use by buildings themselves accounts for much demand for coal and fossil fuel power generation, contributing significantly to atmospheric CO2 levels. Conventional building practices have impact at the scale of the individual as well. Buildings contain chemical and biological irritants and since we spend 90% of our time inside buildings, poor air and light have measurable health effects. Asthma incidence and related mortality have sharply increased in the past two decades, particularly among children.

Evaluating and responding to these issues has been mostly the purview of specialists and has not been perceived as an obligation of the entire building design and construction community. On the national level, it has been the U.S. Green Building Council (USGBC) that has provided leadership by creating a means of facilitating broader participation. The USGBC's assessment tool, the LEED rating system, has emerged as an ingenious framework for educating and motivating the wide range of participants in the building industry about alternative approaches to building. LEED has provided a pragmatic solution to fostering massive change by making it easy for the largest number of participants to become engaged in making incremental but effective changes to business as usual in the building industry.

What is Green Building?

Green design and construction practices significantly reduce or eliminate the negative impact of building on the environment and building occupants. A range of best practices has been recognized in recent years. Well-designed, dense development in downtowns conserves land. Places with a mix of living, working and shopping options require fewer car trips, thus limiting CO2 emissions. Well-designed streets encourage walking and biking and further reduce the need for car trips. Innovative landscape design conserves water and provides food and shelter for birds, butterflies and other wildlife. Innovative plumbing can reduce water use dramatically. Efficient lights and appliances

and building designs that provide natural light reduce electricity demand. Solar panels and other alternative energy sources supply a portion of energy demand. Materials such as wood from managed forests and materials with high levels of recycled content protect natural resources. Interior finishes that have low levels of pollutants improve indoor air quality and protect health. Access to views, fresh air and natural light protect the health of occupants and also make people happier.

Leadership in Energy and Environmental Design - LEED

LEED is a certification system that provides independent verification that a building project has been built using best practices that improve upon conventional building in the most important areas: energy and water efficiency, CO2 emissions reduction, improved indoor air and light quality, protection of natural resources. The system was developed by the U.S. Green Building Council to provide building owners with a concise and practical method of integrating solutions with measurable benefits into their projects. LEED is applicable to a range of building project types, from commercial to residential, from the scale of the building to the community, from renovation to operation.

The system works through the award of credits for each best practice successfully integrated into the project. LEED recognizes four levels of achievement based on the number of credits achieved with a tiered rating system beginning with basic Certification and advancing through Silver and Gold to the highest level of achievement, Platinum. Credits are earned for different aspects of efficiency and design in appropriate categories. LEED credits represent the consensus of USGBC members on the types of design features that constitute best practice in each category. Credit is awarded based upon the most objective means of measuring effectiveness in implementing these practices. In each credit category, one or two practices are held to be so fundamental to improved environmental performance that they are designated as prerequisites.

The LEED system has been developed through a consensus process involving a wide variety of building industry members. This has shaped the rating system by determining which practices are awarded credit. Any member of the USGBC is entitled to propose a measure for inclusion in the rating system and the entire membership votes on each credit proposed. Because adversarial positions are frequently taken among members, only those practices that are unassailably and demonstrably beneficial are included, There is no pretense by USGBC that the rating system outlines every measure that can be made to improve the environmental and human impact of building activity. The organization instead offers an impartial and inclusive industry-wide consensus on the practices with which no one can argue.

Credits

The consensus process has yielded a roster of minimum efforts that must be made to improve building performance. These "no argument" areas for improvement include site planning, energy use and atmospheric pollution, water use efficiency, materials and resource use and indoor environmental quality.

The Sustainable Sites credit category addresses site planning issues such as development density and access to alternative transportation, habitat preservation, exemplary stormwater management and reduction of heat island effect and light pollution. Prerequisite in this category is a measure that is required by law in most jurisdictions – control of construction site run-off. As with many LEED credits, this practice is derived from an existing local standard that USGBC members considered at the cutting edge of environmental or health protection and worthy of wider application.

Water management is required to meet a prerequisite level of efficiency. Beyond this required minimum, Water Efficiency credits are earned for compliance with water discharge standards; the efficiency of landscape irrigation; innovative wastewater technologies and for overall water use reduction.

Energy use and atmospheric pollution are addressed in the largest and arguably most important and innovative credit category. As the name *Leadership in Energy and Environmental Design* suggests, energy design is a critical part of the LEED rating system, with a large number of credits available. Achievement of the higher Gold or Platinum ratings is unlikely without the attainment of many credits in this category. The LEED system establishes a minimum energy performance level as a prerequisite. Because it is recognized as a significant means of ensuring energy efficient building operation, LEED also requires that all LEED-rated projects include building commissioning as part of the design process to verify coordination of all aspects of building design related to the building systems. Beyond these minimums, optimization of energy performance is rewarded with additional credits according to the measurable improvement in energy efficiency. In addition, the protection of the ozone layer through the use of non-harmful refrigerants; the use of either on-site or off-site renewable energy sources; energy efficient building operation and maintenance practices; measurement and verification of energy saving; and documentation of cost impacts are rewarded through the Energy and Atmosphere credit category.

The exercise of measuring and monitoring energy use in order to demonstrate eligibility for a LEED credit has introduced a wide range of professionals outside the engineering disciplines to the concept that energy use in buildings is a design problem. Architects, often made aware for the first time that building orientation, glazing and shading have environmental implications, are brought to the table to modify designs in ways that limit energy use rather than leaving it all to the mechanical engineer. The result is often a more sophisticated and innovative design.

Credits in the Materials and Resources category are documented based on materials used during construction and address both the creation of waste and the impact of materials extraction and manufacture. The establishment of on-site recycling capacity is a prerequisite. Additional credit is awarded for more involved recycling programs. The diversion of debris from landfills is recognized with credit for exemplary construction waste management. Sourcing materials that have reduced impact on the environment is encouraged through credits for materials that are derived from sustainable sources, such as rapidly renewable materials or materials made from recycled content of various types. Several credits are available for the use of materials with limited toxic content.

People are a key element of the USGBC agenda and the Interior Environmental Quality credit category outlines a range of measures to protect the health and well-being of occupants by limiting toxicity and optimizing ventilation. No smoking is allowed inside a LEED-rated building. This is a prerequisite. Asbestos and PCBs are also required to be removed from existing buildings if they occur. Several credits are available for ensuring fresh air is brought into the building and monitored for harmful gases. Credit is available for limiting indoor chemicals and other indoor pollution sources. This category also rewards design that benefits building occupants psychologically, improving productivity,

health and learning. These include rooms with natural daylight and views; ventilation that permits occupants to adjust it to comfortable levels; and feedback from building occupants to building management about the comfort of the building.

Certification

The LEED rating is organized around the accumulation of credits through an impartial certification process overseen by the USGBC's *Green Building Certification Institute* (GBCI). This process has been rigorously perfected through several years of trial and error to be as efficient as possible but is sufficiently technical that USGBC has established an incentive to entice the building industry to learn how to do it. USGBC offers training and accreditation through its credentialing system to prepare professionals to guide building owners through the process. The LEED Accredited Professional is recognized as an invaluable member of a design team for his or her familiarity with the LEED process itself. There is naturally a credit available for including one on a project team. In the course of attaining this credential, tens of thousands of professionals have been introduced to the LEED system as well as to the principles and strategies that underpin the individual credits, often for the first time. This alone has been instructive for the industry.

The main responsibility of the LEED Accredited Professional is to manage the process of submitting a project for review by GBCI. The whole design team, however, is involved in achieving LEED certification. Architect, Landscape Architect, Civil Engineer, Mechanical, Electrical and Plumbing Engineers, Structural Engineers, Interior Architects, Building Owners, Facility Managers, Broker, Banker and Insurer normally convene a meeting or "charette" to plot out a strategy for achieving certification and continue to coordinate efforts as needed through the design and construction process. The LEED Accredited Professional takes responsibility for overseeing the process and the appropriate technical discipline takes responsibility for individual credits. Registration of a project entitles members of the design team to request interpretation of a proposed design strategy to determine before submittal if it meets the requirements of the credit being sought. Team members may also review previous Credit Interpretations, which have evolved into a data base of design approaches that have enriched the design vocabulary of the industry.

The certification process requires design strategies to be demonstrably better than standard practice. This goal of the USGBC – to cause the building industry to become demonstrably better than the status quo – has translated into sometimes elaborately technical measurement and verification methods for each aspect of the building process. The emphasis on measurement imposes a discipline on design teams by requiring results in place of what is widely called "greenwashing." It becomes impossible to pitch a design strategy as better for the environment if there is no measurable impact. Strategies that are showy but ineffective or insignificant in their benefit to the environment or building inhabitants are not accepted.

Certification requires submittal of documentation that demonstrates effective implementation of the design strategy being presented for credit. Landscape architects, for example, must document the amount of irrigation water that would have been used according to standard practice and the overall reduction generated by their innovative water-saving design strategies. The design team submits a certification package to GBCI that includes this documentation as well as a scorecard summarizing the credits requested and indicating the certification level being sought. The simplified framework depicted in the scorecard functions both as a strategic outline and a concise communication tool – allowing the team to organize its approach and communicate its intentions. The scorecard also establishes the LEED rating as a competitive activity easily accessible to the business mindset.

GBCI conducts a preliminary review of the technical support for the requested credits and issues a preliminary determination of the number of credits to be awarded. The team is permitted to provide corrections for any credit that has been requested and denied. Following another review, GBCI notifies the team of the project's certification status and the level achieved – Certified, Silver, Gold or Platinum – and issues a plaque to affix to the building. The plaque is, of course, made from a recycled resin product.

Innovations and Traditions

There is an orthopedic quality to the LEED rating system. It was conceived as a tool to guide a distorted building industry toward a more responsible building process. A global economy divorces actors from the consequences of their decisions and without a feedback process of some kind there is no mechanism for the building industry to intuitively control its ill-effects. This is where the use of a tool like LEED finds its place in the design of the built environment. Once upon a time, builders were forced to respond to climate, human comfort and resource availability. As we have become more technologically sophisticated, it has become possible to ignore limits imposed by nature and people have forgotten how to design with the environment in mind. Techniques for naturally cooling a building and ensuring occupant comfort went out of the architect's repertoire in the fifties with the advent of air conditioning and with the ascendance of mechanical engineers as the specialists responsible for the ventilation of buildings. The Under the Sun Symposium addresses the art of building in response to place, a tradition that has a renewed relevance as an appropriate response to the host of environmental and health problems caused by conventional building. But because the vast majority in the building industry is not attuned to the capacity of the natural world to sustain us, a tool such as LEED is needed.

LEED was developed to provoke change. It was designed with a pragmatist's acknowledgement that the building industry works according to a set of rules that have little to do with the poetry of architecture and more to do with human ambition. Left to its own devices, the industry would not be likely to evolve toward greener building methods at a pace or at a scale that is appropriate to the impending consequences of its current practices. Hence, LEED was devised to speak the language of industry and business. It is methodical, quantifiable, and marketable. LEED's particular genius has been in concocting a method by which decision makers with little interest in environmentalism or innovation are able to participate in improving building performance. This reflects the USGBC premise that it is better to have everyone doing a little than to have a small vanguard innovating change at the extreme end of the market with the vast majority maintaining the status quo.

LEED has been remarkably efficacious in giving the industry a way into the process of change. A large part of the success has been the result of making better building performance a bit of a sport. The driver of the business brain is an urge to win and LEED taps this basic motivator with its sly score card format. The act of seeking LEED certification has had a salutary effect on the way design teams operate, too. The process becomes a joint undertaking of the entire team and this alone provokes the innovation in problem solving that the building industry needs.

Florida architect's Peter Jefferson, George Reed, Sonia R. Cháo, Alfred Browning Parker, Thorn Grafton, and Jan Hochstim at the *Under the Sun: Sustainable Innovations and Traditions Symposium* hosted by the University of Miami Center for Urban & Community Design on January 25th to January 27th, 2007.

Participants view a presentation during the *Under the Sun: Sustainable Innovations and Traditions Symposium* at the University of Miami School of Architecture's Jorge M. Perez Architecture Center's Glasgow Hall designed by architect and urban planner Léon Krier.

Copy Editor
Lauren Stark

Graphic Designers
Anthony Calzadilla
Ivonne de la Paz

Research for this book was partially funded by:
The J.M. Kaplan Fund

Publication of Research and Symposium papers was funded by:
The National Endowment for the Arts (N.E.A.)
The Center for Urban & Community Design (CUCD)
University of Miami, School of Architecture
University of Miami, School of Architecture

For their professional encouragement of related research, special thanks to:
Conn Nugent
Elizabeth Plater-Zyberk

For their collegial collaboration, heartfelt thanks to:
Ivonne de la Paz
José Gelabert-Navia
Jan Hochstim
Isabel León-Candelaria
Julia Leon-Lâcher
Leonor Pol
Isabel Rigol
Eduardo Luis Rodríguez
Ana Santana
Roberto Segre

Thanks to *Under the Sun* symposium participants and co-sponsors:
Peter Brown
Alfred Browning Parker
German Brun
Jaime Correa
Jose Gelabert-Navia
Thorn Grafton
Mark Hampton
Denis Hector
Rob Hink
Jan Hochstim
Michael Larkin
Peter Jefferson
Carolyn Mitchell
Michael Myers
Elizabeth Plater-Zyberk
George Reed
Gustavo Sanchez-Hugalde
Luis Trelles
Bernard Zyscovich
University of Miami Law School's
Center for Ethics & Public Service
U.S. Green Building Council (USGBC) -
South Florida Chapter

For their generous archival and photographic contributions or access, many thanks to:
Steven Brooke
Celia García Acosta
Olivia Choy
Krisstian de Lara
Thorn Grafton
Jan Hochstim
Rich Hochstim
Raúl Rodríguez
Roberto Segre

Research Assistants
Carolina Calzada
Olivia Choy
Krisstian Alvarez
Elma Felix
Anthony García
Stephen Johnson
Emma May
Kathy McQuillen
Elena Roth

Staff Support
Andrea Cole
Isa García
Brian Lemmerman
Elienai Maldonado
Marietta Mont
Carolina Moscoso
Ana Santana
Gilda Santana
Elaine Segrera
Dominic Sevald
Luis Valdez Bartolis

Photographic and Footnote Credits & Research
Gabriella Alegre

UNIVERSITY OF MIAMI
SCHOOL of
ARCHITECTURE

ART WORKS.
arts.gov